LB
1139.4
D49
2002

Developing
constructivist
early childhood

This Book is due...	This Book is due...	This Book is due...
SEP 1 6 2002		
OCT 0 7 2002		
JUN 2 '03		
MAR 0 4 '05		
NOV 2 8 '05		
MAY 2 4 2007		

D0962159

Mt San Jacinto College Library
1499 N. State Street
San Jacinto CA 92583
(909) 487-6752
ext. 1581

EARLY CHILDHOOD EDUCATION SERIES

Leslie R. Williams, Editor **Millie Almy, Senior Advisor**

ADVISORY BOARD: Barbara T. Bowman, Harriet K. Cuffaro, Stephanie Feeney,
Doris Pronin Fromberg, Celia Genishi, Stacie G. Goffin, Dominic F. Gullo,
Alice Sterling Honig, Elizabeth Jones, Gwen Morgan, David Weikart

(Continued)

Developing Constructivist
Early Childhood Curriculum

PRACTICAL PRINCIPLES AND ACTIVITIES

Rheta DeVries
Betty Zan
Carolyn Hildebrandt
Rebecca Edmiaston
Christina Sales

TEACHERS
COLLEGE
PRESS

Teachers College
Columbia University
New York and London

Published by Teachers College Press, 1234 Amsterdam Avenue, New York, NY 10027

Copyright © 2002 by Rheta DeVries, Betty Zan, Carolyn Hildebrandt, Rebecca Edmiaston, and Christina Sales

All rights reserved. No part of this publication may be reproduced or transmitted in any form or by any means, electronic or mechanical, including photocopy, or any information storage and retrieval system, without permission from the publisher.

Library of Congress Cataloging-in-Publication Data

Developing constructivist early childhood curriculum : practical principles and activities / Rheta DeVries . . . [et al.].
    p. cm. — (Early childhood education series)
  Includes bibliographical references and index.
  ISBN 0-8077-4121-3 (cloth) — ISBN 0-8077-4120-5 (pbk.)
    1. Early childhood education—United States—Curricula. 2. Constructivism (Education—United States. I. DeVries, Rheta. II. Early childhood education series (Teachers College Press)

LB1139.4 .D49 2002
372.19—dc21   2001026689

ISBN 0-8077-4120-5 (paper)
ISBN 0-8077-4121-3 (cloth)

Printed on acid-free paper

Manufactured in the United States of America

09   08   07   06   05   04   03   02   8   7   6   5   4   3   2   1

Contents

Acknowledgments

Our examples of classroom events come from work with teachers in seven schools: University of Houston (Texas) Human Development Laboratory School (HDLS); Plainfield (Iowa) Community School Preschool; Child Development Center, Malcolm Price Laboratory School, University of Northern Iowa; Audubon Elementary School, Dubuque, Iowa; Grant Early Childhood Center, Cedar Rapids, Iowa; Roosevelt Elementary School, Waterloo, Iowa; and Tri-County Head Start at Gates School, Waterloo, Iowa. The teachers in these examples are Beth Anderson, Amy Hird, Val Dolezal, Gwen Harmon, Christina Sales, Coreen Samuel, and Karen Wohlwend. We gratefully acknowledge the teachers, staff, and children at these schools whose work enriches our own and without whose help this book would not have been possible.

In addition, teachers from across Iowa in the Regents' Center for Early Developmental Education's Teacher Practitioner Council gave us valuable feedback, for which we are grateful. We also acknowledge the photography, videotaping, and extensive technical assistance of Cathy Richey, as well as the photography of Rebecca Edmiaston, Carolyn Hildebrandt, Shari McGhee, Christina Sales, Thos Sumner, Pat Wehr, Karen Wohlwend, and the University of Northern Iowa Archives. We acknowledge Lynn Zahrobsky for her original artwork. Once again, Susan Liddicoat at Teachers College Press served as our invaluable editor. Finally, we want to express our deep appreciation to Theresa Johnson for her infinite patience in making seemingly endless changes to the manuscript.

Developing Constructivist Early Childhood Curriculum

PRACTICAL PRINCIPLES AND ACTIVITIES

Introduction

Rheta DeVries

Four-year-olds Quenisha, Donell, and Ryan build a complex block structure that incorporates ramps made of several lengths of cove molding. They want their balls to roll from one ramp to the next and are surprised to see them stop time after time at a sharp-angled junction between ramps. They make small adjustments between the ramps, but still the balls stop at the junction. The teacher observes their difficulties and asks Ryan to show her with his finger where he wants his ball to go. As he traces the sharp angle of the ramp path, the children see the need to straighten it and do so together. They exchange smiles and cheers as their ball rolls down both ramp segments in a straight line.

This vignette illustrates how children's interests can lead them to experiment and cooperate to solve a new problem. It also shows how teachers can come up with interventions that foster new and more adequate reasoning. We hope this and other stories we tell in this book will help teachers construct a more elaborated vision of constructivist early education.

Our book provides a constructivist interpretation of developmentally appropriate curriculum in preschool and kindergarten. It has two aims. The first is to extend descriptions of constructivist teaching beyond those offered in my previous books on physical-knowledge activities and group games (Kamii & DeVries, 1978/1993, 1980). In those books, the activities described were conducted only once with children. What is missing is an account of how activities are transformed over time and how children's reasoning is transformed in the course of extended experience with a physical phenomenon or group game. In this book, we provide accounts of transformations over time in materials, activities, teacher interventions, and children's reasoning. We show how the teacher's thinking about children's thinking influences modifications and extensions of activities. As in the past, we are inspired especially by the research and theory of Jean Piaget.

The second aim of this book is to put these accounts of constructivist teaching in the context of the play-oriented curriculum advocated by the

National Association for the Education of Young Children (NAEYC). My coauthors and I identify with the position statements of NAEYC that advocate developmentally appropriate practice (Bredekamp, 1987; Bredekamp & Copple, 1997; Bredekamp & Rosegrant, 1992, 1995). We believe that these position statements reflect the constructivist view that learning is the result of efforts to make sense of the world. In their discussion of "Principles of child development and learning that inform developmentally appropriate practice," NAEYC authors state that these principles "are based on several prominent theories that view intellectual development from a constructivist, interactive perspective" (Bredekamp & Copple, 1997, p. 13) and cite Piagetians (Piaget, DeVries, Kohlberg, Kamii, and Ewing) and Vygotskians (Vygotsky, Berk, Winsler, Bodrova, Leong, and Rogoff).

Piaget's constructivist theory provides the research base and theoretical underpinning for the constructivist interpretation of curriculum presented in this book. Part I focuses on theoretical and practical foundations for developing constructivist early childhood curriculum, and Parts II and III offer detailed descriptions of classroom activities (using pseudonyms for children's names) and principles of teaching followed by constructivist teachers. We try to show how teachers we know transform their teaching so as to enable children to transform themselves. Part II presents examples of physical-knowledge activities, and Part III focuses on group games. Throughout, we emphasize the importance of a sociomoral context of mutual respect, the focus of a previous book (DeVries & Zan, 1994).

In this book, we write about how teachers transform curriculum in a constructivist direction and how this curriculum transforms children. Our effort to illustrate how to transform curriculum takes off from NAEYC's third position statement dealing with transforming curriculum (Bredekamp & Rosegrant, 1995). This statement moves beyond previous ones to show how a developmentally appropriate integrated curriculum can foster knowledge of content in subject matter disciplines. It attempts to resolve the tension between the

> "early childhood error" (inadequate attention to the content of curriculum in preschool programs) and the "elementary error" (overattention to curriculum objectives, with less attention to the developmental characteristics of young learners or the specific needs and interests of young children). (p. 174)

In the NAEYC statement, however, learning processes remain general and are not elaborated within the context of specific activities. We hope to supplement the NAEYC effort by showing how to meld the teaching of content with children's construction of the relationships that constitute intelligence.

PART I

UNDERSTANDING CONSTRUCTIVIST EDUCATION

Rheta DeVries

The position statements of the National Association for the Education of Young Children support the constructivist view of play as critically important for children's development and education: "An essential component of developmentally appropriate practice" is "child-initiated, child-directed, teacher-supported play" (Bredekamp, 1987, p. 3; Bredekamp & Copple, 1997, p. 14). This emphasis on play carries on a long tradition in early education and child development (for example, beginning with the ancient Greek Aristotle, trans. 1932, and progressing in modern times through Froebel, 1826/1999; Dewey, 1913/1975; Freud, 1913/1950, 1920/1974; Isaacs, 1930/1966; Klein, 1932/1975; Piaget, 1945/1962; Pratt, 1948/1970; Smilansky, 1968; Erikson, 1977; Fein, 1981; and Fein & Rivkin, 1986). Our book builds on the current scientific consensus about the role of play in high-quality early education and attempts to move the discussion a bit further.

As we take up this task, it is important to acknowledge the political problem for advocates of a play-oriented curriculum. This problem is due in part to the failure of both critics and advocates to distinguish between developmental and maturationist worldviews. It is also evident that too often early childhood educators rely on global justifications of play that leave the impression that it is trivial. These ideas are discussed below.

THE POLITICAL PROBLEM WITH PLAY-ORIENTED CURRICULUM

We see our book in part as a response to the political problem encountered by advocates of developmentally appropriate and constructivist practice. That is, the historic advocacy of a play-oriented curriculum has unfortunately had the

result of attracting criticism from those who view play as "aimless" (noted by
Fein & Rivkin, 1986), "of little importance" (Montessori, 1936/1956), or
as "irrational," "dangerous," "a nuisance," "disorderly," or "subversive"
(Montessori, 1916/1965; 1949/1967; noted by Sutton-Smith, 1986). Weber
(1969) suggests that "acceptance or rejection of the educative value of play is
rooted in the Puritan ethic" (p. 221). Similarly, Rubin, Fein, and Vandenberg
(1983) point out that "The Puritan ethic dichotomized work and play," viewing work as "an extension of God's work" and seeing play as "the province of
the devil" (pp. 697–698). They note that although this idea is less pronounced
now, it still "contributes to the relative disregard of play as an important topic
for study" (p. 698). Piaget (1945/1962) acknowledged the problem this way:

> In spite of the prophetic visions of the great educationists, play has always been
> considered, in traditional education, as a kind of mental wastematter, or at least
> a pseudo activity, without functional significance, and even harmful to chil-
> dren, keeping them from their homework. (p. 151)

As shown below, Piaget did not agree with the traditional view. He saw play
as an important and necessary vehicle for children's cognitive development
and provided scientific evidence for his views.

Unfortunately, some contemporary writers associate play with entertainment rather than with education. For example, Damon (1995), a developmental psychologist, notes that implementation of child-centered, constructivist education "generally means a laissez-faire approach" (p. 102) and that
"early education in most places has become a grab bag of loosely structured
story telling, singing, untutored arts and crafts, play activities, and frequent
partying" (p. 104). This kind of erroneous characterization could lead to the
demise of developmentally appropriate and constructivist education. That
is, if play is viewed as trivial, then play-oriented curricula will also be considered trivial and of little or no educational value. I begin by examining the
issue in terms of a failure to distinguish developmental and maturationist
worldviews of learning and development.

Failure to Distinguish Developmental and Maturationist Worldviews

The controversy over play-oriented curriculum reflects in part a confusion
between two streams in educational thought noted by Kohlberg and Mayer
(1972): (1) maturationist, and (2) cognitive-developmental. The romantic
maturationist stream is based on the idea that the child's naturally occurring
development should be allowed to flower without adult interventions in a
laissez-faire, permissive environment. In contrast, the cognitive-developmental

or constructivist stream is based on the idea that the dialectic or interactionist process of development and learning through the child's active construction should be facilitated and promoted by adults. A third stream in educational thought conceptualized by Kohlberg and Mayer is the cultural transmission or behaviorist stream reflecting the view that all knowledge results from information coming from outside the individual to the inside and thus requires didactic adult transmission. (See also DeVries & Kohlberg, 1987, for a discussion of these three streams.)

Criticism of the play-oriented curriculum is most commonly heard from behaviorist critics of the developmental approach who mistakenly assume that developmentally appropriate and constructivist education falls in the maturationist stream. For example, Stone (1996) describes the developmental view as valuing "naturally occurring developmental progression" where "frustration and delayed gratification are to be minimized while immediate success and satisfaction are to be maximized" (pp. 16, 18). On the basis of these mistaken ideas about developmentalism, Stone goes on to criticize educational efforts that seek to be "child centered," "progressive," and "developmentally appropriate," through efforts to promote "reflective thinking," "authentic learning," "hands-on experiences," "discovery learning," "cognitive apprenticeship," "whole language," and "emergent literacy" (pp. 20–21). These terms, so dear to developmentalists, are summarily dismissed by Stone as "obscure but pervasive restriction on educational improvement" (p. 2). Further, he states that "developmentalism discourages teachers and parents from asserting expectations or otherwise acting to induce more mature behavior" and "encourages tolerance and acceptance of immaturity, irresponsibility, and failure" (pp. 7–8).

Developmentalists certainly do not recognize themselves in this preposterous portrayal of their views as leading to permissive programs of frivolous play in which teachers take a "hands-off" attitude. Consider the following statement of Piaget (1948/1973) in which he also criticizes giving children complete freedom:

> A few years ago the main trend, especially owing to the widespread influence of psychoanalysis, was carefully to avoid frustrating the developing child in any way. This led to an excess of unsupervised liberty which ended in generalized play without much educational benefit. (pp. 6–7)

This remark introduces the matter of concern in this book. We need to develop a way of thinking that helps us distinguish what is of educational benefit to children and what is not. A barrier to this goal is the tendency of early childhood educators to rely on global notions of play to justify and describe their play-oriented curriculum.

Reliance on Global Notions of Play

Global notions of play include vague general statements to justify the play-oriented curriculum and vague characterizations to describe play in early education.

Vague General Statements about Play. I would like to point out that we developmentalists are partly responsible for the false accusation that developmentalists are romantic maturationists who let children waste their time in frivolous play. We often articulate our views vaguely in ways that make us seem like maturationists. For example, one easily finds popularized slogans such as the following in books on early education:

> The primary program is designed to incorporate play as a way of learning for all primary children. (Nebraska Department of Education et al, 1993, p. 27)

> Play is the child's work. (Turner & Hamner, 1994, p. 195)

> Children play to discover and master experience. . . . Children play to learn. (Read, 1976, pp. 25, 200)

> Play promotes the development of both mental and social abilities in children. (Bodrova & Leong, 1996, p. 57)

> Teach in the context of the child's play. (Kamii & DeVries, 1975/1977, p. 383)

Similarly, in its first position statement on developmentally appropriate practice, NAEYC states that "children learn most effectively through a concrete, play-oriented approach to early childhood education" (Bredekamp, 1987, p. 1) and asserts that "Children need years of play with real objects and events before they are able to understand the meaning of symbols such as letters and numbers" (p. 4).

These vague general statements, of course, are not wrong and may be a good starting point. Certainly, many developmentalists, including those cited above, have discussed developmentally appropriate and constructivist practices in ways that go beyond slogans to provide detailed examples and principles of teaching. Yet, when teachers do not go beyond the slogans, their superficial understanding may lead them to implement a play-oriented curriculum that at best may be nothing more than entertainment. More often the play activities provided simply reflect an underestimation of what children can do.

The problem is that when teachers are not given detailed descriptions of activities and explanations of how development and/or subject matter learning arises from them, misinterpretations are bound to occur. Just such misunderstanding led to efforts to clarify the 1987 NAEYC statement. In 1992, Bredekamp and Rosegrant say that "the worst misinterpretation of developmentally appropriate practice is that if teachers just let children play, at Grade 3 they emerge literate" (p. 5). The necessity for this kind of clarification stems partly from the fact that developmentally appropriate practice and constructivist education are not intended to be curricula. They are approaches that offer a general philosophy and principles of teaching that must be interpreted by teachers in the course of life with children in classrooms. Therefore, constructivist education and developmentally appropriate practice are always open to misinterpretation. We therefore need clearer descriptions of exactly what *is* developmentally appropriate and constructivist practice at the level of daily experiences of teachers and children. We hope this book contributes to such clarification.

Vague Characterizations of Play. Play is often characterized in early education only in global, vague ways. These correct but incomplete characterizations include the following:

1. Play is active.
2. Play involves manipulation of concrete objects.
3. Play is interesting.
4. Play is the child's work.

Consider now how these incomplete characterizations fall short of developmentally appropriate and constructivist ideals.

Play Is Active. We developmentalists are fond of insisting that children in early education must be active. This notion is grounded solidly in Piaget's theory of the development of knowledge and intelligence. It is an important starting point. However, many early childhood educators reduce the idea of action to mere physical action and assume that as long as children are moving and talking, they are learning. For Piaget, however, action is not just physical but mental. If we are satisfied with an uncritical acceptance of any physical movement as educational, then any approach that allows children to move around and talk may claim the "developmentally appropriate" label. Instead, we must be specific about the kinds of activity that lead to specific benefits. Throughout this book we present activities in terms of their specific possibilities for promoting children's development and learning.

Play Involves Manipulation of Concrete Objects. Developmentalists in early education have emphasized the importance of children's engagement with concrete objects. Some cite as rationale Piaget's work on concrete operations that are brought to bear on thought about manipulable objects. Unfortunately, this idea is often watered down to the trivial recommendation that children simply manipulate objects. However, for Piaget, it is the capacity for *mental* manipulations that is important for development. In discussing active methods in education, Piaget (1969/1970b) noted that "although the child's activity at certain levels necessarily entails the manipulation of objects and even a certain amount of actual physical groping," operations "are derived, not from the objects manipulated but from the (mental) actions of the child and their coordination" (p. 68). Dewey (1933) was even more critical of the related maxim for educators to move from concrete to abstract, from things to thought. In his view, dealing with things without thought could not possibly be educative. Piaget and Dewey inspire us to understand *how children are thinking about objects* while manipulating them and how to promote the development of thinking about them. We follow their lead throughout this book by describing materials, activities, and interventions that inspire mental activity.

Play Is Interesting. NAEYC addressed the difficulty in knowing when children are interested by amending its statement and clarifying that its endorsement of play should not have been interpreted as supporting practices simply because they are fun.

> Sometimes teachers seem to use as their primary criterion for selecting curriculum, "But the children just love it!" Enjoying the curriculum is an important but insufficient criterion for curriculum selection. Worthwhile curriculum does not have to entertain children; instead, children's enjoyment can derive from positive findings about self and meaningful learning as they realize their own progress and growing competence. (Bredekamp & Rosegrant, 1992, p. 22)

Our developmental emphasis on the importance of children's interests is also well grounded in the work of Piaget and Dewey. Piaget (1954/1981, 1969/1970b) referred to the element of interest as the "fuel" for the constructive process. However, interest may be fleeting and shallow. Dewey (1913/1975) criticized "a false identification of interest and play with trivial amusement" and contrasted this with interest as "whole-hearted identification with what one is doing" (p. 80). If children are not interested, they do not think very deeply.

We extrapolate from Piaget and Dewey the idea that *children's purposes* must be engaged if an activity is to contribute to development and learning. Piaget indicated that the challenge is to identify content that intrigues children and arouses in them a need and desire to figure something out. He wrote sympathetically of the challenge facing teachers who want to appeal to children's interests and purposes when he said, "There is nothing more difficult for the adult than to know how to appeal to the spontaneous and real activity of the child or adolescent" (Piaget, 1948/1973b, p. 105). According to Piaget, interest is central to spontaneous mental actions by which the child constructs knowledge, intelligence, and personality. Without the affective element of interest, the child would never make the constructive effort to make sense out of experience. Without interest in what is new, the child would never modify the instrument of reasoning. Interest performs a regulatory function, freeing up or stopping the investment of energy in an object, person, or event. Thus, for Piaget, methods aimed at promoting this constructive process must arouse the child's spontaneous interest that is inherent in purposeful activity. We must not forget that such interest is not mere entertainment. It is expressed as seriousness of purpose and perseverance.

Constructivist teachers thus encourage the development of children's interests and values through fostering their purposes in activities. In this book, we try to show how to appeal to children's interests and purposes.

Play Is the Child's Work. "Work" is often associated with academics—serious business having nothing to do with play. Some teachers who believe their approach is developmentally appropriate emphasize play to the exclusion of work, justifying it by stating that play is the child's work. This kind of apology for play fails to communicate the value of a play-oriented curriculum for children's learning and development.

Developmentally appropriate practice was originally conceptualized by NAEYC as a reaction to inappropriate programs of work emphasizing "teacher-directed instruction in narrowly defined academic skills" (Bredekamp, 1987, p. iv). One result of this movement away from narrow academic skills was that many people then interpreted developmentally appropriate practice as unstructured free play having little to do with academics such as reading, writing, and arithmetic. In my opinion, the exclusion of work from early childhood curriculum was unfortunate. It is useful on this point to consider how the relation between play and work was addressed by Piaget, Dewey, and Vygotsky—authors cited as inspirations for developmentally appropriate early education.

Piaget saw the capacity to work not as something opposed to play or having to be imposed on the child by adult instruction, but as something developing out of the play interest. That is, he saw symbolic play becoming more and more reflective of reality, developing "in the direction of constructive activity or work" (1945/1962, p. 112). For example, a child who pretends that a piece of wood is a boat may later really make a boat replica. Addressing the educational issue directly, Piaget wrote:

> In the course of its own internal development, the play of small children is gradually transformed into adapted constructions requiring an ever-increasing amount

of what is in effect work, to such an extent that in the infant classes [for children ages 3 to 7 years] of an active school every kind of spontaneous transition may be observed between play and work. (1969/1970b, p. 157)

Note that in this view exploration and experimentation aimed at finding out something new are not considered to be play. Some of what is called "play" might be considered "work" in that it is not always pleasurable and may require intense effort and involve initial failure.

As Dewey pointed out, young children do not divide activities into utilitarian "work" and "play." Rather, "whatever appeals to them at all appeals directly on its own account" (1933, p. 215). Dewey commented:

From a very early age, however, there is no distinction of exclusive periods of play activity and work activity, but only one of emphasis. There are definite results which even young children desire, and try to bring to pass. (1916/1966, p. 239)

Vygotsky (1933/1966) viewed play as fantasy that provides "a means of developing abstract thought" (p. 17) and as "the leading source of development in preschool years" (p. 6). He saw in fantasy play the use of implicit rules in acting out roles and, like Piaget, saw value in wish fulfillment and deferred gratification. Also like Piaget, Vygotsky saw the school-age child as moving from fantasy play to games with rules. Vygotsky emphasized the importance of fantasy play for children's practice of self-regulation skills. (See also Bodrova & Leong, 1996.)

In light of these ideas, it is not really accurate to say that play is the child's work. Evolution in forms of play reflects developmental advances that should be valued. Play is useful to children as they try to understand the world in which they live. Piaget, Dewey, and Vygotsky not only provide educators with a strong rationale for the value of play as well as work in early education, but also lead us to appreciate how work can evolve from play. This work is interesting to the "workers," engages them in reflecting on meaning, brings consciousness of purpose, leads to a search for means of realization, and moves toward coherence in thought. Thus we should expect to see all kinds of play and work in children's activities in developmentally appropriate and constructivist classrooms.

CONCLUSION

My colleagues and I approach the task of elaborating constructivist teaching by considering it in relation to three other interpretations of developmentally appropriate early childhood curriculum. Chapter 1 describes four types of classrooms reflecting these different interpretations. In Classroom Types A and B, the emphasis is on academics. In Classroom Type A, play is peripheral to academic work and learning. In Classroom Type B, play is disguised academic exercises. In contrast, Classroom Types C and D share the goal of development. In Classroom Type C, play is integrated with social and emotional developmental goals. In Classroom Type D, play is integrated more broadly with social, emotional, moral, and intellectual developmental goals. Our principal aim for the book is to show how to transform the activities in the Type C classroom into the constructivist activities of the fourth type. In doing so, we hope our principles and examples will serve as guides to the creative work that reflective teachers must do to provide constructivist early education for young children.

Chapter 2 addresses the question "What is constructivist education?" by offering a definition and eight general principles of teaching. Chapter 3 takes up the issue of assessing and documenting learning in constructivist classrooms.

Early in this introduction to Part I, I said that wide misunderstanding of the nature of constructive and educational play could lead to the demise of constructivist and developmentally appropriate early education. I fear that if educators do not provide play-oriented curriculum that clearly leads to development and learning, those responsible for administering schools will turn away from developmentally appropriate and constructivist education, and the pendulum will swing back to traditional behaviorist approaches. We must conceptualize and describe what kinds of play/activities contribute to children's development and knowledge and how they do so. General justifications are not enough. It is up to developmental educators and researchers to present clear rationales for educational play/activity, and to be specific about the differences between generalized play and play that contributes to development.

Chapter I

Play in the Early Education Curriculum: Four Interpretations

Rheta DeVries

Over the course of observing many preschool and kindergarten classrooms, I have been struck by the wildly diverging range of practices flying the flag of developmentally appropriate practice (DAP) or constructivist education. With the widespread acceptance of DAP as the definition of the best early education, the advocacy of a play-oriented curriculum has become "politically correct." Yet many teachers do not really understand or accept the developmentally appropriate approach with its emphasis on play. Consequently, teachers assimilate the politically correct notions into their own beliefs and understandings. The problem, as I see it, is that teachers often interpret the idea of play-oriented curriculum in different ways and express these interpretations in a wide variety of often contradictory classroom practices—all of which they label "play-oriented curriculum," even though they often depart in significant ways from DAP. The result is agreement at the level of rhetoric but disagreement at the practical level of children's experiences in classrooms. It is with a desire to foster more focused dialogue on what is desirable for children to experience in high-quality early education that we write this book.

As an aid to reflection, I present four types of classrooms that show four different interpretations of how to incorporate play into the curriculum:

Classroom Type A: Play is peripheral to learning and academic work.
Classroom Type B: Play is disguised academic work.
Classroom Type C: Play is integrated with social and emotional development.
Classroom Type D: Play and work are integrated with social, emotional, moral, and intellectual development.

While the following descriptions of these types are based on numerous classroom observations, the types are composites and not descriptions of any single, particular classroom. One finds many classrooms that are pure examples of each type, but it is perhaps more common to find classrooms that are mixtures of types. Although I try to characterize the classroom type as a whole, I focus on how center time is implemented. At center time, many different activities are simultaneously available to children. Descriptions of the four types deal with materials and activities and the teacher's role in promoting reasoning. In addition, I include a commentary on each from my constructivist perspective in which I show how the Type A, B, and C goals may be realized by transforming activities into alternative Type D activities. Table 1.1 summarizes the differences among classroom types in terms of goals, teacher's role, and materials and activities.

CLASSROOM TYPES A AND B:
EMPHASIS ON ACADEMICS

In Classroom Types A and B, the emphasis is on academics. These types are rooted in the history of elementary education where the mainly academic goals focus on the acquisition of correct subject matter knowledge. This tra-

TABLE 1.1. Four interpretations of play in the early education curriculum.

Classroom Type	Primary Goals	Teacher's Role	Materials & Play Activities
A: Play is peripheral to learning academic work	Academic	Authoritarian	Limited; reward for academic work
B: Play is disguised academic work	Academic	Disengaged	Mostly shallow; trivial arts and crafts
C: Play is integrated with social and emotional development	Social and emotional development	Noninterventionist; warm and nurturing; sometimes mildly authoritarian	Abundant; often below children's capabilities
D: Play and work are integrated with social, emotional, moral, and intellectual development	Development and reasoning – social, emotional, moral, and intellectual	Interventionist; warm and nurturing; democratic	Abundant; challenging

ditional approach reflects a behaviorist view of knowledge and learning as resulting from the direct transmission of information coming from outside the individual to the inside through the senses.

Classroom Type A: Play Is Peripheral to Learning and Academic Work

In Classroom Type A, the emphasis on academic work leaves little room for play, and play is not integrated with academics. Type A teachers either do not have a developmental perspective or they are required by administrative policy to teach in a behaviorist way, with a focus on drill and practice, reward and punishment. In fact, Teacher A's school district usually emphasizes performance on standardized tests as the only acceptable evidence of children's achievement, and there seems to be little choice about how to teach.

Materials and Activities. Children in Type A classrooms spend almost the entire day in a steady stream of academic work, leaving the classroom to go to physical education, art, music, or library. For example, one might observe children being drilled on the color names of paper circles, time on a clock face, the number of cents in pictured coins, or letter sounds. They might recite the days of the week and the months of the year. They do a lot of worksheets on letter sounds and addition algorithms as they sit at their desks. In one Type A classroom, when children lined up to go to the bathroom, the teacher held a letter card for the child at the head of the line to identify. If correct, the child went down the hall to the bathroom. If incorrect, the child went to the end of the line. Art activities are teacher-directed, sequenced lessons that instruct children on how to create identical products such as rabbits with cotton tails. The result is an atmosphere in which children produce products such as worksheets and crafts that depend on teacher direction.

Center time is reserved for the last 20 or 30 minutes of the day as a reward to children who have finished their work. During this period these children may play with available materials:

1. They build with blocks.
2. They play with toy cars and trucks.
3. They dress dolls and engage in pretend play.

Lesson plans in Type A classrooms typically label this as "self-selected free play," and these are not considered educational activities. Limited materials offer children few choices. Inadequate resources in both materials and time often result in an unfriendly and destructive competitive attitude among the children who vie for the opportunity to play with scarce materials.

The Teacher's Role. The teacher's relation to children is generally authoritarian in Type A classrooms. The teacher is the boss, makes all the rules, and expects children to be submissive. For example, in one lesson on *s*, when a child said "Ssss" when not asked to do so, the teacher said, "How many times do I have to tell you not to talk unless I tell you to?" After intense work on *s*, children were told to get out their pencils. This signal of a transition led them to stretch and whisper a bit. The teacher then began counting menacingly, "1, 2, 3, 4, 5," and immediate quiet ensued.

The teacher's involvement with the children during free play time is limited to monitoring children's behavior and disciplining children in conflicts by forcing them to leave their play and sit at their desks.

Commentary from a Constructivist Perspective. Several years ago, a teacher new to our constructivist program observed that the difference between what we were doing and what she saw in most classrooms was that we did not have free play. She commented that *free play* in early education meant that the teacher is free from teaching responsibility while children are free from adult interference to do what they want. Wien (1995) found such teachers in her study who understood developmentally appropriate practice to mean that child choice belongs only to free play, reflecting a view of practice as "deeply split into two compartments or conflicting spheres held in tandem as separate frameworks for conducting practice" (p. 106). The teachers in Type A classrooms seem to take this view. They view play and academics as two entirely different sorts of activities and see no role for themselves in children's play. Play is barely acknowledged as having any place in school, and is considered useful only to give children a break from work and to motivate them to get work done. It is notable that the centers in this type of classroom are usually crowded against the walls in the least space possible, with most classroom space taken up by individual desks and chairs. Play is truly peripheral in Type A classrooms—literally and figuratively.

While children may have some choice of activities during free play in Type A classrooms, they do not have enough time to develop and pursue in depth the complex problems that can arise when children go beyond superficial use of materials into enriched exploration and experimentation. Such investigations are not facilitated by the Type A teacher who provides no materials that lend themselves to experimentation and who takes no interest in what the children are doing unless conflict or misbehavior occurs. Teacher

Type A's understanding of the teacher's role in children's play is that a responsible teacher must monitor and control children's behavior.

Unfortunately, too many teachers (or their administrators), especially in early primary grades, believe that a period of free play after academic work is an acceptable compromise between academics and developmentally appropriate practice. Such a compromise distorts the idea of play-oriented developmentally appropriate education.

The problem with play and work in Type A classrooms is not so much a problem with objectives as with how to promote the objectives. Constructivist teachers take many of the same aims but approach them in different ways. For example, to learn about coin values, children in a Type D classroom might play a Piggy Bank card game (see Kamii, 2000, pp. 180–181; Kamii & DeVries, 1980, p. 55) in which children use cards with pictures of one, two, three, four, or five pennies, or a nickel to figure out which combinations make 5 cents. In this game, children do a lot more reasoning and spend much more time actively thinking about coin values than in teacher-directed drills. Math games and discussion of math problems arising from everyday life are more powerful ways of teaching number and arithmetic than drills and worksheets (see Kamii, 1982, 1989, 1994, 2000). Color names are more easily learned in the context of conversation during art and other activities where children are more personally invested in working with colors. Letter sounds are more solidly learned as children listen to books and discuss the words in the stories as well as names of children in the class.

In addition, considerable research has shown that when children are rewarded for doing something, they devalue it and lose any interest they might have had in it (see review in Kohn, 1993). The use of play as a reward for completing academic work thus defeats a teacher's (or parent's) hope of motivating children to learn academics.

From a constructivist perspective, a major shortcoming of Type A classrooms is that children do not have adequate opportunities to interact with each other or to engage their reasoning in activities in which they want to figure out how to do something. We do not see a community where children engage with others to pursue meaningful purposes. The children are clearly acting in terms of the teacher's interests, not their own. Coercion keeps children at what Dewey (1913/1975) might call "uneducative and miseducative" tasks that "deaden and stupify" (p. 55).

Classroom Type B: Play Is Disguised Academic Exercises

In Classroom Type B, children also work on academics, but these are disguised by the use of colorful materials intended to appeal to children's interests. Instead of using worksheets, the teacher offers workbook content in a format that allows children to be more active. This format is more appropriate for young children than the academics in Classroom Type A. However, while the teacher thinks of these activities as play, children do not share this view.

Materials and Activities. Children in Type B kindergarten classrooms may spend some time in large group activities such as listening to stories and watching informational videos on topics such as farm animals (also found in classroom Types C and D). In contrast to center time in Type A classrooms, their center time activities are integrated with academic goals. Children typically do not have free choice but are assigned and follow some kind of daily or weekly rotation through the following types of centers:

CLASSIFICATION/MATH

- They match paper cutouts of flowers and flowerpots by putting together those of the same color.
- They count the number of watermelon seeds drawn on one watermelon-shaped card to match the numeral on another watermelon-shaped card.
- They put cutout, numbered bees in numerical order.
- They make graphs of the numbers of pink, yellow, and blue cutout flowers placed on a table by the teacher.

LITERACY

- They match the halves of paper butterflies, one half with an uppercase letter and the other with its lowercase equivalent.
- They cut out the four sections of a sheet of paper with schematic drawings of a story and put them in an arbitrary, predetermined order.

FINE MOTOR SKILLS/ART

- They cut out petals outlined by the teacher on construction paper for precut flower stems.
- They glue tufts of tissue paper flowers on precut, construction paper trees.
- They paint at an easel where the teacher has outlined on the paper a large butterfly shape.

Children are allowed to use the woodworking, colored rice, manipulatives, puppet theater, or housekeeping centers only in the beginning of the year when the teacher feels children need a transition into work.

The Teacher's Role. The teacher intervenes little except to instruct children on how to do the activities and usually remains rather disengaged. She or he mainly observes as children obediently do assigned tasks, and checks their work from time to time to correct errors. After about 30 minutes, the teacher sings a clean-up song, and children put materials away in order to go to a "special" class (physical education, music, art, or library) outside the classroom.

Commentary from a Constructivist Perspective. Teacher Type B, like Teacher Type A, places priority on academics as the goal. However, in an attempt to introduce an element of play, the teacher sugarcoats academic exercises with cute materials presumed to appeal to children. The problem with Type B activities is not with providing appealing materials—which teacher Types C and D also do. The problem is that the appeal is superficial when the materials disguise a basically uninteresting exercise. Such an activity does not inspire children's real interest in their own purposes. They are doing the activity only because the teacher wants them to. When focused on producing right answers and specified products in these tasks, children in Type B classrooms know that they are not playing. Often, such tasks unnecessarily make something dull out of content that children would in more authentic contexts find extremely interesting. Dewey (1913/1975) criticized efforts to "make things interesting" when he stated that "it reduces method in instruction to more or less external and artificial devices for dressing up the unrelated materials, so that they will get some hold on attention" (p. 23). Dewey argued for a more authentic approach in which the child sees the connection of new material to what the child already values.

In one instance in a Type B classroom, a teacher was perplexed when she reported, "Children complained that they didn't have anything to do!" The teacher seemed to be asking, "Weren't the children active? Weren't they engaged in hands-on activities? Hadn't I provided thematic centers as recommended by early childhood educators?" It seems that the thinly disguised work did not fool children into thinking that what they were doing was meaningful. From their point of view, it was not play. It is no wonder that the children in Classroom B feel they have nothing to do! What they mean is that they don't have anything they *want* to do. Csikszentmihalyi (1975) comments on the striking phenomenon of children—and adults— who "complain that 'there is nothing to do' when they are surrounded by innumerable stimuli" (p. 204). He accounts for this in terms of deprivation of the kinds of activities that so capture complete absorption that the sense of time is lost.

In Type B classrooms, children are able to move around more than in Type A classrooms. However, they do not choose but are assigned to activities. Research by Apple and King (1977) shows that if the teacher requires children to engage in an activity, children tend to think of it as work and undesirable, even when the content is something they would enjoy if freely chosen. Fein and Wiltz (in press; also Gupton & Cooney, 1997) point out that it is important to consider children's perceptions of whether an activity is play or not. As noted by Jackson (1968), King (1979), and Wing (1995), children are not fooled by work presented by teachers as play.

"Play" in Classroom Type B is mainly a combination of trivial arts and crafts and thinly disguised work (or rather, as Dewey would probably say, "labor") that requires little thought. Especially in light of the fact that children are required to do them, these would be better characterized as "tasks" that children do to oblige the adult rather than "activities" that children do out of their own interests and purposes. Cutting out petals for the flower stem is "busy work" in the sense that no challenge is involved and no apparent use is to be made of these materials later. While gluing tissue paper requires a certain technique of twisting the eraser end of a pencil to create tufts, this also seems to present no challenge. Sequencing the drawings is arbitrary when the "correct" sequence is not the only one a child might imagine. The matching (colors and letters) and counting and ordering (numerals) tasks might be termed "tests" in the sense that the teacher wants to know if the child knows the answers. Or perhaps the teacher thinks of these as "practice." However, in these tasks one cannot practice what one does not already know, and if one knows it, practice is not necessary. How much more effective it is, for example, to teach number by engaging children in a game of High Card (commonly known as War; Kamii, 2000, p. 154) in which they not only think about numerical seriation but reason to compare the relative values of numbers. Art, story reading, personal writing, and group games provide more effective contexts in which children may construct knowledge of colors, number, and written language.

The value of graphing cutout flowers in the Type B classroom is attenuated by the teacher's arbitrary decision about what children are to graph and by the lack of genuine need or purpose for the graphs. How much more effective it is in a Type D kindergarten where children create a graph of magnetic name cards every morning to indicate lunch choices. The useful result is the daily attendance and lunch count.

In Classroom Type B, children are fed mainly a diet of trivia and busy work that neither appeals to their personal interests and purposes nor challenges them to figure out how to do something. "Stultifying tasks" might also describe many of children's activities in this classroom. They have little more opportunity than do children in Type A classrooms to interact with other children or to engage in meaningful, purposeful activities that promote reasoning. While coercion may be more masked than in classroom Type A, children still feel its presence and experience little autonomy.

CLASSROOM TYPES C AND D:
EMPHASIS ON DEVELOPMENT

In contrast to the focus on academics in Classroom Types A and B, Classroom Types C and D share the goal of development. These have their roots in the early history of American early education (what I call the "child development tradition") when the fundamental concern was to facilitate the play and social interaction of the child in a way that would promote ego strength or positive mental health. Curriculum stressed self-selected, self-directed activities in centers of interest (such as housekeeping, blocks, sand, water, art, books, puzzles, science, and woodworking). According to Spodek (1977), the teacher's role up until the early 1960s was noninterventionist:

> The noninterventionist view held that the teacher's role was to provide a stimulating, attractive environment in which young children could play. The teacher would then step aside and let children play without adult interference. The teacher was supposed to support development, not intervene in the processes. (p. 7)

Concerns with promoting the school success of disadvantaged children in the 1960s and 1970s led to a new stress on cognitive and linguistic competencies. However, when trying to facilitate children's learning and intellectual development, child development teachers often reflected behaviorist theory and practices without realizing this contradiction with their emotional and social theory and practices. An appreciation of Jean Piaget's research and developmental theory led to efforts to change the child development approach, especially in its cognitive aspects, in order to bring it more in line with this new perspective.

Classroom Type C: Play Is Integrated with Social and Emotional Developmental Goals

In Type C classrooms, teachers view play as mainly intended for social and emotional development, and work is deemphasized if included at all. What is described here for Classroom Type C is a watered-down version of a child development approach. Play in these classrooms fits the general image of what a developmentally appropriate classroom should look like. Many early childhood teachers have progressed to this level in their ability to foster children's development through play.

Materials and Activities. Children in Type C kindergarten classrooms can choose to play alone or together and move freely among the following kinds of center activities:

SENSORY EXPERIENCES

- They pat and roll pink playdough.
- They smell small jars containing pieces of lemon, onion, and other things, to learn that the nose is to smell with.
- Using funnels, they pour water into different containers, then empty them; then wash dolls.

LITERACY

- They look at books in the library area.
- They listen to stories read by the teacher or on audiotape, write or draw stories, and dictate stories to an adult.
- They write however they wish at the writing table.

CONSTRUCTION

- They build structures with blocks.
- They build with Legos.

PRETEND PLAY

- They wear dress-up clothes and pretend to cook and eat dinner and feed the baby in the housekeeping center.

ART

- They paint at the easel.

COOKING

- They help the teacher make muffins by pouring ingredients as the teacher directs. Each child who is observing gets a chance to stir. They help to fill the muffin cups and go with the teacher to put them in the oven.

CLASSIFICATION

- They sort plastic bears by color.

SCIENCE

- They watch steam from a kettle, to learn that water evaporates into the air.

- They watch as the flame of a candle is extinguished when a glass is placed over the candle, to learn that fire needs air to burn.

Like children in Classroom Types A and B, children leave the classroom to go to "special" classes for physical education, library, art, and computers.

The Teacher's Role. Teachers in Type C classrooms vary widely on the degree to which they take a controlling role in relation to children. Many are warm and nurturing, but many are sometimes arbitrarily controlling (and thus at least mildly authoritarian). They provide many of the types of activities recommended as developmentally appropriate, but the teacher's role at center time is limited to that of observer, director, materials manager, and order keeper. Frequently, teachers more or less leave children to play by themselves until a problem arises. Except for the occasional reprimand, Teacher Type C is usually relaxed and pleasant with children, although in some Type C classrooms the teacher may sometimes be emotionally disengaged. The teacher spends center time observing, directing the cooking activity, and reminding children to put materials away when they are finished. Posted rules are made by the teacher and given to children. When conflict over the use of objects occurs, a typical response is, "If you can't share nicely, I'll put it up and nobody can play with it." Children are exhorted to share.

Commentary from a Constructivist Perspective. Children in Type C classrooms undoubtedly gain a great deal from many of their activities. In fact, Teacher Type C has moved far beyond Types A and B in providing developmentally appropriate activities for children. An approach emphasizing social and emotional aspects of play may be a necessary step on the way to implementing play in more comprehensive ways. Yet many Type C teachers often hear people criticize their programs as "just play." How can Type C teachers improve the value of play and integrate work in their programs? Our purpose in this book is to show how educators can improve the value of these classroom activities and, by doing so, address the concerns of critics who see little value in the play they observe in Type C classrooms.

Whether an activity is Type C or Type D depends on the ways in which children are able to engage in it. In assessing the value of an activity for children's development and learning, the teacher must consider the developmental levels of children. Some of the activities (such as playdough) described in Classroom Type C are high in value for 2-, 3-, and even some 4-year-olds but are not sufficiently challenging to hold the interest of older or more advanced children. Some activities (such as pretend play, blocks, writing, and book reading) are appropriate and beneficial for both younger and older children because the materials lend themselves to use at a range of developmental levels. No matter what else children experience in a classroom, these activities, given adequate time, are rich in developmental possibilities that are not limited to social and emotional benefits.

While the activities in Type C classrooms do promote child choice and engage to some extent children's interests and purposes, many are below children's capabilities. They fail to challenge children to figure out solutions to new problems and develop new ways of thinking. Many of the activities underestimate what children could do with more challenging or complex materials and situations. For example, most 5-year-olds who have been in preschool are old hands at playdough, and it offers few new possibilities. Mixing playdough for younger children to use might confront children with the need to think about the relative effects of adding more flour and more water. However, this also may be too simple for older children unless they are given a recipe with pictures to "read" and are encouraged to experiment, perhaps even to develop their own recipes. Challenges may also be created by introducing many different modeling materials and implements. Children can work to create particular effects, experiment with different kinds of modeling substances, study sculptures made by artists, and collaborate with others on projects such as making a sculpture museum. Similarly, water play can be dramatically transformed into more challenging investigation and experimentation with the provision of materials and interventions that encourage children to figure out how to create new effects with water (see the description for Classroom Type D below).

Pretend play is valuable for children's construction of representations and their further development of symbolic thought and reasoning. It can be expanded and enriched by engaging children in deciding whether they want to change their house center to another pretend context—flower shop, restaurant, grocery store—then in preparing the materials they will need and discussing how to use them. Such pretend centers can provide opportunities for writing the names of flowers, prices, and menus, for calculating bills and using number to figure out how to make change with pretend money, and for organizing their respective roles; the children thus exercise and develop literacy, numeracy, representational ability, and symbolic thought.

Cooking can be turned over to children by providing recipe books illustrated to aid reading (see Kamii & DeVries, 1978/1993; Chapter 6 in this book), and by supporting children's autonomy and cooperation as they take turns and work together in pairs to make snacks for the class. This experience is far more educational than observing the teacher do most of the food preparation.

Sorting plastic bears is another example of disguised, purposeless work (except when a child invents the idea of sorting on his or her own). Many teachers think they are teaching classification through such sorting activities; however, this kind of sorting involves simple groupings of subclasses and does not require thinking about relations between superordinate and subordinate classes, the hallmark of classification. Piaget (Piaget & Szeminska, 1941/1952) defined classification as a system of inclusions and discussed the development of the logic of classification as hierarchical inclusion of subordinate classes in a superordinate class. For example, the class of "flowers" may be composed of "roses" and "tulips." If there are more roses than tulips, young children respond to the question, "Are there more flowers or more roses?" by saying there are more roses than flowers. This indicates the inability to think about the roses as both a separate class and a part of the class of flowers.

While most kindergarten children are not yet capable of hierarchical classification of subordinate classes into a superordinate class, they can profit from the use of materials in which hierarchies can be made. With this as the long-term goal, open-ended activities to promote thinking about class relations are much better than simple sorting for the sake of sorting. For example, card games such as Making Families and Go Fish (see Kamii, 2000, pp. 146–147; Kamii & DeVries, 1980, pp. 133–142) involve classificatory reasoning that young children can do even before they are capable of the class inclusion necessary for true classification. Children must think about making sets of two, three, or four cards that are alike in some way but not identical (for example, four sheep in each of four colors, or four different animals of the same color). In such games, children are motivated by their interest to think again and again about class membership by constructing similarities and differences in the course of playing the game. Such intellectual activity is more likely to promote the construction of class relations than simple sorting for the sake of sorting. As Piaget pointed out,

> The child can certainly be interested in seriating for the sake of seriating, and classifying for the sake of classifying, etc., when the occasion presents itself. However, on the whole it is when he has events or phenomena to explain or goals to reach in an intriguing situation that operations are the most exercised. (Piaget & Garcia, 1971/1974, p. 26)

The challenge for teachers is to figure out how to select events and phenomena that will intrigue children and lead to development of reasoning.

When subject matter content is included, Type C teachers sometimes take a behaviorist approach to teaching. For example, many Type C teachers believe that children learn by absorption through their senses and by association. In the activity where children smell different objects, the assumption is that children will associate the smell with the object. This type of classroom activity is not very helpful to older preschool and kindergarten children because they already know how these objects smell. In this case, the content is too easy. Moreover, it is closed-ended and cannot go any further. In contrast, Type D constructivist teachers view sensory activities as guided and organized by the intelligence. That is, when the child actively reasons about sensory experiences, what is known comes from the organizing intelligence and not from perception alone (see Piaget, 1961/1969).

Other examples of a behaviorist approach to selecting science activities are found in the planned observations of a steaming kettle and the extinguishing of a candle. In these activities, children are expected to learn that water evaporates and that fire needs air (or oxygen) to burn. The problem with these activities is that children cannot observe the physical interactions causing these phenomena. Because they cannot understand these events, they can at best only parrot what the adult says. Most likely, the events will be regarded as incomprehensible "magic." These are examples of content that is impossible for young children to understand. From the constructivist perspective, trying to teach such subject matter not only fails to teach the content but also has a possible harmful effect: When children have to try to understand too much content that is beyond them, they may lose confidence in their abilities to learn or may "tune out" to school entirely.

Type C teachers generally underestimate children's capacity for reasoning in work and play. They seem to believe that it is enough to let children engage in activities that from a constructivist perspective fail to lead development and learning forward.

Classroom Type D: Play and Work Are Integrated with Social, Emotional, Moral, and Intellectual Development

Type D teachers represent the ideal constructivist teacher. They extend their developmental goals beyond social and emotional development to include a conscious focus on moral and intellectual development as well. Constructivist teachers expand the Type C notions about social and emotional development by conceptualizing the development of personality and the child's hierarchy of personal values as constructions the child elaborates in the course of everyday experiences (see DeVries, 1997; Piaget, 1954/1981, 1928–1964/1995). They include the specifically moral and intellectual development of children as important aims.

Materials and Activities. Type D constructivist teachers engage children in making rules to live by and some decisions about life in the classroom, ask what children want to learn about, center the curriculum around children's interests, and engage children in social and moral discussions of issues that arise in the classroom as well as issues that are found in children's literature. Compare the classrooms described above with a Type D classroom in which kindergarten children engage in both work and play activities, as listed below, according to their free choice during center time. In addition to a number of activities found in Type C classrooms such as block building and play with other construction toys, reading books, and using standard art materials that are always available, they use the following types of centers:

GROUP GAMES

- They play the classification game *Guess Who?* in which they have to conceptualize and pose yes-no questions to a partner, eliminate possibilities, respond to the other's questions, and try to guess the identity of a mystery card (similar to the game Animal, Vegetable, Mineral).
- They play the Cover Up game (see Kamii, 2000, p. 173), in which players roll a die to determine how many of the squares to fill on their 12-square card.
- They play the card game Making Families to try to figure out what card to ask for in order to make sets.

PRETEND PLAY

- They make a shoe store in the pretend play area and pretend to buy and sell shoes, write price signs and receipts, and answer the telephone.
- Using a wolf puppet and a red sweater for a hood, they cooperate to act out *Little Red Riding Hood* for other children in the library corner.

PHYSICAL KNOWLEDGE/COOKING/ART

- Two children negotiate how to follow a written and illustrated recipe to make something for the class snack.
- They experiment at the water table with a variety of transparent plastic glasses that have small, medium, and large holes drilled into sides and/or bottoms. The teacher provides a pegboard on a stand over the water table that is sitting on the floor (with its legs removed). Children can arrange cups in metal cup holders that hook into the pegboard, then observe the draining that occurs when they pour water into the cups (see Chapter 7 for pictures and further description).
- They work with strips of construction paper (plain, fringed, accordion-pleated, and so forth) to create three-dimensional sculptures on a base.

- They work with pattern blocks and tangrams, using Cuisinaire's plastic shape frames (see Sales & Sales, 1994, 1995). Once a frame is filled, it can be lifted to leave the block design on the table, and then reused to create the same shape with different blocks (see Chapter 8 for detailed discussion).
- Individual children survey the others and make graphs on something the surveyor wants to know (such as what are the favorite TV programs of the class members).

LITERACY

- They write in personal journals at the writing table, writing (or pretending to write) stories which they illustrate, or making a list of things they did over the weekend, or dictating a story for the teacher to write down.

In all activities, children engage in conflict resolution with the teacher's help or by themselves. Many of the activities extend over several days or even weeks. Like Classroom Types A, B, and C, children in a Type D classroom also go to "special" classes that include physical education, art, library, and computers.

The Teacher's Role. The teacher not only observes but also engages with children in activities, wondering aloud and posing questions to promote reasoning (for example, "I wonder why the water stays in that cup [with side hole only]" or "Do you think you can get the water to flow from one to another and then another and another?"). Sometimes he or she takes part in a game as a player alongside children. As children work with the shape frames and pattern blocks, the teacher asks questions such as "Do you think you can make that shape with other colors?" and "Could you make it all yellow? Would that work?"

Conflicts occur, and the teacher intervenes to facilitate children's resolutions and self-regulation, emphasizing that the conflict is theirs and they must figure out what to do. He or she helps children listen to each other and makes sure all agree to a resolution (see DeVries & Zan, 1994, for other principles of teaching in conflict situations). For example, during a game of Cover Up played by two 4-year-old girls and the teacher, a problem arises with regard to the order of turns. Both girls think they are next, and there is a long impasse during which the teacher refrains from settling the problem and asks again and again what they can do to solve the problem, making it clear that responsibility for a solution belongs to the children. Finally, one girl suggests they each take a die and roll them at the same time! This is what they do. Later, the teacher confided that she was astonished and pleased with their solution, one that would never have occurred to her, illustrating how children's solutions to their conflicts are often different and work better (because the children feel ownership of the solution) than what teachers might suggest. In another Type D classroom, a child complains that another called him a name. The teacher responds, "Have you told him how you feel about that? What can you say to him?" The child goes away to assert his feelings and, if not satisfied, returns to ask the teacher's help in communicating. In cases where many children want to do a new activity at the same time, the constructivist teacher introduces the idea of a sign-up list.

Recognizing that group games could, if too easy, fall into the category of mere entertainment, Teacher Type D selects games he or she expects to offer intellectual challenges, and observes to see whether, in fact, children's reasoning is challenged. If a game turns out to be too easy or too difficult, the teacher learns that it does not offer educational possibilities to children and either retires the game, modifies it, or encourages children to modify it.

The teacher promotes literacy development by integrating the need to read and write throughout many activities in print-rich classrooms. For example, each game has a set of written rules, and the teacher makes a "big deal" out of reading the rules to find out how to play the game. In the shoe store, children have opportunities to read and write. They read class rules as they illustrate them. Children have to "read" recipes in order to find out how to make snacks. Like Type C teachers, Teacher Type D reads stories aloud, encourages children to write or draw stories of their own, and takes down children's dictated stories, thus developing their appreciation for literature and writing. By having children reenact a story they know well, the teacher facilitates the consolidation of their knowledge of sequential temporal events and their knowledge of "story," an important component of literacy. The teacher encourages children to engage in a variety of writing activities so that children come to conceive of themselves as writers.

The Type D teacher promotes children's reasoning about number by providing materials involving number in group games and pretend play, and by conducting discussions of everyday issues involving number. For example, when children make the "logical error of addition" in a path game by counting as "one" the last space on which they landed on the previous move (rather than going forward on the count of "one"), the teacher provides a die with four 1s, a 2, and a 3 so that children will have many experiences of confronting the unsatisfying situation in which they count "one" and go nowhere! As they begin to have a feeling of logical contradiction in this situation, children often stumble and stutter in their count, saying, "one" (going nowhere) . . . "one" (hesitatingly moving the marker forward). At a certain point in their development, children feel something is wrong. Such a feeling of internal conflict is the beginning of a feeling of logical necessity that eventually leads to self-correction of this error. Other areas also involve reasoning about number. In making snack, for example, children must figure out how many crackers to spread if everyone is to get two. Or, if they had six balls when they went outdoors and only four when they are ready to come inside, the teacher encourages children to think how many they need to look for.

In physical-knowledge activities (see Kamii & DeVries, 1978/1993) such as water and cooking, the teacher provides opportunities for children to construct knowledge about the world of objects, making comments and asking questions to draw children's attention to its many spatial and causal problems in the hope that children will be inspired to find their own purposes as they pursue questions that interest them. In the water activity, the Type D teacher views the child not as just playing, but as making progress in constructing knowledge about the properties of water and its containers, even constructing greater intelligence with increased capability to reason. In cooking, the teacher encourages children to think about irreversible physical changes (such as what happens when flour is mixed with a liquid). They also learn about health-related issues such as the importance of cleanliness and food values. With pattern blocks and tangram frames, the teacher fosters children's construction of relations of equivalence by encouraging children to discover, for example, that two triangles can make a parallelogram.

Commentary from a Constructivist Perspective. In the course of trying to show how to transform the activities in Classroom Types A, B, and C, I have shared a lot of the Type D constructivist approach and perspective. The reader will therefore not be surprised to read that two characteristics emphasized in Type D classrooms are often missing in Type C (as well as Types A and B) classrooms. First is the conscious effort of Type D teachers to create a certain kind of sociomoral atmosphere (discussed in Chapter 2) in which the teacher respects children and takes their perspectives into account. Some—perhaps many—Type C classrooms are characterized by a positive interpersonal dynamic but do not reflect a conscious effort to cooperate with children and create a feeling of community. Second is the constructivist focused effort to facilitate children's intellectual development by microanalyzing children's thinking in activities and by providing materials and suggestions that lead children into play and work with more complex materials and situations.

Let us consider in more detail the rationales for activities provided in Type D classrooms. In *Guess Who?* and Making Families games, children have the opportunity to use classificatory reasoning to think about classes and their relations. In Making Families, the problem is a matter of thinking of the superordinate category of sheep with its subordinate subclasses of colors. The child has to think of one subclass (such as the red sheep) that is missing from his or her hand (and thus not observable at that moment). In *Guess Who?* the problem is even more complicated and challenging for 4- and 5-year-olds because of the difficulty of turning affirmations into negations. Piaget (1974/1980) showed that negations are especially difficult. For example, if the partner says yes to the question "Does your person wear glasses?" it is necessary to turn the affirmation into a negation and think, "I have to push this face down because this one does *not* wear glasses," and to perform the action of negating or eliminating the faces *without* glasses. A common error is for the child to hear "yes" and turn down all the faces wearing glasses, a failure to think of the opposite of wearing glasses. In this game, children are motivated to use more mobile thinking in order to master this "mind twister."

The less challenging game of Cover Up offers no opportunity for strategy, but children who have had little experience with games can become committed to the reciprocity of turn taking and think about number. Continued assessment of one's standing in the game can involve thinking about the number of spaces yet to be filled, comparing the number filled on one's own card with that of the opponent, and thinking what would be the ideal number to roll on the next turn.

Art frequently provides opportunities to construct knowledge about the properties of objects as well as opportunities for reasoning. For example, creating paper sculptures presents children with the problem of how best to attach the end of a paper strip firmly to the base (with paste, glue, staples) and with the spatial problems in arranging strips in relation to each other. In the case of illustrating the pages in their class rule book, children have the opportunity to take further their ownership of the rules they made to regulate their relationships in the classroom, thus promoting moral development of a system of values.

Making graphs involves solving the logico-mathematical problem of the unit of measurement (for example, using a cube or inch-square on a paper to represent each child) and offers children the opportunity to take a scientific approach to finding answers to their own questions.

All these self-chosen activities offer children in Type D constructivist classrooms the opportunity to exercise autonomy as they pursue their interests, create their own purposes, and pursue intriguing questions raised by themselves or the teacher, as well as the opportunity to exercise reasoning to figure out how to accomplish various personal goals. In all interactions with children the Type D teacher shows respect to them and cooperates with them, minimizing the exercise of unnecessary coercion (for discussion of how the teacher accomplishes this, see DeVries & Zan, 1994; Chapter 2 in this book).

The constructivist Type D teacher also includes academic goals in planning activities, but these are embedded in the context of play and work in which children find personal interest and value. Play merges into work as children develop a seriousness of purpose and desire to create high-quality work characteristic of older children and adults whom they admire.

CONCLUSION

The National Association for the Education of Young Children has taken a courageous stand in support of developmentally appropriate practice as the standard in early education from birth through third grade. The NAEYC position statements advocating a play-oriented approach have had enormous influence, especially in communicating the inappropriateness of "teacher-directed instruction in narrowly defined academic skills" (Bredekamp, 1987, p. iv). NAEYC's descriptions of appropriate practices have gone a long way toward creating an attitude of acceptance of these practices among preschool and elementary administrators and teachers. Unfortunately, however, research on teachers' implementation of DAP (for example, Cole, 1996) reveals a lack of consensus about its practical implementation. This may be due, in part, to the fact that while the position statements attempt to give examples of DAP, they are limited in their description of specific practices. Thus the reader is left to interpret (and misinterpret) how general ideas are reflected in practices.

My descriptions of how play-oriented curriculum is actually implemented in four classrooms dramatize the vastly different experiences offered to children under the DAP flag. In Classroom Type A, play is viewed as peripheral to learning and academic work, and Type A teachers seem to believe that a short period of free play after a day of academic work is an acceptable compromise between academics and DAP. In Classroom Type B, what is called play is really academic exercises disguised with colorful materials, and what is really trivial busy work is thought to be a way of meeting DAP guidelines. In contrast to Classroom Types A and B where academics are the goals, Classroom Types C and D take development as their goal. The Type C classroom offers what is usually thought of as DAP, a program where social and emotional goals are integrated in center-based play that is a mixture of activities rich in developmental possibilities and activities with little intellectual challenge. Type D constructivist classrooms go beyond Type C classrooms by adding challenging intellectual and moral goals in both play and work.

It is important to recognize that developmentally appropriate practice is being misunderstood by some educators to include the notions of play as peripheral to learning and as disguised work. It is more difficult and, in my view, more crucial to recognize that developmentally appropriate and constructivist education are being misunderstood by many educators to be what Piaget (1948/1973b) called "generalized play without much educational benefit" (pp. 6–7). Many of the current definitions of play, such as intrinsic motivation and freely chosen activity, distinguish the differences between Classroom Type B, on the one hand, and Classroom Types C and D, on the other. However, these definitions do not distinguish between Classroom Types C and D.

To identify an activity as "play" does not automatically mean that it is constructive or educational. Play can be at a low level, without much value (for example, when children play a game that is too easy and holds no new intellectual or social challenges). "Constructive" or "transformational" play is justified by the contribution it makes to some aspect of the child's development and learning. While constructive or transformational play can occur without the teacher, the teacher can enhance the value of an activity through insightful interventions that extend children's interest, exploration, and experimentation by helping children see new possibilities in what they are doing. To know whether an experience is educational, we must assess the child's purpose, interest, and engagement; the worthwhileness of the content; and the value for the child's development and learning.

The examples of activities in Type D classrooms provide a glimpse of what teachers do in constructivist classrooms. In Chapter 2, constructivist education is defined in more detail, with principles of teaching and examples.

Chapter 2

What Is Constructivist Education?
Definition and Principles of Teaching

Rheta DeVries, Rebecca Edmiaston, Betty Zan,
and Carolyn Hildebrandt

Constructivist education takes its name from Piaget's research showing that children actively interpret their experiences in the physical and social worlds and thus construct their own knowledge, intelligence, and morality. We know that children construct knowledge because they have so many ideas that are never taught to them. For example, when 5-year-olds were making their own bubble wands, one child made a U-shaped wand and was puzzled when it did not work. Other children made triangular and square-shaped wands. It was clear that they expected to see triangular and square bubbles! The day after one child failed to make a square bubble, he excitedly proclaimed to the teacher, "I know how to make a square bubble! I was thinking about it all night, and what you've got to do is blow each corner real fast!" When he tried this, he concluded, unconvinced, "I just have round breath today." These ideas were created by the children themselves, and even though wrong, they were ingenious efforts to explore the world of bubbles and construct their knowledge.

According to DeVries and Zan (1994), the best ways to promote children's construction of knowledge are to

1. Engage their interest
2. Inspire active experimentation with all its necessary groping and error
3. Foster cooperation between adults and children and among children themselves

This definition of constructivist education can be summarized in three words: interest, experimentation, and cooperation. These characteristics are embedded in the general principles of teaching discussed below.

GENERAL PRINCIPLES OF TEACHING

Teachers moving to Type D constructivist teaching inevitably reconsider their own role in the classroom. The questions they ask are "What do I say?" and "What do I do?" This chapter is an attempt to respond to these concerns. One common misconception of the teacher's role in constructivist education is that the teacher is simply an observer who passively watches children construct knowledge (see DeVries & Edmiaston, 1999, for discussion of misconceptions about constructivist education). Teachers who have been mainly observers of children's play must shift into a more active role. Teachers who have been accustomed to teaching by telling and by directing children's work must shift from seeing themselves as central in producing learning to seeing the child as central. Yet at the same time, they must see themselves as playing a crucial role in promoting children's learning and development. We offer seven general principles of teaching that relate to the definition of constructivist education given above.

1. Establish a Cooperative Sociomoral Atmosphere

The first principle of constructivist education is to create a cooperative sociomoral atmosphere in which mutual respect is continually practiced. All other principles rest on this first principle. By *sociomoral atmosphere*, we refer to the entire network of interpersonal relations in a classroom. These pervade every aspect of the child's experience in school and profoundly influence social, moral, intellectual, personality, and emotional development. Every classroom has a sociomoral atmosphere that may be viewed along a continuum from coercion to cooperation. While it is not possible to present a detailed discussion of the sociomoral atmosphere in constructivist education here (see DeVries & Zan, 1994, 1995), we want to engage the reader in considering briefly the rationale drawn from Piaget's work.

Piaget (1932/1965) distinguished two types of morality corresponding to two types of adult-child relationships, one that retards children's development and one that promotes it. The first type of morality is a morality of obedience. Piaget called this "heteronomous" morality. The individual who is heteronomously moral follows moral rules given by others out of obedience to an authority who has coercive power. Heteronomous morality is conformity to external rules that are simply accepted and followed without question.

The second type of morality is "autonomous." The individual who is autonomously moral follows moral rules that are self-constructed, self-regulating principles. The individual who is autonomously moral follows internal convictions about the necessity of respect for persons in relationships with others.

Our constructivist goal for children is the development of autonomous morality, partly because without belief that rises from personal conviction children will not be likely to follow moral rules. How do adults help children construct autonomous morality? Piaget suggests the general answer in his discussion of two types of adult-child relationships that parallel the two types of morality.

The first type of adult-child relationship is one of coercion or constraint in which the adult prescribes what the child must do by giving ready-made rules and instructions for behavior. In this relation, respect is a one-way affair. That is, the child is expected to respect the adult, and the adult uses authority to socialize and instruct the child. The adult controls the child's behavior. In this sociomoral context, the child's reason for behaving is thus outside his or her own reasoning and system of personal interests and values. Piaget calls this type of relation "heteronomous." Heteronomy can range on a continuum from hostile and punitive to sugar-coated control.

While in adult-child interactions heteronomy is often appropriate and sometimes unavoidable, well-meaning teachers often feel that it is their responsibility to manage every detail of children's behavior. Unfortunately, when children are governed continually by the values, beliefs, and ideas of others, they practice a submission (if not rebellion) that can lead to mindless conformity in both moral and intellectual life. Piaget warned that coercion socializes only the surface of behavior and actually reinforces the child's tendency to rely on regulation by others. Tragically, obedience-based schools simply perpetuate qualities needed for submission. Intellectually, the heavily coerced child may react with a passive orientation to the ideas of others, an unquestioning and uncritical attitude, and low motivation to think, being satisfied instead with parroting rote-memory answers.

Piaget contrasted the heteronomous adult-child relationship with a second type that is characterized by mutual respect and cooperation. The adult returns children's respect by giving them the possibility to regulate their behavior voluntarily. Piaget argued that it is only by refraining from exercising unnecessary authority that the adult opens the way for children to develop minds capable of thinking independently and creatively and to develop moral feelings and convictions that take into account the best interests of all parties.

Mutual respect means that the constructivist teacher considers the child's point of view and encourages the child to consider others' points of view. While cooperation is a social interaction in which individuals regard themselves as equals, children and adults are obviously not equals. However, when the adult is able to respect the child as a person with a right to exercise his or her own will, one can speak about a certain psychological equality in the relationship. This is not to suggest, of course, that children have complete freedom because such freedom is inconsistent with moral relations with others.

The sociomoral atmospheres of the four classrooms described in Chapter 1 are very different. In one Type A classroom, the teacher responded to a child's answering out of turn with a reprimand, and to children's stretching and whispering during a transition with counting in a warning tone. These interactions suggest that the teacher's control is based on intimidation. Teacher Type A makes no effort to develop a spirit of cooperation or community in the classroom. She is the boss and expects children to be submissive.

In Classroom Type B, the atmosphere is a mixture of cooperation and coercion, but is weighted more toward coercion. Certainly we do not see a community where children pursue personally meaningful purposes. The effect of coercion is often hidden by the compliant surface of children's behavior. A hint about the degree to which children's compliant behavior is coerced can be seen when the teacher leaves the room. We have seen a quiet, calm atmosphere quickly dissolve to some children running around, poking and teasing others, with other children threatening to "tell the teacher."

In Classroom Type C, we see an example where the teacher sometimes takes a hands-off approach and sometimes takes a directive approach toward children. The one glimpse of reaction to conflict over an object shows the teacher solving the problem for children in a conflict situation. This unhelpful response reveals an underestimation of children's conflict resolution ability.

In Classroom Type D, the teacher succeeds in creating a sociomoral atmosphere in which children are encouraged to cooperate with one another as well as with the teacher. For example, the teacher gives children a strategy for turn taking (a sign-up list) and responds to a child having interpersonal difficulty by interpreting his complaint not as tattling but as an opportunity to help him deal with the situation himself. Teacher D minimizes the unnecessary exercise of adult authority by engaging children in making classroom rules. Teacher interventions in this classroom aim to make children reflective and autonomous. Conflict resolution, for example, is considered part of the curriculum, and considerable time, especially at the beginning of the year, is devoted to helping children develop the interpersonal understanding necessary for negotiation competence.

It goes without saying that the teacher must make the environment physically safe. When children are endangered by an aggressive peer or threatening adult, they can become preoccupied with protecting themselves. Beyond physical safety is the psychological safety that is necessary for activity that promotes growth. The teacher's respect for children is the foundation for creating the kind of safe and secure environment in which children can relax and pursue their intellectual and social interests. Part of creating the socio-moral atmosphere is to develop with children a feeling of community in which rules made by children reflect the ideal of treating people with care.

2. Appeal to Children's Interests

The importance of interest is discussed in the introduction to this book. On a practical level, the Type D constructivist teacher observes what children do spontaneously to identify interests, proposes enticing activities, solicits children's ideas about what they want to learn, and provides ample opportunities for children to make choices. These are discussed below.

Observe What Children Do Spontaneously. The most important questions of all are *children's* questions. Young children do not always express these in words, but by observing carefully, teachers can often figure out a child's question. Identifying children's questions can inform the teacher's interventions and planning. For example, when Christie Sales watched her 4-year-old children experimenting with a ramp connected to a track, she noticed that they kept trying to readjust the arrangement of their zigzagged tracks each time the marble rolled off, without much success. It was clear from their actions that their question was "How can we get the marble to roll to the end of the track?" Christie wanted to draw attention to the cause of the problem, so she asked one child to take his finger and show how the marble would go on the track. When he got to a right angle, he suddenly realized the problem and straightened out the track. He then worked with his companions to straighten out the rest of the track.

Propose Enticing Activities. Proposing enticing activities can take the form of putting out materials and suggesting purposes to children, then observing to see whether these catch and hold children's interest and become children's own purposes. It can also take the form of planning with the class by proposing possible activities and consulting children about what they prefer.

Solicit Children's Ideas about What They Want to Learn. Young children often do not know how to think about what they want to know. When this is the case, the teacher might pick up on one child's interest in ladybugs and ask what others want to know about ladybugs. Then the teacher's responsibility is to find resources (e.g., books about ladybugs, live ladybugs to observe, and so forth). Four-year-olds who are accustomed to being consulted are often able to suggest topics they want to know more about. For example, at the Grant Early Childhood Center during a shoe project the children wanted to know how shoes are made, especially how the colored words and logos were put on. Thinking that shoes were made at shoe stores, the children decided they needed to visit a shoe store to get answers to their questions. The teacher agreed and organized a class trip. The children were quite surprised to find out that shoes were not made at the store. Because their teacher respected and accepted children's ideas, they felt comfortable enough to say what they honestly thought. When this is the case, children's thinking is more observable to the teacher.

Provide Ample Opportunities for Children to Make Choices. Providing ample opportunities for children to make choices is essential to appealing to children's interests. Children should be able to choose from a variety of possibilities during activity time. The constructivist teachers we know usually include at least one special physical-knowledge activity, art activity, and group game in addition to blocks, pretend play, cooking, and writing centers. In addition, children are free to choose other art activities, games, books, other construction materials (such as Legos), and puzzles.

3. Teach in Terms of the Kind of Knowledge Involved

Piaget's distinction among three kinds of knowledge is helpful to constructivist teachers. These are physical knowledge, logico-mathematical knowledge, and arbitrary conventional knowledge. Briefly, physical knowledge is constructed when children observe the reactions of objects to their actions; for example, the baby pushes a ball and observes that it rolls. As children observe objects' reactions, they also construct logico-mathematical knowledge. For example, the baby pushes a cube and notices that it moves *differently* from the ball. The relation of "difference" exists in neither the ball nor the cube but in the mind of the knower who puts them into this relation. One can think simply of a ball and a cube without thinking of the difference relation. Such logico-mathematical relations can be said to constitute the general framework of intelligence, the entire system of relations of which the individual is capable. Therefore, physical-knowledge activities (the focus of Chapters 4–7) are not just for the purpose of learning about the physical world, but are also for the purpose of developing the intelligence. A third type of knowledge, arbitrary conventional knowledge, is knowledge that can only be gained through transmission from other people in some form. Examples of arbitrary knowledge include names of objects and concepts (for example, colors, days of the week), rules (for example, red means stop and green means go), and dates (for example, holidays or special events).

The significance of these three types of knowledge for teachers is that one teaches differently, depending on the type of knowledge. If it is arbitrary, one tells or shows children. If it is physical, one assists children in finding opportunities to act on objects and find out their reactions. ("How could we find out?" "Would you like to see if that works?") If it is logico-mathematical, one provides experiences through which children can reorganize their own knowledge. (See DeVries & Kohlberg, 1987; Kamii & DeVries, 1978/1993; Piaget, 1964, 1970a.)

As pointed out above, the children who believed in the possibility of a square or triangular bubble were not left to be satisfied with these wonderful but wrong ideas. They learned from the results of their actions on the objects that their expectations were not borne out. Children are more likely to accept negative feedback from objects than from people, without feeling put down (for example, when an object sinks rather than floats as expected). If the teacher says, "That's wrong," or "That won't work," children are more likely to be discouraged from trying out their ideas. And they will not be convinced their ideas are wrong until they try them.

When logico-mathematical knowledge is involved, the teacher has to decide whether simply to note erroneous reasoning or provide experiences in which children themselves can correct their reasoning. For example, if a child believes that a sandwich cut into four pieces is more to eat than an identical sandwich cut into two pieces, a correction might not be understood because knowledge of number depends on construction of a system of numerical relationships. If the teacher corrects this error, the child will simply be confused and may lose confidence in his or her own thinking. However, when elementary number (values below 10) is involved, the teacher may be able to provide experiences (for example, board games or card games) that lead a child to revise his or her logic and make progress toward understanding or constructing a system of number.

4. Choose Content That Challenges Children

Constructivist teachers create a culture of inquiry and evaluate curriculum content in terms of the following questions:

- Does the activity promote open inquiry? Or do I wish to *lead* my children to comprehend a specific idea?
- Is the activity appropriate to the intellectual abilities of my children? Is it too difficult, abstract, or sophisticated? Or is it too simple?
- Does the activity allow for a wide range of possible responses? Or does it lead to a single, correct answer?
- Will the activity lead to new insights and awareness? Or does the activity stay with material that is familiar and well known?
- Will the activity provoke the children's curiosity, engage their attention,

and sustain interest? Would *I* be interested in it? Or is the activity boring or of only momentary interest?

- Does the activity allow the *children* to do most of the thinking? Or is the activity teacher-centered?

Challenging content focuses on "big ideas" that allow children to go into depth in their study. In order to be challenging to children, the content, as well as the materials and activities related to the content, must be accessible to a wide range of developmental levels. It is useful to analyze activities and materials in terms of regularities and relationships children can construct. These are discussed below.

Focus Experiences on Big Ideas That Allow In-Depth Study. When planning activities, it is useful to ask, "Is this activity worth thinking about?" Does the content have substance, depth, and significance? Or is it thin, trivial, or banal? Names of colors is one example of content that is useful to know yet does not deserve special lessons devoted to its acquisition. Color names can be learned in the course of art activities and other situations where reference to color is embedded in purposeful activities. Mixing colors sometimes has value as experimentation and opportunity to discover regular effects of combinations. However, this experimentation does not usually lead to complex relationships because when more than two colors are combined, children generally do not remember what they have done and therefore cannot think about complex combinations. An example of experimentation of greater value involves working with water and plastic cups with holes of various sizes in various positions (see Chapter 7). A topic such as this can easily be expanded into more in-depth study of water flow. All the activity chapters in this book are examples of how to teach with big ideas in mind.

Provide Activities and Materials Appropriate to a Wide Range of Developmental Levels. One of the advantages of constructivist education is that its activities appeal to a range of developmental levels. This makes the approach appealing to many early childhood educators who find they have children from many different backgrounds, with many different languages, experiences, and skills. In addition, as increasing numbers of children with disabilities are included in early childhood classrooms, the expected range of developmental levels is becoming even wider. Type D teachers accommodate activities to a variety of developmental levels. For example, in a kindergarten classroom that includes children with severe disabilities, the water table includes materials for dumping and pouring as well as materials appealing to more complex purposes.

During a recent investigation of ramps in a preschool classroom, some children experimented with how fast a marble went down a board and how far it went when different numbers of blocks were used to elevate the ramp. Other children with more experiences in working with ramps were engaged in setting up an elaborate marble run structure. All the children were making discoveries about the relationships between elevation and distance traveled, but at different levels of complexity.

Analyze Activities in Terms of Regularities and Relationships Children Can Construct. From a constructivist perspective, development involves the gradual construction of simple regularities in the course of experimentation, as well as more and more complex logico-mathematical relationships. A *simple regularity* is that, under certain conditions, something always happens. For example, the child may notice that whenever an object is dropped, it falls. Or the child may observe that whenever he hits someone, the other usually objects in some way (social regularities are not as perfect as physical regularities, and social regularities may thus be more difficult to construct).

It is important for an activity to have the possibility for the child to move beyond regularities to construct more complex relationships. Examples of logico-mathematical relationships include knowing that the harder one throws a ball, the farther it goes (implying a continuum of force in relationship to a continuum of distance), and that negotiating generally has a more satisfactory outcome than hitting.

The construction of logico-mathematical relationships is important because these constitute intelligence in Piaget's theory. Thus an increase in coordination of relationships is an increase in intelligence as well as specific knowledge. In activity Chapters 4–10, we discuss the regularities and relationships children have the opportunity to construct through participating in specific activities.

5. Promote Children's Reasoning

An important part of the role of the Type D constructivist teacher is to use questions and other interventions that will move children's thinking forward. With this goal in mind, teachers should consider the purposes of questions and other interventions, questions to avoid or ask rarely, and questions and comments that inhibit children's reasoning. These are discussed below.

Purposes of Questions and Other Interventions. It is important for the Type D constructivist teacher to consider the following purposes of questions and other interventions.

To Find Out What the Child Honestly Thinks. The constructivist teacher tries to find out how children reason and what they think. For example, to begin their study of shadows, a Type D teacher asked at group time, "What is a shadow?" and "What makes a shadow?" Responses to such questions give valuable information the teacher needs to design follow-up activities. As children become accustomed to the teacher's nonjudgmental interest in their ideas, they feel more and more free to openly share them, including their wrong ideas. In contrast, when the teacher is not open to accepting children's wrong ideas, they are unlikely to be expressed, and the teacher is unlikely even to know about them. Expressing ideas freely requires a certain comfort with risk taking that can be easily discouraged by an environment that values only right answers.

Valuing wrong ideas is a delicate issue because it is possible to conclude erroneously that constructivist teachers think that any wrong answer is as good as a right answer (see DeVries & Edmiaston, 1999). Our aim is, of course, for children to know the right answers, but not at the sacrifice of the development of reasoning and curiosity. The appreciation for wrong ideas is based on the conviction that children's eventual understanding of right answers comes from the development of logic that leads them to discard wrong ideas as inadequate. The problem with avoiding wrong ideas is that they do not go away easily, a fact to which high school and college physics teachers can attest as they confront their students' still incorrect intuitive ideas about phenomena of the physical world. Appreciation for wrong ideas is also based on confidence that with adequate opportunities for experimentation and reflection, children will construct correct logic. The child's construction of logic takes more time than memorizing the teacher's logic, yet it is a much more solid acquisition.

To Provide Counterexamples and Promote Disequilibrium. In an interview, Piaget commented that:

> Teachers should select materials that make the child become conscious of a problem and look for the solution himself. And, if he generalizes too broadly, then provide additional materials where counter-examples will guide him to see where he must refine his solution. (in Evans, 1973, p. 23)

At another time, Piaget (1948/1973b) elaborated on the teacher's role:

> [The teacher] is needed to provide counter-examples that compel reflection and reconsideration of over-hasty solutions. What is desired is that the teacher cease being a lecturer, satisfied with transmitting ready-made solutions; his role should rather be that of a mentor stimulating initiative and research. (p. 16)

Counterexamples are designed to provoke a feeling of contradiction in the child. In Piaget's theory, feelings of contradiction play an important role in the child's construction of more and more adequate (correct) knowledge and forms of reasoning.

The constructivist teacher is always on the lookout for opportunities to provide counterexamples that will help children refine their ideas. For example, if a child is satisfied that "heavy things sink," the teacher can offer something heavy that floats. It is for testable ideas that counterexamples should be suggested.

Some ideas should not be contradicted directly by teachers. For example, when a child says the unseen shadow is "in my tummy," this idea cannot be proven or disproven. If a teacher simply contradicts it, the child may not really understand. In this case, the teacher can only provide many opportunities for the child to think about shadows. The more the child reflects on causality of shadows, the more likely the child is to abandon this erroneous notion.

To Obtain Needed Information. Some questions in a Type D classroom are asked to get needed information: "Do you want to take a walk or play on the playground?" "Do you want to keep the restaurant in the pretend center or change it to something else?" "How many children are buying lunch today?" "Who is next on the sign-up list?" Constructivist teachers often ask children for information, in contrast especially to teacher Type A who gives virtually all information to children.

To Inspire Children's Purposes. The constructivist teacher hopes to inspire in children their own purposes for engaging in an activity. Sometimes the very presentation of materials (such as ramps and toy cars) inspires children to experiment and try to figure out how to do something. Piaget (1973a) said, "I'd rather ask questions that lead to a practical task and then, once the child has succeeded in this, go on to the question of how it happened" (p. 24). We can derive two general kinds of questions from this statement: questions about practical problems (how to accomplish a task) and questions of understanding (how something happened). This distinction is particularly relevant to questions in the context of experimentation in physical-knowledge activities. Sometimes a question orients children to certain possibilities in materials. For example, the teacher might set up several blocks and ask children if they can figure out how to knock them down by throwing a ball.

To Focus Children's Thinking. Once children are engaged in their purposes, the teacher may help to extend these by focusing children's thinking on a particular aspect of their activity. After children have sufficient experience in a certain activity, this might take the form of asking for a prediction (for example, in an activity involving shadows, asking children where they expect to see shadows of a block when a flashlight is turned on from various positions). Again, it might take the form of suggesting a new comparison. For example, in a Target Ball activity, the teacher might ask if it would be easier or harder to knock down their tall, narrow arrangement of blocks than their low, wide target. After children have succeeded in knocking down some blocks, the teacher might probe their understanding by asking, "How did you know how to knock those down? First you missed, but then you knocked them down. What did you do differently?" Such questions may prompt children to reflect on what they are doing, leading to more consciousness and understanding.

To Enrich Children's Efforts with Suggestions. One type of suggestion is to offer new materials. In a ramp activity with three girls in a Head Start classroom, Christie Sales asked if they would like to see how far a matchbox car rolls off their ramp. She taped a strip of adding machine paper on the floor so they could mark where each car stopped. She also suggested they might try putting more blocks under the top of the ramp. Soon the girls were intensely engaged in studying the effects of various numbers of blocks on the distance the car rolled. They had taken up the teacher's suggestions as their own purposes.

Sometimes, of course, children do not find a suggestion interesting. If the teacher has succeeded in creating an atmosphere in which children are autonomous thinkers, they will simply ignore or reject a teacher's idea in which they are not interested. Then the teacher should back off.

To Model a Higher Level of Reasoning. It is possible for the teacher to model a higher level of reasoning that may be within the children's ability to grasp. If it is not, the children can simply ignore it. For example, in playing Tic Tac Toe, the teacher may think aloud, "If you put your X there, you'll have three in a row, so if I put my O there, I can block you." Sometimes children who do not yet understand blocking as a strategy will reject this idea and insist that the teacher put her marker elsewhere. In this case, of course, the teacher should respect the child's way of thinking and do as instructed. In other cases, however, this intervention will open up a new world of interesting possibilities for a child.

With all these interventions, it is important to remember that it is possible to ask so many questions that children lose interest in an activity. The danger of intervening too much or in ways too distant from children's purposes is that children may lose their purposes. Good interventions flow into what children are trying to do. Nevertheless, there are times when the teacher may want to deliberately shift children's focus. Such times include those when children are in a rut, beginning to lose interest, or misusing materials.

Questions to Avoid or Ask Rarely. It is not possible to say *never* ask a particular question, but the following questions should be avoided or asked rarely.

"Why" Questions. Young children usually find it difficult to answer "why" questions, especially with regard to physical causality (for example, "Why does the cork float?" "Why does the marble sink?"). As discussed in the introduction to physical-knowledge activities, children often do not know why, and trying to respond interrupts the child's activity and reasoning. "I *wonder* why the marble sinks" invites children to reflect but does not put pressure on them to verbalize a difficult concept. Children often respond to "I wonder why" with, for example, "Because it wants to" or "Because it's heavy," and such replies give the teacher valuable information about how children are reasoning.

Closed-ended Questions. Closed-ended questions are questions that have only one right answer. One type of closed-ended question is the test question, such as "How many pictures of apples are there?" "What color are they?" Constructivist teachers avoid closed-ended questions because these generally do not inspire children to think. In fact, they can kill interest and discourage children's thinking.

One type of closed-ended question can be answered with a simple yes or no. Such questions often lead to a dead end. However, some yes-no questions can be useful in obtaining needed information (e.g., to find out what the child wishes, or to find out what the child honestly thinks). These are not closed-ended questions, because they have more than one right answer. Examples of appropriate yes-no questions include "Do you need some help?" "Do you want to sign up to use the computer?" "Is it all right if I write on your paper so that I can remember what you wrote [where the child has used invented spelling]?"

There is one precaution about asking yes-no questions: If the child really has no choice, it is better not to ask the question at all. Teachers sometimes make the mistake of asking children the question "Do you want to clean up now?" when they mean "You *need* to clean up now." In this case, it is better to ask "What would you like to clean up now?" or "Would you like to clean that up by yourself, or would you like some help?"

Another type of yes-no question sits midway between a test question and a question to promote reasoning. These are questions such as "Do you think the toy car will sink?" and "Will the red car roll across the room as far as the blue one did?" These invite prediction and comparison and may be appropriate questions. However, they may not reveal or inspire as much thinking as questions reworded by prefacing them with *what, how, where,* or *which.*

Questions likely to be more productive are "What do you think will happen to the toy car if we put it in the water?" or "Which car do you think will roll the farthest?" or "What happened when you rolled the cars down the ramp?"

Questions for the Teacher's Benefit. In considering questions that are for the teacher's benefit, it is important to identify the function of a question or the intention behind it. Sometimes the sentence form does not match the speaker's intent. Some questions are really disguised commands, such as "Will you sit down?" Adding *please* makes it no less a demand although it is more polite. When the purpose is a demand, it is better to state it as a polite command: "Please sit down." We recognize the cultural differences in wording commands (direct or indirect). The solution we propose is to phrase commands unambiguously as commands, so that children are not confused.

When behavior commands are couched as questions, children may think they really have a choice; however, these questions are meant to tell the child what to do (for example, "You need to pick up the game before you get out another one, don't you?"). Statements followed by "OK?" with a questioning intonation are similar (for example, "I need you to sit in circle, OK?"). Such ambivalence on the part of the teacher can confuse children about what is optional.

Reminders for correct behavior in the form of questions are often heard in Classroom Types A and B: "How do we walk through the hall?" "How do we sit in a circle?" "What do we do when someone else is talking?" These are coercive reminders of rules usually prescribed by the teacher. In contrast, the constructivist teacher talks with children before going in the hall about the reason it is important to be quiet. As to sitting in a circle, we know that many Type A, B, and even C teachers require children to sit cross-legged with their hands in their laps. Type D teachers feel this is an unnecessary regulation of children's bodies and that it really does not affect the goals of group time if children sit in other ways. If noise is the issue, the Type D teacher might ask, "Do you like it when you can't hear the story?" and emphasize the reason for asking children to be quiet during group time.

Interventions That Inhibit Children's Thinking. In addition to the questions to avoid or ask rarely, it is useful to take note of a number of ways in which a teacher can inhibit or "short-circuit" children's reasoning. These points are based in part on an article by Wasserman and Zola (1977) and are discussed below.

Giving Indiscriminate Praise. Teachers often think they should heap praise on children in order to boost their self-esteem or encourage them. Sincere praise that acknowledges a child's special efforts or accomplishments can serve a positive purpose. However, when praise is given too frequently and indiscriminately, it can lessen the value of the activity for its own sake in the child's eyes. Considerable research (reviewed by Kohn, 1993) shows that when children are praised for an activity they already value, they become less interested in the activity and less likely to engage in it later. Moreover, indiscriminate praise can make children dependent on praise. They may turn to the teacher for approval of everything they do. Such dependency is heteronomous and operates against the child's development of autonomy.

Negating Children's Ideas. It is important to respect children's ideas, whether they are right or wrong. Even wrong ideas are the result of intelligent efforts to figure something out. Teachers often feel it is their responsibility to correct children's every mistake. This occurs particularly in didactic classrooms where there is considerable direct instruction on academics. While it is appropriate to correct or disagree with children at times, relentless correction can destroy a child's confidence, motivation, and reasoning, as well as stifle a child's interest.

Putting a Child on the Spot, Threatening, or Making a Child Defensive. "Why did you do that?" "Didn't I tell you not to do that?" "Do you want to stay in for recess?" Questions of this type are used in Classroom Types A and B when the teacher is angry with a child. They are not intended to serve as real questions, but are admonishments and tend to make children feel humiliated. Children in constructivist classrooms who are accustomed to real questions sometimes do not respond to a teacher's disguised threats as the teacher expects. For example, two children from a constructivist first-grade class were misbehaving during their art class, and the art teacher asked, "Do you want to go back to your classroom?" Thinking this was a real choice, the children left!

Rushing Ahead without Waiting for a Child to Reflect. When teachers are sincerely interested in what a child has to say, they wait after a question or other intervention to give the child time to think and formulate a response. However, some teachers inadvertently allow too little wait time, not understanding how long it can take a child to formulate a response. Many teachers have to work on not talking too much.

Children also need time to reflect when they first encounter new materials or a new problem in order to figure out what to do. The teacher needs to refrain from rushing ahead and inundating the child with questions before the child has had adequate time to become acquainted with the material or problem.

6. Provide Adequate Time for Children's Investigation and In-Depth Engagement

"Adequate time" refers to the amount of time during the day that is provided for children's investigations, as well as time over weeks and even years. Children cannot be expected to construct complex relations when their exploration is limited to 15 to 30 minutes a day. Children require a minimum of 1 hour each day in a half-day program and 2 hours a day in a full-day program to pursue freely chosen activities and engage in in-depth explorations. Particularly when children have limited experience with materials, they need sufficient time to develop their interests, explore the possibilities, and try out their own ideas.

Children also need sufficient time over weeks to revisit topics as their understanding deepens. Too often in early childhood classrooms, teachers change themes weekly. Children may study insects one week, autumn leaves the next week, and clowns the next. However, one week is usually not long enough for children even to identify their questions, let alone engage in in-depth exploration and experimentation. As pointed out in Chapter 4, after children in Val Dolezal's kindergarten classroom spent one week studying shadows, their investigations did not appear to be driven by complex questions. However, with additional time and materials, the children soon began to address important questions regarding relationships among the object, the screen, and the light source.

At a national conference Howard Gardner (1997) stated that the greatest enemy of understanding is *coverage*. Teachers often feel pressured to cover a multitude of curriculum topics in the classroom, and sacrifice depth for breadth. Constructivist teachers recognize that the development of children's understanding is a long, drawn-out process. Adequate time and opportunities for in-depth engagement support children's construction of knowledge.

7. Link Ongoing Documentation and Assessment with Curriculum Activities

Assessment should be part of teaching and not separate from it. In constructivist classrooms assessment has two foci—assessing children's performance and assessing the curriculum. Teachers regularly document children's growth, development, and academic progress. In addition, constructivist teachers strive to better understand children's reasoning by identifying the relationships and regularities they are constructing. Assessment of children's performance and reasoning occurs as children engage in daily routines and activity times within the classroom. Therefore, it follows that the teacher must assess the curriculum, particularly with regard to the possibilities for constructing regularities and relationships. Chapter 3 is devoted to this important aspect of teaching.

CONCLUSION

Eleanor Duckworth (1972, 1996) wrote an excellent piece titled "The Having of Wonderful Ideas" that has become almost a mantra for many constructivist teachers. She considers the having of wonderful ideas to be the essence of intellectual development. In the case of the wand making described at the beginning of this chapter, the teacher responded to children's wrong ideas by encouraging them to find out from the results of their actions whether their ideas were correct. As Duckworth points out, wonderful ideas may not look wonderful to the outside world. In fact, they may be quite wrong! "Having confidence in one's ideas does not mean 'I know my ideas are right,' it means 'I am willing to try out my ideas'" (p. 5). In constructivist classrooms, one often hears children exclaim excitedly, "I have an idea!"

Constructivist teachers are constantly searching for new ways to promote children's development by stimulating their interest, experimentation, and cooperation. In this sense, constructivist teaching is an experimental undertaking. Each intervention is an experiment. The teacher observes reactions to an intervention and, if children do not respond, drops or modifies it. Type D teaching is never boring because children continually bring new material for the teacher to work with. The unexpected is a daily occurrence in constructivist classrooms!

Chapter 3

Assessing and Documenting Learning in Constructivist Classrooms

Rebecca Edmiaston

Policy makers, school administrators, parents, and community members want to know how well children are doing in our schools. In this time of increasing attention to children's achievement, constructivist teachers must document the knowledge, skills, and abilities of the children in their classrooms. As pointed out in the introduction, commonly held misconceptions about constructivist education—that children just play or that these programs do not contain academic content (DeVries & Edmiaston, 1999)—compel constructivist educators to provide strong evidence of program effectiveness.

In constructivist classrooms assessment is a dual process that centers upon both children and the curriculum. It can be defined as the process by which we observe, document, and interpret what children know, what they do, how they reason, and how the activities and instructional practices in the classroom facilitate or impede their learning. According to Hills (1992), assessment in preschool programs has been underemphasized and neglected. In past years, assessment in elementary schools has been equated with high-stakes testing and has not been used to assist teachers in making curriculum decisions that will better meet the needs of children. Because assessment is embedded in constructivist curriculum, it plays a primary role in the design and implementation of classroom activities. This chapter will describe how assessment operates in Classroom Types A, B, C, and D; identify principles for conducting assessments in early childhood programs; and discuss approaches for communicating assessment results with different audiences.

ASSESSMENT AND DOCUMENTATION IN CLASSROOM TYPES A, B, C, AND D

Teachers carry out assessments in Types A, B, C, and D classrooms in very different ways, as described below.

Classroom Type A

Reflecting the academic focus of Type A classrooms, assessment is seen as the culminating event, or the outcome, of instruction. Documentation of children's learning is product-oriented and typically centers upon achievement as measured by standardized norm-referenced assessment instruments. These consist of narrowly focused tasks requiring children to identify colors, recognize numerals and letters, count to 20, and so forth. Because teachers naturally attempt to link assessment and instruction, standardized test items have unfortunately become the curriculum of many preschool and kindergarten classrooms. Numerous critiques point out the limitations and negative effects of standardized testing on young children (Fleege, 1997; Kamii, 1990; Kohn, 2000). The Association for Childhood Education International (ACEI; Perrone, 1991) and the National Association for the Education of Young Children (NAEYC, 1988) have taken a strong stand against the use of standardized testing in early childhood programs. Nonetheless, standardized testing continues to be prevalent across educational programs in the United States.

Classroom Type B

Teachers in Type B classrooms also view assessment as a product-oriented activity. However, recognizing the possible deleterious effects of standardized testing on young children, teachers in Type B classrooms limit the use of norm-referenced standardized tests and may rely instead on criterion-referenced assessments. *Norm-referenced tests* compare children's performance to the performance of other children (the norming group) while *criterion-referenced tests* determine whether a child has achieved an identified task such as stacking seven blocks. As Goodwin and Driscoll (1980) have pointed out, a serious problem exists with criterion-referenced instruments in that the identification of the standard to be reached is generally an arbitrary decision and may or may not be appropriate for the children being tested. Teachers in Type B classrooms also try to disguise tests as "fun" activities. Children might be asked to match pictured cars with a certain number of dots to numbered garages to assess their ability to match the appropriate numeral with a set of objects reflecting that numeral. As in Type A classrooms, documentation of children's learning does not change instructional practices. If a child cannot perform the previously described task, teachers in Type B classrooms would most likely assume that the child simply needs more drill and practice to meet this objective. Children's errors would not be analyzed to identify their underlying understanding.

Classroom Type C

Teachers in Type C classrooms understand assessment of children's learning to be both product- and process-oriented. They take seriously the position toward assessment voiced by ACEI and NAEYC that teachers should utilize multiple ways of documenting children's learning. Teacher observation, checklists, assessment activities embedded in classroom activities, and collections of children's work over time may all be part of the documentation process. Teachers and children may contribute to an ongoing portfolio containing children's work. However, teachers often find themselves with an overload of data (Chen, Krechevsky, & Viens, 1998). As O'Donnell and Wood (1999) have so aptly pointed out, "Without a clear organization plan, the portfolio can become an all-inclusive storage bin" (p. 293). In many Type C classrooms teachers lack a systematic process for collecting and reflecting upon children's reasoning and abilities. Assessment then becomes peripheral to the program because teachers do not use portfolio samples to inform their instructional practices.

Classroom Type D

Assessment in Type D constructivist classrooms engages teachers in systematic reflection on children's knowledge, reasoning, processes of inquiry, and ability to apply understanding across contexts. Although documentation of children's learning is a goal of the assessment process in constructivist classrooms, equally important is the assessment of the curriculum that is to inform and guide teaching. In fact, assessment and curriculum become reciprocal components—two sides of a coin. Teachers recognize the necessity of keeping assessment and documentation procedures congruent with daily instructional practices. Because constructivist classrooms engage children in interactions with materials (the object world) and with their classmates and teachers (the social world), assessments must evaluate children as they engage in real-life classroom situations. Teachers seek answers to questions such as the following:

- What do my children know?
- What are they doing?
- What are they noticing?
- How are they reasoning?

While assessment in Types A and B classrooms relies on artificially contrived tasks that children must perform on demand, constructivist teachers document children's "authentic" performance as they actively participate in the daily activities of the classroom.

At the same time that teachers study children's understanding, skills, and abilities, they also question their own role in relationship to the curriculum and learning environment. They ask questions such as the following:

- What knowledge can children construct here?
- Are these worthwhile goals?
- Have I provided materials, activities, and experiences that are of interest to my children?
- What do I need to change to better facilitate their learning?

As these questions demonstrate, constructivist teachers do not distinguish between curriculum and assessment because assessment is embedded in the ongoing activities and routines of the classroom.

PRINCIPLES FOR CONDUCTING
MEANINGFUL ASSESSMENT

Accurate assessment of children requires that teachers have knowledge of child development and the typical or atypical characteristics of children within the age ranges of those being assessed. They must also have knowledge of and the ability to implement a variety of alternative assessment techniques for documenting growth and development and assessing the curriculum. The following seven principles guide assessment and documentation of children's learning. Although these principles are not new (see Bredekamp & Rosegrant, 1992), the discussion here stems from a unique constructivist orientation that integrates the physical-knowledge activities common to constructivist classrooms (such as physical-knowledge and group games).

1. Embed Assessment in Classroom Activities

Assessment in constructivist classrooms mirrors the curriculum content and instructional practices in the classroom. According to Dichtelmiller, Jablon, Dorfman, Marsden, and Meisels (1994/1997),

> Performance assessments that focus on classroom activities allow teachers to learn about these processes [children's analyzing, synthesizing, evaluating, and interpreting facts and ideas] by documenting how children interact with materials and peers in real-life "authentic" situations. (p. 4)

This information is most useful to teachers when it increases their understanding of children's reasoning. For example, children's understanding of measurement can be observed as they make muffins in the cooking center where they may become more conscious of a cause and effect relationship between the accuracy of the measurement and the resulting baked-good (see Chapter 6). One commercial instrument, *The Work Sampling System* (Meisels et al., 1995), provides systematic procedures for assessing children as they engage in classroom activities.

2. Use Multiple Sources to Collect Assessment Evidence

Teachers can best make sound evaluation decisions by relying on a variety of sources of information about a child. Teacher observation is the most effective source for getting close to children's learning, and it allows teachers to collect assessment information without disrupting the daily activities of the classroom or requiring "on-demand" behavior of children. Cohen, Stern, and Balaban (1997) discuss in-depth practices for observing and recording young children's behavior. Teachers can record observations in the form of narratives or anecdotes in daily logs or journals. Checklists provide a convenient and efficient means of recording children's acquisition of conventional knowledge such as knowing the names of letters and numerals as well as other kinds of knowledge. Other ways to document children's understanding and performance include collections of children's products (artwork, writing samples, constructions, stories) or photos of their products (block constructions, ramps, marble pathways). Voice-activated audio recorders are useful for audiotaping classroom discussions and conversations. Video cameras allow teachers to videotape children as they engage in classroom activities, conflict resolutions, discussions, and so forth. Helm, Beneke, and Steinheimer (1998) provide a vast array of suggestions and practices for documenting young children's learning.

3. Set Time Aside for Systematic Observation of Children

Documenting children's learning in an organized, systematic fashion is one of the most challenging aspects of assessment. Having too much data to review leaves teachers feeling overwhelmed; having insufficient data or sporadically collected data prevents teachers from presenting an accurate picture of a child. Teachers are continually observing children and mentally noting their actions and words. However, these informal observations are not sufficient for assessment purposes. Fleege (1997) considers this informal type of observation lacking "the purposefulness and the documentation needed to be considered thorough and valid for making important decisions about children" (p. 317). Both spontaneous and planned observations provide valuable insights, but the latter are necessary to insure comprehensive documentation of all children in the classroom.

Teachers sometimes feel guilty about taking time just for observing. However, the important information gleaned from systematic observation enhances teachers' abilities to be responsive to children's needs and is just as important as the time they spend interacting with children. To facilitate the observation process, teachers in Type D classrooms determine ahead of time what child or children are to be observed, what type of information is desired (for example, the relationships or regularities children have constructed), in what type of activities children will most likely demonstrate their knowledge, and how this information will be recorded. The following example illustrates a planned observation.

For several weeks, three boys in Gwen Harmon's preschool class had been building pathways and ramps for cars to travel on with strips of 2-inch cove molding. Gwen wished to identify children's construction of the regularity that if the boards do not connect, the cars will roll off the path, and the relationship between the height of the incline and the distance the car will go. To document the boys' knowledge, she decided to observe them in the ramp center, photograph the boys' constructions, write anecdotes about their actions, and place these on a printed sheet listing the regularities and relationships the boys had constructed. To increase the possibility of observing these, she placed in the ramp center toy racecars and 2-inch cove molding that had been cut into lengths of 1 to 2 feet. She found that all three of the boys understood these relationships at a practical level. Her findings were filed in their portfolios to be shared during parent conferences.

4. View Assessment as a Process That Takes Place Over Time

As pointed out by Wiggins and McTighe (1998), "assessment of understanding should be thought of in terms of a collection of evidence over time instead of an event" (p. 13). Drawing conclusions about a child based upon a single point in time may result in a distorted or incomplete view of a child. Children's individually produced work samples are one source of documenting children's growth over a period of time. Helm et al. (1998) suggest that children's representational drawings provide a window into their development. They discuss the usefulness of having children revisit topics by drawing new pictures or editing previous drawings—what they refer to as "Time 1, Time 2 drawings" (p. 87). Children can also draw symbolic pictures to represent their understanding of relationships. Val Dolezal, a teacher in an inclusive kindergarten at Grant Early Childhood Center, Cedar Rapids, Iowa, used this strategy to document children's understanding of shadows. She asked children in her classroom to represent their understanding of making shadows in their daily journals. Figure 3.1 shows the Time 1, Time 2 drawings done by Shelby. In her first drawing, completed a few days after the set-up of the shadow studio, Shelby emphasized the presence of her friends and their opportunity to play together. Her second drawing, done two days later, shows that she is now focused upon the relationships among the light, the screen, and an object. Her Time 2 representation clearly demonstrates her growing understanding of shadow phenomena. (See Chapter 4 for further discussion of children's understanding of shadows.)

5. Examine Children's Reasoning Through Their Actions and Words

In this book the reader will find many examples of children's reasoning and numerous strategies for promoting reasoning. Chittenden (1991) defines the examination of children's reasoning as the "finding out" stance or attitude

Me and Hailey making our shadows.
This is our shadows.

FIGURE 3.1. Shelby's Time 1, Time 2 shadow drawings

toward assessment. The teacher's role is one of inquiry in which he or she is genuinely engaged in finding out how children think as opposed to asking children test questions to "check up" on them. Teachers can then implement interventions in response to children's actions and questions. Thus assessment and teaching are so intertwined that it becomes impossible to separate them.

An obvious source for documenting children's reasoning is observation of their actions. For example, in the process of making dinosaur shadow puppets, children in Val's kindergarten class drew eyes, fierce-looking teeth, and spikes on the dinosaur's backs but did not cut out these features. They were quite surprised when they held their puppets in front of the light source and could not see any of these details. Their surprise informed the teacher that they did not fully understand the role of light in creating shadows. Val's response was, "Can you make eyes or teeth in another way?" The children's errors thus provide invaluable assessment information and suggest a direction for interventions.

Webbing a map of important ideas and their relationships is an effective technique for documenting children's ideas and understanding, their questions, and even their suggestions for future activities they would like to pursue. Webbing is a familiar activity in Val's kindergarten classroom (example shown in Figure 3.3). She uses webs not only to identify children's thoughts but also to see how their thinking changes throughout a given study. She sometimes uses plastic overlays on top of previously constructed webs so that she and the children can see how their thinking has changed. The information children share during webbing helps her determine the direction of future activities. When Val first webbed with children about shadows, she was surprised to find they did not have much to say. She observed children to determine whether children lacked sufficient experiences with shadows or whether they were simply not interested in shadows. She added additional materials to the shadows center—cardboard tubes, solid blocks, and blocks with holes—and read to children a number of books about shadows. She also decided to pose some specific problems for children to solve in the shadow studio. After reading *Me and My Shadow* (Dorros, 1990) to the class, she suggested they might want to explore how to make big and little shadows in the shadow studio. The next time children webbed about shadows, they had much more to share and began to identify numerous questions to investigate.

A more formal method of documenting specific levels or stages in children's reasoning is to use *Guttman scales*. Such scales order items from easy to hard and, if they meet certain criteria, permit assigning a scale score that reflects a child's particular developmental level. According to Kohlberg and DeVries (1987), Guttman scaling and other criteria can be used to test Piaget's belief that children's reasoning develops in qualitatively different stages that follow a sequential order and are hierarchical—that is, a later stage incorporates the one before. Although development of such scales requires rigorous research efforts, Guttman scales have been developed by DeVries (1986) on children's conceptions of shadows (see Appendix) and by DeVries and Fernie (1990) on Tic Tac Toe. These scales can provide a basis for ongoing documentation of children's stages in reasoning about shadow phenomena and Tic Tac Toe.

6. Examine the Curriculum Through Children's Actions and Words

The driving questions that guide teachers' ongoing scrutiny of curriculum are:

- Does this activity continue to capture children's interest?
- What are children figuring out how to do?

Children's actions and words best answer these questions. As noted above, children's interests and questions determined the content of the shadows investigations in Val's kindergarten class (see Chapter 4). Through careful observation of children's actions, teachers can identify next steps and changes that need to be made in materials. An example of this was demonstrated in Gwen's Head Start classroom as Christie Sales joined Zachery at the water table where he was investigating water flow. He had arranged on a pegboard three clear plastic cups that had holes of different sizes drilled in the bottom. Zachery had arranged the cups so that the cup with the smallest hole (1/8") was on top; water poured into it drained into the cup with the medium-size hole (1/4"), which then drained into the cup with the largest hole (1/2"). He was pouring water from two pitchers at the same time into the cup with the smallest hole in order to fill up the two cups beneath it. Of course the water was not draining quickly enough to fill the other two cups. He soon lost interest and started to leave the water table, but Christie exchanged the top and bottom cups so that the one with the largest hole was on top. She said, "Look, Zachery, the bottom cups are filling." Zachery smiled, picked up a pitcher, started to pour, and observed the results. He continued at the water table until activity time ended. Christie's intervention with the materials extended his ongoing exploration. (See Chapters 2 and 7 for additional strategies for promoting reasoning in this water activity.)

Constructivist teachers must also document children's progress in meeting school district goals or performance standards. As a rule, constructivist curriculum not only meets but exceeds district expectations. However, when teachers are just beginning to implement constructivist practices, one of their greatest concerns is whether they will be able to meet district curriculum requirements. To this end, before implementing the shadows project, Val Dolezal, Mary Campbell (the studio teacher), and I constructed the web shown in Figure 3.2 to identify the children's learning experiences and the corresponding kindergarten district standards that were addressed. Out of 16 standards of performance, all but 4 were addressed. In addition, children had the possibility of constructing many regularities and relationships. The teachers then used observation, structured and unstructured child interviews, children's work samples, videotapes of children's actions in making shadows, and Time 1, Time 2 drawings to document children's mastery of district requirements and their construction of regularities and relationships.

7. Make Assessment a Collaborative Endeavor

Observing, recording, and interpreting children's understanding and action in the classroom is a very demanding task. Assessment should not be a solitary process. Colleagues, parents, and children themselves can and should be included in the assessment process. Collecting and discussing documentation data with others who are familiar with the children can enrich and extend the interpretation of data. In fact, it is important that all the adults in the classroom—teaching assistants, volunteers, parents, preservice educators—contribute to this process because it is impossible for one teacher to observe all of the learning that occurs. For example, one day in a preschool classroom I was building a structure with Kimball in the block center. When we finished, I asked if he wanted me to draw a picture of his structure so we could rebuild it if it was accidentally knocked over. He thought that was a good idea. Upon completing the drawing, I suggested that he put his name on it. A classmate informed me that he could not write his name. I showed him how to make the first letter of his name, and for the first time that year, he began signing his work with a *K*. This accomplishment was an important moment in his beginning understanding of letters that I was able to share with his teacher.

Parents are also important collaborators who can provide examples of children's application of learning. For example, in Gwen's Head Start classroom, we found that our efforts were extending to home activities. I had been making books with a number of children in the classroom about their physical-knowledge activities. Latrice's mom came in one morning with a book that Latrice had made at home about her favorite singers, NSync. She had drawn the pictures in her book and asked her mother to write the words for her. She proudly read her book to her classmates at grouptime.

Finally, children themselves are collaborators in the assessment process. In classrooms where teachers regularly record children's words, children understand that their ideas and thoughts are valuable and are more willing to share and perhaps even initiate ways of informing teachers about their

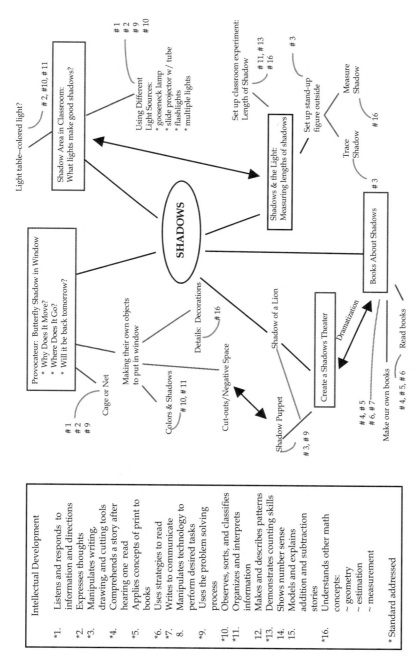

Intellectual Development

1. Listens and responds to information and directions
2. Expresses thoughts
3. Manipulates writing, drawing, and cutting tools
4. Comprehends a story after hearing one read
5. Applies concepts of print to books
6. Uses strategies to read
7. Writes to communicate
8. Manipulates technology to perform desired tasks
9. Uses the problem solving process
10. Observes, sorts, and classifies
11. Organizes and interprets information
12. Makes and describes patterns
13. Demonstrates counting skills
14. Shows number sense
15. Models and explains addition and subtraction stories
16. Understands other math concepts:
   ~ geometry
   ~ estimation
   ~ measurement

* Standard addressed

FIGURE 3.2. Kindergarten standards of performance addressed in shadows project

63

learning. For example, during the shadows project in Val's class Alicia, who understands that letters make up words but does not yet know sound/symbol relationships, decided that she would make her own web so Val would know what she knew about shadows. In her web (see Figure 3.3) she described actions that she created with her shadow puppet in the shadow center such as jumping, moving, and talking. She also identified future activities that she wanted to explore such as making big shadows and making flower shadows.

COMMUNICATING ASSESSMENT FINDINGS

Sometimes others do not understand the complexity of the learning experiences embedded within activities in constructivist classrooms. Teachers must think carefully about others' understanding or lack of understanding when sharing assessment findings. Val Dolezal and Mary Campbell find displays

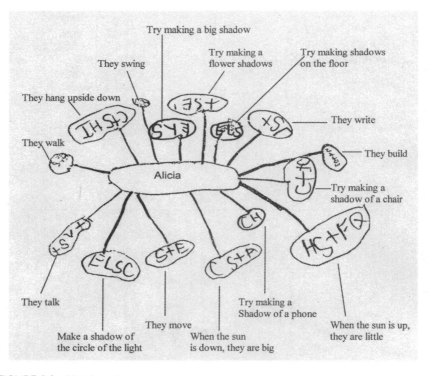

FIGURE 3.3. Alicia's web

patterned after the documentation displays of the Reggio Emilia approach (Edwards, Gandini, & Forman, 1998) helpful in sharing assessment information. Teachers and children construct documentation panels using children's work samples, teachers' and children's drawings, photographs, transcripts of classroom conversations, and so forth.

As the culminating activity of a 6-week study of shadows, children in Val's kindergarten classroom decided to invite parents to the classroom one evening to share what they had learned about shadows. Val and Mary prepared several documentation displays to familiarize parents with the scientific relationships children had developed. Figure 3.4 is a photo of one sec-

FIGURE 3.4. Will see-through things make shadows?

tion of a display panel that addressed the question "Will see-through things make shadows?" In this photo Alicia demonstrates that a clear plastic bag has a shadow. Another panel, titled *What We Have Learned About Shadows*, included children's thinking about shadows in general and specifically examined the role of light in relationship to shadows. Some of the children's comments were

> Shadows are all around us.
> Shadows do not move by themselves. They have to copy you.
> Shadows require light.
> When we are close to the light, our shadow is big.

Also displayed on this panel, the following conversation demonstrated children's global understanding of the role of light in making shadows:

Maria: It has to be light to have a shadow.
Teacher: If you went into a very, very dark place, would you see a shadow? (The children suggest going into the dark closet and closing the door. They did and saw no shadow.)
Sandy: The whole room was really dark!
Maria: You can't see your shadow when it is totally dark.
Alicia: 'Cuz there is no light for a shadow.

Under their child's tutelage, parents had the opportunity to make shadows in a shadows center using shadow puppets constructed by their child. Parents were surprised to find that the children in this classroom had extended their study to the comparison of similarities and differences between shadows and reflections, a topic generally too difficult for kindergarten science curriculum.

CONCLUSION

Standardized testing common to Types A and B classrooms is not appropriate for children in preschool and kindergarten classrooms. A lack of interest in answering test questions, an inability to understand test directions, and feelings of anxiety about pressure to perform well are all factors that may impede young children's performance on standardized tests. In addition, as Gullo (1994) has pointed out, standardized tests do not tell us how children apply their knowledge to situations in or out of the classroom. Teachers in Type C classrooms recognize that teacher observations of children and their work in the classroom provide the most accurate picture of the child. However, they lack a well-organized system for collecting and interpreting children's work and behavior. Assessment in Type D classrooms centers on children's reasoning and its relationship to the curriculum that they experience in the classroom. Type D teachers understand that assessment is an ongoing component of their program because the development of children's reasoning is a process, not an event. Constructivist educators want to know how children are reasoning and applying their understanding. Reflection and interpretation of organized, systematic observations guide teachers in deciding how to change and extend classroom activities to better meet the needs of children. The combination of careful teacher reflection upon children and curriculum enables teachers to transform children's learning in constructivist classrooms.

PART II

PHYSICAL-KNOWLEDGE ACTIVITIES

Rheta DeVries

In *Physical Knowledge in Preschool Education: Implications of Piaget's Theory* (Kamii & DeVries, 1978/1993), *physical-knowledge activities* are defined as those in which children act on objects and observe their reactions. Such activities appeal to children's interests, inspire experimentation, and often involve cooperation. We conceptualize two types of physical-knowledge activities—those that involve the movement of objects (physics, especially mechanics) and those that involve changes in objects (chemistry). Some of the phenomena in physical-knowledge activities focus on inclines, parachutes, bubbles, tops, shadows, making musical instruments, and cooking. The rationale for physical-knowledge activities is found in Piaget's distinction among three types of knowledge: physical knowledge, logico-mathematical knowledge, and arbitrary conventional knowledge (explained in Chapter 2). In physical-knowledge activities the constructivist teacher promotes the child's construction of logico-mathematical relationships and observes to see whether children are experiencing contradictions in their activities. The objectives of physical-knowledge activities include learning properties of objects and causal factors in phenomena of physics and chemistry. Constructivist teachers find it useful in implementing physical-knowledge activities to know about stages in children's reasoning about physical objects, criteria for good physical-knowledge activities, and general principles of teaching. These are discussed below.

STAGES IN CHILDREN'S REASONING ABOUT PHYSICAL OBJECTS

In physical-knowledge activities, children are developing their conceptions of causality. Piaget (1937/1954) traced the origins of causal reasoning to the first months of life when the infant has a feeling of effort, expectation, desire, and efficacy in reproducing some event (sucking the breast or bottle, pulling a string and shaking a mobile above the crib). This adaptation reflects the young child's practical intelligence that is for a long time oriented to success (what one can do with an object) and not to conceptual intelligence involved in explanation. On a practical level, a child may be able to act consistently on an object to achieve a desired effect without understanding why an action causes a reaction, or even without being conscious of what he or she does to achieve the effect. It is notable that children's understanding of physical phenomena generally proceeds from *knowing how* to *knowing why*—from the practical to the conceptual. When children are asked for explanations, their answers reflect stages in reasoning. For example, Piaget (1971/1974) reported a study in which children were shown how a Ping-Pong ball may be pushed but given a reverse spin so that after traveling forward a short distance, it reverses and comes back. While children as young as 5 years of age can succeed in reproducing this effect, it is not until age 10 to 12 that a complete explanation is given. Piaget describes the stages as follows:

> In stage 1 the return of the ball is attributed to its lightness, speed, etc., to the table, to the air that pushes it, etc. In stage 2 it is due to the movements of the experimenter, but described in broad terms without the clear-cut distinction between the two movements in question as is the case when the subjects reach age 10 to 11. (p. 69)

Because causality of physical phenomena is tied closely to the specific nature of each phenomenon, stages in children's developing conceptions are different for each phenomenon. (See, for example, DeVries's stages in children's conceptions of shadows given in the appendix.)

CRITERIA FOR GOOD
PHYSICAL-KNOWLEDGE ACTIVITIES

Kamii and I (1978/1993) propose four criteria for good physical-knowledge activities that were considered in developing the activities in Chapters 4–7. These were originally conceptualized for activities involving movement of objects, but they apply, at least in part, to other types of physical-knowledge activities. Briefly, the criteria are as follows.

- *The child must be able to produce the phenomenon by his or her own action.* As noted above, the essence of physical-knowledge activities is the child's actions on objects and observation of the objects' reactions. The phenomenon selected must therefore be something the child can produce by acting on an object.

- *The child must be able to vary his or her action.* When the variations in the child's action result in corresponding variations in the object's reaction, the child has the opportunity to organize—that is, to construct—these relationships.
- *The reaction of the object must be observable.* If the child cannot observe a reaction to his or her actions on objects, there is no content to be organized.
- *The reaction of the object must be immediate.* Correspondences are much easier to establish when the object's reaction is immediate.

PRINCIPLES OF TEACHING

The constructivist teacher plans and provides materials for at least one physical-knowledge activity a day. In addition to this special activity, children also are involved with physical knowledge in block building and art activities. The special activity might be experimenting with ramps, water, rollers, parachutes, or kites. Often a cooking activity is an additional regular part of the activity time. In these activities the constructivist teacher uses the following general principles of teaching:

1. Provide Materials That Invite Children's Interest and Experimentation

Materials that interest children in a sustained way are usually those with which experimentation is possible. Children may immediately have ideas to try with unfamiliar materials, such as a pendulum or boards and rollers. When materials are familiar or when the teacher wants to focus children on certain types of experimentation, purposes may be suggested to children. Suggestions may even be implicit in materials, such as cups with holes in them placed in the water table. Or they may be explicit, such as when the teacher proposes that children try blowing through a straw on various objects to see if they will move across the floor.

2. Ask Questions Related to Four Ways of Engaging With Objects

In order to promote the child's construction of knowledge about the physical world and the construction of intelligence, Kamii and I (1978/1993) recommend keeping in mind four ways, or levels, of acting on objects physically and/or mentally. These are useful because they suggest questions that are especially conducive to promoting children's reasoning and construction of relationships.

Acting on Objects to See How They React. The first actions on unfamiliar objects may be simply to find out how they react. Babies often go through their entire repertoire of actions (shaking, turning, squeezing, dropping) and in the course of these actions learn something about the properties of an object. Such experimentation is useful throughout childhood (and beyond), especially with novel materials. This way of acting on objects suggests questions and interventions like "What can you do with these?" or "See whatever you can think of to do with these." The teacher may also suggest actions and encourage children to anticipate what will happen by asking, "What will happen if you (do X)?"

Acting on Objects to Produce a Desired Effect. While toddlers, preschoolers, and older children sometimes act on objects without an expectation of a particular reaction, they also frequently act on objects to produce a desired effect they have in mind beforehand. Activities of this sort suggest questions like "Can you (do X)?" and "Can you find anything else that you can (do X) with?" Children often try to imitate each other in order to produce a particular effect, and the teacher can call attention to a child's feat: "Look at what Kim is doing. Does anybody else want to try to do that, too?" The aim is for children to have in mind effects they want to produce before they act. This promotes a sense of purposiveness.

Becoming Aware of How One Produced a Desired Effect. By the age of 4 or 5 years, children are able to do many things at the level of practical intelligence, but they are not aware of *how* they produced a result. A first step toward conceptual intelligence is awareness of how one achieved an effect. Once children have mastered an action at the practical level, the constructivist teacher offers opportunities for them to reflect and become conscious of how they produced a result: "How did you do that?" (in an admiring tone). "Can you show (child X) how to do that too?" "Can you do that again?"

Explaining Causes. If the correct description of actions is difficult for children, how much more so is explaining why something occurs. Explanations of most phenomena are impossible for 4- and 5-year-old children because explanations must go beyond what is observable. It is therefore best to avoid asking why something happens. If asked why shadows are sometimes in front and sometimes in back of one, a child may say, "The wind blew it there" or "It's when I lean that way." Frequently, children interpret "why" questions as "how" questions and respond in terms of their own action. Although "why" questions should be asked sparingly, they may occasionally be useful to encourage a child to reflect and to stimulate discussion among children. Often it is more effective not to directly ask why but to wonder aloud: "I wonder why your shadow stays on that side of you?" This may prompt children to notice and begin to wonder about this aspect of shadows. Many other interventions and examples are found in Kamii and DeVries (1978/1993).

3. Understand and Assess Children's Reasoning by Observing Their Actions

Assessing children's reasoning involves figuring out what children are thinking, what they notice and wonder about. Children's actions are a window into their thinking. For example, Tom's surprised squeal when a plastic cup with a hole in its side spurts on his arm (described in Chapter 7) showed the teacher that this event was unexpected. Surprise is often a clear indicator of thinking. A child's effort to make something happen can reveal how a child is reasoning. For example, a child may try to make an object's shadow bigger by moving back as far as possible—even behind the light—and waving it around while looking expectantly at the wall!

4. Encourage Children to Notice Regularities and Construct Logico-Mathematical Relationships

In Chapter 2 we discuss three types of knowledge and emphasize that physical-knowledge activities are not only for children's learning about the physical world but also for children's construction of logico-mathematical knowledge—the organization and adaptation of their intelligence. The process by which children do this involves noticing regularities and constructing logico-mathematical relationships. An example of a regularity is that water always flows from plastic cups with holes in the bottoms. An example of logico-mathematical relationships is that the smallest flow comes from the cup with the smallest hole. This knowledge implies a whole set of relationships, as described in Chapter 7.

5. Support Children's Ideas, Even Those That Are Wrong

Construction of correct ideas frequently is preceded by incorrect ideas that must be tested in order to be rejected. Type D constructivist teachers therefore support children's ideas, even when these are wrong. With the child who tries to make a shadow by waving an object behind the lamp, the teacher can reflect his puzzlement and encourage further action: "I wonder where the shadow went! What can you do to see it again?"

6. Model and Suggest New Possibilities

It is appropriate for the teacher to model and suggest possibilities, especially when children need to know how to use equipment, when they run out of ideas, and when the teacher has in mind a particular type of experimentation children may be interested in. The teacher may simply model an action to make children aware of a possible effect. Part of the teacher's responsibility is to provide intriguing problems that children have not thought of before.

7. Back Off If a Child Does Not Respond to an Intervention

An intervention is an experiment that sometimes inspires children's further reasoning and sometimes does not. In Chapter 7, for example, when Christie suggests experimenting with hanging cups on a pegboard, Tom eagerly takes up this idea. However, when Christie's "wondering aloud" later elicits no response, she lets it go.

8. Create a Forum in Which Children Can Discuss Their Ideas and Share Their Discoveries with Others

Children are often so excited about figuring something out that they spontaneously share it with other children. A child can thus become a teacher. Providing a time for such sharing at group time frequently has the effect of inspiring imitation and further investigation. Chapter 4 describes how children sometimes experiment during group time.

CONCLUSION

Physical-knowledge activities are particularly important for the construction of logico-mathematical relationships. In addition to constructing knowledge about the physical world, children are increasing their intelligence—that is, their general abilities to organize experiences. The optimal construction of knowledge and intelligence in physical-knowledge activities depends on a cooperative sociomoral context described in Chapter 2. In chapters to follow, we focus on shadows, musical sounds, cooking, water, and pattern blocks. We hope to show with very specific examples how children construct knowledge and develop their reasoning in physical-knowledge activities.

Chapter 4

Casting Shadows

*Rheta DeVries, Betty Zan, Rebecca Edmiaston, and
Karen Wohlwend*

Children are often surprised by shadows. They appear and disappear, grow larger and smaller, are dark and light, are sometimes on one side of you and sometimes on the other, and sometimes look like an object and sometimes do not. The potential of shadows to intrigue children and inspire experimentation thus makes them good educational "materials." In this chapter we first consider some ways in which early childhood curriculum guides suggest teaching about shadows. These activities can be characterized as reflecting a Classroom Type A, B, or C approach. Following a brief rationale for including shadows in the constructivist curriculum as good physical-knowledge activities, we refer to the research bearing on children's developing conceptions of shadows. Finally, we discuss practical matters in conducting shadow activities and describe activities in Type D classrooms that illustrate principles of teaching specific to shadow activities.

SHADOW ACTIVITIES IN CLASSROOM TYPES A, B, C, AND D

Classroom Type A

Shadow activities in Classroom Type A consist of worksheets and prescribed "experimentation," modeled after elementary science manuals. One sample manual designed for K–1 students consists of a series of "hands-on" lessons in which the teacher poses scripted questions. The children's responses are scripted as well. In the introductory lesson, a typical script is presented:

> Ask, "How would you explain what a shadow is?" Students should be able to say that a shadow is a dark shape cast upon a surface by something that blocks the light from that surface. Ask the students, "What three things are needed to

produce a shadow?" Students should mention sunshine (or a light), an object (in this case, their bodies), and the ground or other surface where the shadow is seen. (Allen, 1996, p. 9)

One would suppose that if a 5- or 6-year-old child could verbalize and truly understand the answers to these "introductory" questions, there would be little need to continue the unit of study!

The Type A goal is to move efficiently through each lesson by explaining shadows to children and reinforcing or correcting children's responses to questions about shadows. For example, in one kindergarten guide, the teacher is instructed to proceed as follows: Show a book with pictures of shadows and "Explain that light helps to make shadows"; have children draw each other's shadow on the ground and "Explain that as the position of the sun in the sky changes, a shadow changes"; and read another book about a shadow "friend" and "Explain that when a person gets in the path of light, the person's shadow is made" (Mallinson et al., 1993, pp. 203, 204). A lesson on hand shadows and shadow play may be added in the last lesson of the unit, after all the "real work" has been covered.

Classroom Type B

In Classroom Type B, the teacher follows the same manual as Teacher Type A but dresses up the worksheets with colorful drawings and substitutes small toys for the plain blocks in the directed science "experiments." Children's actions are often tightly controlled by the teacher. Here is an activity from Allen (1996):

> *Science and the Arts*
>   Let each student draw a picture of the class watching the cloud shadows. Instead of simply drawing the clouds, students could glue cotton batting to the paper. To contrast with the white cotton, students should first color the sky blue, or you could have them work on light blue paper. (p. 62)

Another suggested activity is for the teacher to demonstrate the shadows of several objects, then have the children guess the identity of an object from its shadow or drawing of its shadow (Mallinson et al., 1993). In our view, children can do this "busy work" without learning anything about shadows.

Classroom Type C

Teachers in Type C classrooms select their activities from a wealth of materials that support children's play in the shadows center: tracing silhouettes, creating shadow box puppets, coloring groundhogs. However, little if any attempt is made by the teacher to set up situations that will cause the children to question their misconceptions about shadow phenomena. Sometimes an activity includes a cognitive goal beyond free exploration, but aims at objectives having nothing to do with shadows. For instance, a shadow box activity is used to teach directional words to 3-year-olds as they move a shadow puppet up, down, and sideways (Williams, Rockwell, & Sherwood, 1987).

Shadow tag is another frequently suggested activity (Gammons & Kutzer, 1997). However, while children may find shadow tag entertaining, it violates the observability criterion of good physical-knowledge activities (see the introduction to Part II). That is, although children can judge their own success at tagging someone else's shadow, they are unlikely to see when someone has tagged their shadow. A typical result is frustration, conflict, and simple running around.

Classroom Type D

In Classroom Type D, the constructivist teacher engages children in active experimentation with shadows. Because shadows often surprise them, children are interested in figuring out how to make shadows behave in particular ways. For example, when a 5-year-old noticed a shadow accidentally cast on the ceiling, the teacher encouraged children to try to figure out how to make it happen again. Other examples of interest, experimentation, and cooperation in constructivist classrooms are given in the discussion of principles of teaching later in this chapter.

SHADOWS AS PHYSICAL-KNOWLEDGE ACTIVITIES

Activities involving shadows fall strictly in neither of the two categories of physical-knowledge activities, movement of objects or changes in objects. Rather, they are unique, sharing some characteristics of both categories. Like phenomena of basic mechanics, shadows obey some laws related to their movement. These are actions at a distance, however, and are not "actions on the object" in the strict sense. Moreover, the same action (from the child's perspective) does not always lead to the same result. For example, the action of pushing a ball gives the child the same result each time. However, walking up to one wall may produce a shadow whereas walking up to another (or even the same one again) may not. Such experiences are likely to be felt by children as contradictions.

Like phenomena involving changes in objects, shadows themselves change in some respects (size, shape, density). But unlike, for example, the transformation of flour when liquid is added, these are not irreversible changes in the substance of shadows. In mixing flour and water, the direct interaction of the objects is most responsible for observable reactions. With shadows, however, interactions among the objects involved are not direct but occur over a distance.

Nevertheless, shadow activities do meet the criteria for good physical-knowledge activities: Children can produce shadows, observe them, vary them, and get immediate reactions to their actions at a distance. Shadows are thus amenable to experimentation.

CHILDREN'S CONCEPTIONS OF SHADOWS

An understanding of how children's thinking about shadows progresses can help the teacher who is trying to design and implement activities more in line with constructivism. Research by Piaget (1927/1960; 1945/1962) brought to light the psychological and developmental nature of children's conceptions of shadows. DeVries (1986) extended Piaget's research by identifying developmental stages in children's reasoning about shadows (see the appendix for complete descriptions of stages). In this chapter we present only a brief summary of the progression of children's reasoning about shadows. Following a description of the regularities and relationships that children can construct, we describe contradictions that inspire children to reason.

Regularities and Relationships

Development in thinking about shadow phenomena is a progressive construction and coordination of relationships among four elements—object, shadow, screen, and light (Figure 4.1). This progression begins with a simple awareness of the object and the shadow. When 2-year-olds notice shadows at all, they tend to think simply in terms of "me and my shadow."

When children first become conscious of the screen on which the shadow falls, they tend to think simply in terms of proximity. That is, in order to cause a shadow to appear on a wall, they walk up to the wall—never mind the light! As children begin to coordinate relationships among these three elements—object, shadow, and screen—one can observe misconceptions in their reasoning. For example, DeVries (1986) describes having children sit on the floor and observe their shadow on one side of them. When she asks children if they can make their shadows appear on the other side, they turn around 180 degrees. They think that the relationship between the object (their bodies) and its shadow can be manipulated (that is, rotated) simply by changing the relationship between the object and the screen (the floor).

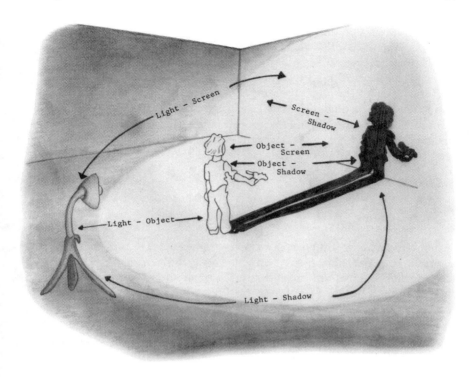

FIGURE 4.1. Spatio-causal relations constructed by children in their efforts to understand and explain shadow phenomena

The last (and most difficult) element to appear in children's thinking about shadows is the light. At first, children's thinking about light is relatively global—an awareness that light accompanies shadows. As children add the light to their relations among object, shadow, and screen, their thinking does not at first include notions of causality. Rather, they have the notion that the light and the object must be present to make a shadow but do not consider the spatial relations. They may notice that a shadow is usually surrounded by a lighted area, and state that to make a shadow, you need to turn on a light. Even when they begin to take the directionality of the light into account, their thinking is still relatively static. That is, they do not think about what occurs between the light and the screen or between the light and the object. We often see children wave an object outside the path of light, expecting to see a shadow.

Children's thinking about shadows is dramatically transformed when they begin to think of the light as active. This is evident when they use active verbs (for example, "The light *goes* from here [lamp] to here [object casting shadow] and *hits* it"). Later, a more interactive conception is evident when children think of the object reacting to the light, for example, "The light hits it and can't go through it." When this happens, they can begin to construct causal relations among the light, object, and shadow. The entire system of relations among light, object, screen, and shadow becomes dynamic. Children think about what occurs between the light and the object and realize that the object is blocking the light, thus causing the shadow to appear on the screen.

Contradictions

As children experiment with shadow phenomena and grapple with the relations among light, object, screen, and shadow, their erroneous reasoning becomes evident. Does this mean that teachers should avoid shadow activities with young children? We think not. Piaget inspired our conviction that children's errors are intelligent and necessary in moving toward scientific knowledge. This is a very long process in the case of coming to understand shadows, incomplete even at age 9 for most children. Because shadows are full of possibilities for contradicting children's anticipations and surprising them, they are an excellent source of activities. Consider now some of the contradictions that teachers may observe in the course of children's activities.

1. Movement of Shadows Does Not Require Direct Contact. Children's experiences with objects lead them to expect movement as a result of a certain kind of direct contact with an object. Shadows' violation of this expectation is a source of difficulty and intrigue to children. For example, in the mistaken notion that the object and screen must somehow connect physically, young children sometimes go to the screen and touch the shadow or place their objects directly on the screen, thus obliterating the object's shadow from view.

2. Light Makes Something Dark. One 8-year-old whose teacher included shadows as part of their science curriculum struggled with this paradox and concluded, "That's the hardest question I ever had. . . . It somehow turns black. This is just like a mystery, you know. You can't find an answer to it. Prob'ly nobody has." (See DeVries, 1986, for further detail on this child's thinking.) In this case we learn that classroom instruction about shadows has not been understood at all.

3. Proximity to the Screen Does Not Always Result in a Shadow. A child's belief that the action of putting the object next to a screen will produce a shadow is often true. Eventually, however, the proximity hypothesis leads children to awareness of contradictions. This is experienced when children do not consider the light-object relation and the light-screen relation. In DeVries's research, when asked to make a shadow on the wall opposite the illuminated one (and behind the lamp), many children simply walked up to the wall and were surprised not to see their shadow! This contradiction appears in children who do not consider the light as specific illumination of a screen.

4. One's Shadow Does Not Move from Back to Front by Leaning Forward or Turning Around. When a child's shadow is in back, the teacher may ask, "Can you make it in front of you?" Many children respond by simply leaning forward or turning around. Children who make this hypothesis fail to consider the fact that in this case the floor is the screen. They also do not recognize the specific directionality in the light-object-screen relation and think only about the object-shadow or the object-screen relation. Belief that the shadow's location depends on their action alone results from failing to consider the light-object relation. One 5-year-old tried to make his shadow move to his other side by scooting forward a couple of times. Seeing that his shadow was still behind him, he declared, "See, it gets stuck on my shoes. It's hooked up with me." Others are unconvinced by the shadow's failure to move as they expect, and they lean further forward (often nearly falling) or turn around many times, faster and faster.

5. Shadows Unaccountably Disappear. This occurs when children move behind the light but do not consider the light-object relation. One 4-year-old concluded that "It ran out [of] the room," and went to see if it was in the hallway. Three-year-olds and even some 4-year-olds may solve this problem by concluding that when their shadow disappears, it "runs away" or "goes inside my tummy." This can be a very strong conviction because it cannot be disproved.

6. The Configurations of Shadows Do Not Always Correspond to the Special Shape of an Object. In an activity described later in this chapter, one 5-year-old shone the light on a flat wooden elephant that was perpendicular to the light. He denied that the rectangular shadow was the elephant's shadow and was totally perplexed about what had happened to the elephant's shadow he had seen moments before. This event is a puzzle to children who possess the light-object relation but do not consider what the light "sees."

These are only a few of the many contradictions one observes in the course of shadow activities. Others will be highlighted in the activity descriptions below.

INITIATING SHADOWS INVESTIGATION

Practical matters must be considered in selecting and setting up materials for shadows experimentation. Shadows investigation requires screens, light sources, a darkened room, and collections of objects to cast interesting shadows. Getting started on an investigation of shadows also involves capturing children's interest in shadows.

Assembling Materials

Screens. A classroom wall with a smooth surface can serve as a screen, or a screen can be created by hanging paper or sheets. Teacher Karen Wohlwend created a freestanding screen in the kindergarten classroom at Audubon Elementary School, Dubuque, Iowa, from the following materials:

Two wooden child-sized coat trees
A 7-foot length of plastic 1-inch PVC pipe
A white twin flat bed sheet

The PVC pipe was placed horizontally across the pegs of the coat trees. The sheet was then draped over the pipe, making a screen large enough for three children to create shadows. The plastic pipe and small coat trees were of lightweight material to prevent injury if tipped.

Lights. Safety precautions must be considered when selecting light sources. Light bulbs of all kinds get hot and remain hot even after they are turned off. Children should be cautioned about touching lamps, projectors, electrical plugs, and outlets, and the teacher must provide appropriate supervision.

The quality and intensity of light is also a factor to bear in mind. A filmstrip or slide projector is a good choice as it emits a strong beam that will allow sharp, dark shadows. Halogen lamps are too hazardous for use in early childhood classrooms. An overhead projector confuses children by changing the angle of the light beam, allowing shadows to be created by placing objects on a plane perpendicular to the screen. Flashlights vary in the amount of light produced and can create confusing light effects, caused by the diffusion of light in an object's shadow. Yet, flashlights can be valuable in directing children's attention to the perspective of the light source. When children hold the flashlight, they have the possibility to see the object and its shadow as the light "sees" it. It is necessary to test out materials before they are introduced to the children, evaluating them for safety, unforeseen variables, and confusing light effects.

Darkened Room. The degree to which the room must be darkened depends on the intensity of the light source. Flashlights and small lamps require a very dark room. A filmstrip or slide projector with a strong beam can be used successfully in a partially darkened room.

Objects. Children can participate in the collection of objects for the shadows center. It often helps to begin with shadows of simple opaque objects having a unique shape, so that the correspondence between the object and its shadow is obvious. Objects that could spark later investigation might include objects with and without holes, cardboard tubes, objects that vary in transparency, plastic bags, marbles, tissue paper, colored cellophane, and clear containers that can hold a variety of liquids and solids.

Capturing Interest

Getting started requires capturing children's interest in shadows. This may begin with the reading of a story involving shadows. (See Figure 4.2 for a list of children's books containing shadows themes.) One teacher used a

Anno, M. (1988). In shadowland. New York: Orchard Books.
Asch, F. (1985). Bear shadow. New York: Prentice-Hall Books for Young Readers.
Bartalos, M. (1995). Shadowville. New York: Viking.
Dorros, A. (1990). Me and my shadow. New York: Scholastic.
Kent, J. (1981). The biggest shadow in the zoo. New York: Parents Magazine Press.
Lowery, L. (1969). Dark as a shadow. New York: Holt, Rinehart, and Winston.
Munsinger, L. (1984). Nothing sticks like a shadow. Boston: Houghton Mifflin.
Narahashi, K. (1987). I have a friend. New York: Margaret K. McElderry Books.
Paul, A. W. (1992). Shadows are about. New York: Scholastic.
Simon, S. (1970). Let's try it out. . .light and dark. New York: McGraw-Hill.

FIGURE 4.2. Children's literature containing shadow themes

walk on a sunny day to spur children's interest in shadows. The 4-year-olds began noticing their shadows in front of them. As they turned around to return to the school, the teacher called attention to the fact that now their shadows were behind them. "I wonder why now they are behind us." Peering over her shoulder, Trenisha responded, "The wind blew them there!"

Sometimes it is not a question of drawing children's attention *to* shadows, but rather of not diverting children's attention *away from* shadows. Almost every teacher who has ever shown a filmstrip or movie has seen children's hands shoot up to cast shadows on the empty screen. Children have a near compulsion to do this! Instead of racing to switch off the projector, the teacher can seize the moment and allow some exploration or pose intriguing questions.

After just such an experience, Karen set up a slide projector and a free-standing shadow screen (described above) in the corner of her kindergarten classroom. The children's first reaction was to interpret it as a movie theater setting for dramatic play. Children went behind the screen one at a time to experiment with small objects and finger shadows. Other children pulled up chairs on the opposite side and watched as if in a theater.

In an inclusive kindergarten classroom following the Reggio Emilia approach at the Grant Early Childhood Center, Cedar Rapids, Iowa, the teacher, Val Dolezal, placed a paper cutout of a butterfly in the window on an early spring day so that the sun would cast a butterfly-shaped shadow on the floor. This prompted some children to make hand shadows on the floor. The children became interested in shadows and wanted to study them. Thus began a 5-week unit on shadows.

PRINCIPLES OF TEACHING

Seven principles of teaching about shadow phenomena are illustrated below with examples from classrooms.

1. Find Out What Children Notice and What They Wonder About

Children's questions about shadows will help teachers identify the regularities and relationships that children are constructing. During a class meeting of Val's inclusive kindergarten classroom, Amanda shared, "Last night . . . I saw two shadows of me. One was little. One was big." Val responded, "I wonder how that happened?" This prompted a class discussion of the possibility of having two shadows. The following excerpts from the classroom discussion reveal the children's ideas about how someone might have two shadows.

Ricky: Maybe you must have saw [*sic*] your sister.
Amanda: I don't have a sister. My brother was in his bedroom. And I was right by the wall.
Jamie: Maybe there were two suns.
Amanda: If there were two suns that would be outer space.
Kelly: She could have had two lights in the room that she was in.
Amanda: No, I didn't.
Jamie: Um, maybe one was on top, and the other one was on bottom.
Amanda: No, they were beside each other.
Teacher: All right, I think we've got a problem here that we're going to have to figure out.

The teacher suggested that the children explore this problem in the shadow studio. She added a second light so they could explore Kelly's suggestion about using two lights to make two shadows.

2. Base Activities and Interventions on the Regularities and Relationships Children Are Struggling With

Shadow phenomena provide opportunities for children to construct and coordinate multiple and complex relationships among light, object, screen, and shadow. It is important to develop activities that bring these relationships to their attention.

At the Human Development Laboratory School (HDLS) at the University of Houston, the 4- and 5-year old class participated in a 10-week unit on shadows, with shadow activities conducted approximately once per week. A team consisting of the two classroom teachers (lead teacher Coreen Samuel and assistant teacher Karen Amos) and two researchers (Rheta DeVries and Betty Zan) met weekly to review the videotape and field notes taken from the day's activity, analyze children's reasoning, and plan the next activity. Each new activity followed from the previous one and was based on children's reasoning about shadows—the regularities they noticed and the relationships they constructed.

In the first activity, children were given the opportunity to explore shadows freely with a collection of objects, a slide projector, and a sheet hung from the ceiling. At first children's attention was fleeting, and they were generally unaware of problems or contradictions. Their thinking was dominated by the object-screen and object-shadow relationships. Sometimes they placed their objects directly against the screen. Most ignored the light and paid no attention to what was happening between the light and the screen (for example, waving their objects outside of the path of the light or merging their own shadows with the objects' shadows). Over the next nine weeks, the team designed several shadows activities directed toward helping children notice what happens between the light and the screen. These activities presented children with problems that the team hoped would prompt them to think more precisely about the effects of their actions on the shadows they produced.

In the second activity, Coreen created a paper castle with cutout windows and suspended it from the ceiling, midway between a projector and the screen (see Figure 4.3). The teacher cut a fire shape from transparency plastic, colored it red and yellow with markers, and fastened it to the top of the castle. She made a paper cutout of a dragon and glued it to a stick. At group time, she read to the children the book *The Dragon's Cold* (Talbot, 1988), about a dragon who lost his fire. At activity time, Coreen invited children to help the dragon regain his fire by making his shadow appear in the shadow castle windows as he made his way to the top and captured his fire. Because the dragon's shadow was too large to fit in the shadow windows when the dragon was held next to the castle, the problem was for chil-

FIGURE 4.3. Making dragon shadows in the castle windows

dren to figure out how to adjust their actions and move closer to the screen (and away from the light) to compensate. In experimenting with placing the dragon's shadow in the shadow windows, some children began to notice the changes in the size of shadows as they moved back and forth between the light and the screen.

This theme of changing the size of shadows was taken up again 2 weeks later. The teacher set up a slide projector approximately 10 feet from the wall. Children experimented with changing the sizes of the shadows using similar items of different sizes, including large and small giraffes, elephants, and other animals, and hollow paper rolls of different sizes. After their initial explorations, the teacher posed questions such as, "Can you make the big giraffe have a small shadow? How small can you make it?" One child, upon discovering that shadows could be made smaller, said to the teacher, "Try to get it (the shadow) so small that you can't even see it!" The teacher also asked, "Can you make the small giraffe have a big shadow?" By varying the distance between the object and the screen (and therefore also between the light and the object), children had the opportunity to construct the regularity that in this situation, when they increased the distance between the object and the screen, the shadow became larger. While most children grasped this regularity, their actions also demonstrated that some did not think in a very precise way about the role of the light in creating shadows. For example, 5-year-old Brad became excited about making the small elephant's shadow larger and larger by moving back farther and farther away from the screen. He finally moved behind the projector, and the elephant's shadow disappeared. "Darn!" he exclaimed, and then moved up to the wall again (where he knew he could find the shadow) to start over. He did the same thing a second time, then tried putting the elephant on top and to the side of the projector and waved it randomly until he accidentally caught the light on it. Brad's actions told the teacher that he focused primarily on the object-screen relationship and was oblivious to the role of light.

3. Plan Activities Based Upon Children's Interests and Questions

Children's interests and questions drove the investigation of shadows in Val's classroom, where children showed great excitement in testing their individual theories. Their investigations led to deeper thinking and new questions such as: Are shadows always black? Will colored things make colored shadows? Do see-through things have shadows? In their investigation of the color of shadows, the children brought a variety of materials to the shadows studio to test their hypotheses. First they used different colored puppets and other colored objects to make shadows, but to their surprise, the shadows were black. Then they changed the color of the screen with paper of different colors, but still the shadows were black. Next Ricky suggested, "If you put a colored light bulb, like at the theater, if you put like color lens in there (the projector), it'll probably turn a different color." After trying each of these suggestions, the group agreed with Sean's conclusion, "Shadows are black . . . always black."

Children's questions about colored shadows prompted experimentation at the HDLS as well. As mentioned above, some children noticed in the dragon activity that the shadow of the fire cast a colored "shadow." While children experienced this phenomenon as a "colored shadow," this image is technically a result of the semitransparent object selectively filtering light, allowing certain colors to pass though and be seen on the screen. Coreen invited children to share their observations of shadows at group time. Alexa described the shadow of the fire and protested, "I thought we said that all shadows were black! Very funny! Very, very funny!" Coreen invited children to find objects in their classroom and at home that might cast colored shadows. So children brought a large collection of items, and the teacher made a chart listing each item. Coreen also included a few items that she knew would cast colored shadows. Children individually marked their predictions on the chart and then tested their predictions at activity time. Following this activity, they discussed their findings and one child suggested the hypothesis that when you can see through something, it will cast a colored shadow.

4. Help Children Explore Their Ideas About Shadows (Even "Wrong" Ideas)

A common "wrong" idea can be seen when children construct shadow puppets for the first time. They frequently do not anticipate that the details they have so painstakingly glued, drawn, and colored on their puppets will not be visible in the shadows. Several children in Val's classroom made butterfly puppets and lined the wings with sequins and beads. They were puzzled when their decorations were not visible on the shadows. Contradictions such as these can inspire children to figure out ways in which they can make details observable in their puppets' shadows (for example, cutting out features or making a side-view silhouette).

5. Control Variables So Children Will Be More Apt to Observe Regularities

The multiple relationships that exist in shadow phenomena and the potential for complexity create a danger. If children vary too many aspects at once, regularities are difficult to construct. For example, at HDLS, Coreen created a four-sided enclosure with four sheets hung from the ceiling. She invited children to come to this shadows center in pairs. To one child she gave a hanging-style lamp attached to a cord and asked, "What do you have to do to see (child X)'s shadow?" Turning to the other child, she asked, "Where do you have to stand so that you can see your shadow?" This was supposed to provide the opportunity for one child to take the light's perspective and think especially about the light-object relationship. The other child had the opportunity to think about the light-object-screen relationship. Indeed this happened for some children who experimented and were able to coordinate their actions. In one pair, one child had fun deliberately running away from the light so as to make her shadow disappear. However, in another pair, the child with the lamp moved it around randomly, and the other child ran around randomly. The result was that neither child succeeded, and neither figured out anything. When this happened, Coreen realized that she needed to help the children coordinate their purposes. The problem was that the light *and* the object (in this case, a child) were both moving simultaneously. Combined with four times as many screens as children were accustomed to, the resulting problem was that there were too many variables for children to keep track of and coordinate. Seeing this situation, Coreen offered to hold the lamp (thus controlling this variable), aimed it at one wall, and asked the children if they could make their shadows. Terry jumped around to face the other direction and waved his hand at a dark wall. Coreen asked what she should do, and he said to turn it. She aimed the light at a different wall where neither shadow appeared. "Why can't we see your shadow?" Coreen asked. "What do I need to do?" After a period of time, Roberta finally moved her arm and accidentally saw part of her shadow. Then she awkwardly moved in various ways until she could see her shadow. It was only when the teacher held the position of the light constant that children were able to experiment in ways that eventually enabled them to succeed.

The team agreed that allowing children control over the light could be helpful in drawing children's attention to the light-object and light-screen relations, but thought that the next step should involve a stationary light pointed at one screen. They also thought that children might think more precisely about the light-object relationship if the size of the lighted area was reduced. After experimenting with ways to concentrate a small spot of light on a wall, they finally settled on a slide projector to which was affixed a cone made out of black construction paper. Attached to the cone was a paper towel tube approximately 18 inches long (see Figure 4.4).

The tube could be raised and lowered by hand to move the spot of light a bit higher or lower on the wall. Coreen placed a large drawing of a tree with three cutout knotholes on the wall (see Figure 4.5). The children were given a colored plastic cutout of a squirrel on a stick and were invited to try

FIGURE 4.4. The projector modification

to make the squirrel's shadow appear in the knotholes. Coreen volunteered to hold the tube in whatever position the children wanted, so children could adjust the light and then experiment with the squirrel. When children simply held the squirrel in front of an unilluminated knothole, they were confronted with the fact that the squirrel did not cast a shadow in that hole. They had to adjust the light each time they wanted to move the squirrel's shadow. In this way, they made their adjustments one at a time—first they moved the light, and then they moved the object—and became more aware of *how* they were successful.

The children did many shadow activities over 10 weeks. While they experienced lamps, objects, and shadows in many different ways, they still struggled with coordinating the light-object and object-screen relationships. The team decided that children needed more experience from the light's perspective. Coreen took the familiar book *The Biggest Shadow in the Zoo* (Kent, 1981) as the theme and created sketches on butcher paper of four scenes from the story: the elephant house, the moat, the storm at night, and the elephant house again. Each sheet of paper spanned the width of a wall. She then stood a flat wooden elephant upright on a table in the center of the small room. One child at a time took turns holding the light and

FIGURE 4.5. Putting the squirrel's shadow in the knothole

trying to take Goober's (the elephant in the story) shadow to each of the scenes on the four walls. This task differed in important ways from previous shadow activities in that the light was movable but the object had to stay on a table in the middle of the room. To make the shadow bigger, children had to move forward toward the object (and the screen). This was counterintuitive for the children who were accustomed to moving back (toward the light and away from the screen) in order to make a shadow larger. Furthermore, in order to make Goober's shadow on two of the walls, they had to turn the elephant 90° from his original position so as to shine the light on the elephant shape (see Figure 4.6). Otherwise they encountered the problem of a small rectangular shadow when they aimed the light at the edge of the elephant (Figure 4.7).

For Malcomb, the rectangular shadow cast when he moved the light toward a new wall but did not turn the elephant was most puzzling. Coreen asked, "I wonder what happened to Goober's shadow?" Malcomb replied, "Yeah, where is Goober's shadow?" When Coreen asked, "Does that shadow [the rectangular shadow created by the unrotated elephant] come from Goober?" Malcomb insisted that it did not. Later, Malcomb had the opportunity to see another child turn the elephant to change the shadow.

FIGURE 4.6. Making the elephant shadow

6. Get Children to Make Predictions About Shadow Phenomena, and Help Them Become Conscious of Contradictions Between Their Expectations of Shadows and What Happens

One kindergarten teacher set up a pole lamp with three lights in the middle of the area where the large group met. Without turning on the lamp at first, the teacher asked children to make predictions about what would happen if they turned on lamps aimed at a single object. When they turned on the three lamps, they were surprised to see three shadows. The teacher then asked what would happen if they turned off one light, "Which shadow will disappear?" After children's predictions, the teacher turned off one light, asked for predictions about the second and third, and turned off those two. Then children predicted where each shadow would appear if the lights were turned on one at a time.

Children in Karen's kindergarten class also compared predictions with shadow results. The children gathered in small groups around a large sheet of paper. A wooden cylindrical block stood on end in the center of the paper next to a flashlight aimed at the block but not turned on. The teacher asked

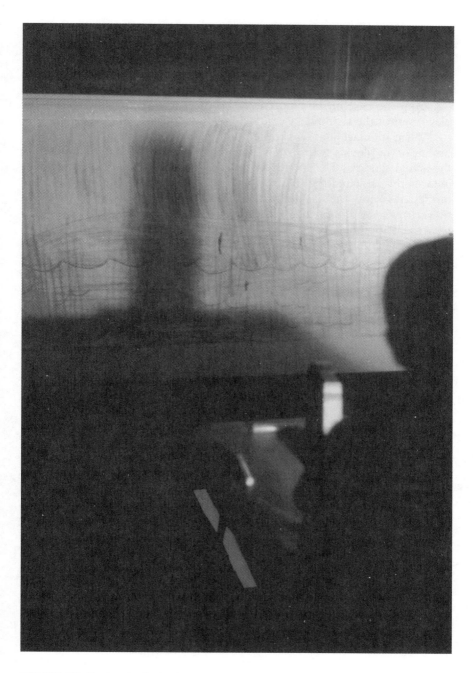

FIGURE 4.7. Elephant's shadow?

the children to predict where the block's shadow would fall when the flashlight was turned on. Each child drew a predicted shadow on the paper "screen" and initialed it. Some drew circles to represent the shadow, reflecting the end or body of the cylinder. Some correctly drew a rectangular shadow out from the base of the block. Few, however, could correctly predict the placement of the shadow.

When the flashlight was turned on, one child in each group traced the outline of the block's shadow. Children then compared their predictions with the actual shadow. The conversation was not focused on who correctly or incorrectly predicted the shadow placement. Instead, the children became interested in how the flashlight could be maneuvered to make their prediction true. This led to further experimentation with the flashlight as children tried to position the light so that the shadow would move to cover their own predicted shadow picture. The initialed papers also served as an embedded assessment that recorded how the children had been thinking about the direction of light.

7. Encourage Children to Figure Out How to Make Shadows "Behave" in Particular Ways

While one goal of all physical-knowledge activities is for children to come up with their own questions and problems, the teacher may sometimes suggest effects that children might try to produce or problems that children might try to solve. This is particularly helpful if children are "stuck" in their thinking and the teacher thinks they need a nudge. In the 8th week of the 10-week unit on shadows at the HDLS, the team noticed that the children still focused mainly on the object-screen and shadow-screen relationships. Most children had a fairly global and imprecise recognition of the necessity of light in the formation of shadows; however, few children seemed to notice what happened between the light and the screen. The team decided to place two additional screens (low, movable room dividers) between the light and the wall. The children had been playing an Uncle Wiggily board game, and Coreen decided to use this as the theme of a new activity. She created a cutout of Uncle Wiggily's house with Uncle Wiggily in the open window with the slide projector's circle of light shining directly on him (shown in Figure 4.8). The challenge to children was to get Uncle Wiggily's shadow to appear first in the forest on the nearest screen, then at the river on the next screen, and then in Rainbow Land (a permanently painted rainbow on the wall). To accomplish this, children had to remove the dividers one at a time. In this activity, many children for the first time began to use active verbs to describe the light. Kim explained that the light "is coming from over there [the projector] and it's coming through Uncle Wiggily." Kerry explained about the

FIGURE 4.8. The screens used with Uncle Wiggily's shadow

shadow appearing in the forest: "See, this is hitting this. The paper's stopping it." The teacher asked, "So how does the light get from all the way over there to here?" Kerry responded, "See, if you put this (she cups her hand around the circular beam of light from the projector and walks toward the screen as though carrying the light), it goes shzzz and it hits Uncle Wiggily's house and then you can see it." Alexa explained to the rest of the children at group time that "There's a beam of light. You might not be able to see it, but it does come right through."

Literature can be a wonderful springboard to investigation. The children in Karen's class were delighted by the antics of Bear as he tried to escape from his shadow in *Bear Shadow* (Asch, 1985) by running away from, nailing down, and burying his shadow. After reading this story, Karen suggested reenacting parts of the book. With the children seated in a circle, she placed a toy bear, blocks, and a flashlight in the center of the floor. She invited children to try to make Bear's shadow disappear as it did in the story when Bear hid behind a tree. Using a block as the tree, individuals tried to position the flashlight so that the toy bear's shadow would disappear. This was accomplished quickly with much advice from onlookers. Then the teacher asked, "Let's take the block away. I wonder if we can make the shadow disappear now? Didn't that happen in the story?" Several children recalled that Bear's shadow had gone away "by itself" in the middle of the story. (Bear's shadow disappeared at noon only to reappear after his afternoon nap.) One child suggested that he walk around the circle with the flashlight to see if at some point the shadow disappeared. Another asked that children pass the flashlight around the circle, but this too only moved the shadow's direction. One child held the flashlight high over his head while seated in the circle. The shadow of the bear shortened slightly. This inspired the suggestion that the teacher hold the flashlight over her head which she did while standing outside the circle. The final suggestion was that this was still not high enough; the teacher must stand on a chair with the flashlight above her head. She followed their suggestion and climbed on a chair, but even this only succeeded in shortening the bear's shadow a fraction. The session ended with the suggestion that the children keep experimenting with the materials at the shadows center and that if anyone discovered a solution that they share it at grouptime.

CONCLUSION

The teachers in the constructivist classrooms described in this chapter saw a great deal of progress in children's reasoning about shadows. Children became more interested and had more ideas about shadows than they had at the beginning, and were aware of problems that they had not been aware of before. Their intuitive ideas decreased, though they reappeared when children were confronted with something they did not understand on a practical level. Through their experimentation both independently and in collaboration with their peers, children increased in their practical intelligence about shadows—their *know-how*. Finally, they constructed many relationships, although in some cases these relationships were sequential rather than coordinated.

Shadow phenomena present children with so many relationships to construct and coordinate that young children should not be expected to have a complete understanding of them by the end of an investigation. However, children develop confidence in their reasoning ability and in their knowledge of concepts when they are encouraged to confront their errors on their own terms. Teachers in Classroom Types A and B tend to rush children to the correct response to meet the objectives of the curriculum guide, leaving children with an understanding that is tentative and frail. Classroom Type C teachers are often content to let errors in children's thinking go unchallenged throughout the course of the unit of study. Teachers in Type D classrooms recognize that the journey to a complete conceptualization of shadow phenomena is a winding path, filled with errors and revisions along the way. Children's interests and questions will chart the course. The teacher's goal is not to race the children through shortcuts or abandon them along the trail, but to draw their attention to the signs and contradictions that may lead them to alter their course. The journey will not end at the conclusion of a 3-, 6-, or 9-week unit, and no one may be at the final destination.

Chapter 5

Exploring the Art and
Science of Musical Sounds

Carolyn Hildebrandt and Betty Zan

Musical-instrument making can provide rich opportunities for learning and development across many domains—music, art, science, literature, drama, and social studies (Chenfeld, 1995). Children can create their own musical instruments, decorate them, and use them to accompany singing, dancing, dramatic play, or readers' theater (where children cooperatively act out a story while it is being read aloud). They can also use them to perform simple rhythm patterns or to create their own songs or improvisations (Hildebrandt, 1998a; Upitis, 1990, 1992).

Musical-instrument making is also a physical-knowledge activity. In the course of making musical instruments, children's interest and experimentation can lead them to create different types of sounds and discover how to change the properties of these sounds (e.g., pitch, loudness, timbre, and duration). Experimenting with musical instruments can help children learn about the physics of sound and lay the groundwork for future development in the art and science of music.

The focus of this chapter is musical-instrument making as a physical-knowledge activity. We begin by describing three approaches to instrument making in the classroom, Type A/B, Type C, and Type D, comparing the strengths and weaknesses of each. Then we give a brief introduction to the physics of sound and describe a system for classifying musical instruments. Next we outline goals and objectives for musical-instrument-making activities, and present some principles of teaching specific to making musical instruments with young children. Finally, we provide examples of two types of musical instruments children can make and simple experiments they can do with them. For each activity, we provide an analysis of the regularities and relationships that children can construct. In focusing on the physical-knowledge aspects of instrument making, we hope to show how teachers can move from Type A/B or C approaches to the study of musical sound to a Type D constructivist approach. In narrowing our focus to physical-knowledge activities, we do not mean to diminish or negate the importance of other musical activities with class-made instruments. In fact, we encourage teachers to make full use of children's instruments in singing, dancing, dramatic play, and readers' theater. Once children have made their musical instruments, they can use them in playing their own music, both alone and in groups, thus maximizing their understanding of both the art and science of musical sound.

THREE APPROACHES TO MAKING MUSICAL INSTRUMENTS WITH CHILDREN

Most teachers have made some sort of musical instrument in their classrooms, be it a drum, a maraca, or a rubber-band guitar. Many books and articles offer instructions on how to make simple instruments with children (e.g., Fiarotta & Fiarotta, 1993; Nelson, 1995; Sabbeth, 1997). Many also include experiments that children can do with their instruments.

Teachers can structure instrument making in at least three ways. Each approach varies according to the individual style of the teacher and what he or she wishes to accomplish with the activity. In a Type A or B approach, teachers provide step-by-step instructions on how to make an instrument and then monitor each step along the way. Every child is given the same instructions and the same materials, and is expected to produce the same results. If the project is within the physical and cognitive abilities of the child, this can be a very gratifying activity. Everybody gets to make a musical instrument and to experience the joy of playing it.

The main limitation of this approach is that children are not free to explore, experiment, or invent. The process of making the instrument is tightly controlled, and the process of playing the instrument is often controlled as well. With this approach, instrument making is essentially an arts and crafts activity where children are expected to look, listen, and imitate the teacher.

A second way teachers can structure the activity is to provide lots of materials and encourage children to make whatever instruments they like. In this Type C approach, children are free to let their imaginations flow. Adult modeling and intervention is kept to a minimum so as not to stifle creativity. If done well, this approach can also be very gratifying. Because children are not constrained by any particular person or model, they are free to explore and invent. If they want to experiment in playing their instruments, they can do that as well.

One problem with this approach is that young children are often better at focusing on things they can see than on things they can hear. If given free reign with such an activity, young children tend to focus on the visual-spatial aspects of the instrument rather than the auditory ones. Furthermore, even though most young children are intrinsically interested in musical sounds, many do not have the knowledge and experience needed to focus on different aspects of these sounds (e.g., pitch, loudness, timbre, and duration) and therefore are less able to discover different ways to manipulate them. Without the help of a teacher or a more knowledgeable child or adult, the learning potential of this approach can be quite limited.

A third approach—Type D—is to provide opportunities for both free and guided exploration. In this approach, children are provided with several examples of musical instruments, a variety of materials, and a question or a problem to solve. The teacher works interactively with individuals or small groups of children, adapting instruction to their level of interest and understanding. Using the type of questioning and observation methods described in Chapter 2, the teacher creates a social and intellectual atmosphere in which children can construct their own knowledge of musical sound. The teacher encourages the children to experiment, invent, and share their discoveries with each other. Each child is an active participant in instrument making, and each innovation and discovery is celebrated with the group.

Although this third approach may involve more work on the part of the teacher than the other two, it has a much greater potential for learning and development. If done well, this approach can lead to important insights into the physics of sound, not just for the students but for the teacher as well.

INTRODUCTION TO THE PHYSICS OF SOUND

Teachers who wish to approach musical-instrument making as a Type D physical-knowledge activity need to know a few things about sound and how it is produced. However, they do not need to have complete knowledge about the topic in advance, since they will have opportunities to learn along with the children. Two useful pieces of information for teachers to know ahead of time are (1) what sound is and (2) what types of things make musical sounds. It is also important to be able to distinguish different aspects of musical sound, such as pitch, loudness, timbre, and duration. Finally, an understanding of five categories of musical instruments can be helpful in planning activities.

What Is Sound?

In order to have a sound, three things are needed: something that vibrates (e.g., a struck tuning fork or a plucked string); a medium to carry the vibrations (e.g., air or water); and something to receive, detect, and interpret the vibrations (e.g., an ear and a brain).

There are a number of ways to demonstrate how sound is produced and transmitted. Children can learn about sound vibrations through tapping a tuning fork on their knee and then putting the tines of the fork in a cup of water. The vibrations from the tuning fork will cause the water to ripple and splash up against the side of the cup. Another way to learn about vibrations is to make a simple stringed instrument with a box, a bridge, and a rubber band (see Figure 5.1). Children can pluck the string, hear its sound, see it vibrate, and even feel the vibrations with their fingers on the box.

Aspects of Musical Sound

Four aspects of musical sound that children can begin to notice are pitch, loudness, timbre, and duration. *Pitch* is related to frequency of vibration, or

FIGURE 5.1. Child making rubber-band guitar

the number of times a sound-making object vibrates in a given amount of time. Pitches can be described as high (as in the sound of a bird or a piccolo) or low (as in the sound of a lion or a bass guitar). *Loudness* is related to the amplitude of vibration, or how large the vibrations are. Sounds can be described as loud (as in the sound of a shout) or soft (as in the sound of a whisper). *Duration* is related to the length of time that a sound-making object vibrates. Durations can be described as long or short. *Timbre* refers to the qualitative differences in sound between two instruments (for example, between a flute and a guitar). Timbre is related to the fundamental vibration of a sound-making object (usually the slowest vibration) in combination with other, faster vibrations, called overtones or partials. Timbre can be described in a number of ways—bright, brassy, twangy, and so forth. (For more information about these aspects of musical sound, including the complex interplay between pitch, loudness, and duration in the production of timbre, see Goldstein, 1996.)

Awareness of these different aspects of musical sound enables teachers to call attention to them as children experiment with their musical instruments. Learning how to distinguish pitch, loudness, timbre, and duration is an ongoing process that can be approached in the context of singing, playing, listening, and experimenting with musical instruments. It is normal for children (and even adults) to confuse different aspects of musical sound with each other, such as pitch with loudness or loudness with duration. Teachers can help children distinguish these aspects of musical sound by controlling variables (for example, having children make a high-pitched note sound loud or soft, or a loud note sound short or long). Such demonstrations can be done vocally or by playing different types of musical instruments, either commercial or child-made.

What Types of Things Make Musical Sounds?

Some people can make musical sounds out of almost anything. A clip from the television series *America's Funniest Home Videos* showed a man playing a complex percussion improvisation on his built-in oven! And a friend of ours, private music teacher Sharon Anway, can make amazing music from a set of tin cans from her recycling bin! Many other professional musicians, such as Peter Schickele ("P.D.Q Bach"), Margaret Leng Tan, and the musical group Stomp make music from everyday objects such as garden hoses, drinking glasses, vacuum cleaners, soda pop bottles, and trash can lids.

Children's instrument making often begins in the bedroom with a rattle hit against a crib or in the kitchen with a spoon hit against a cup or bowl. Once children start making musical instruments, it is easy to keep going until everything in the world is a potential instrument. Our friend Sharon Anway enjoys making musical instruments with her students. One day, a 5-year-old boy said, "Do you wanna hear me play my coat?" He plucked a button on his coat and sure enough, it made a great sound. After teaching Sharon how to play it, a look of wonder came across his face. "Now I get it!" he exclaimed. "*Anything* can be a musical instrument!"

Five Types of Musical Instruments

Musical instruments can be classified into five basic groups: aerophones, idiophones, membranophones, chordophones, and mechanical/electronic instruments. This classification system is particularly useful in thinking about musical-instrument making. In the paragraphs that follow, we offer a brief description of each type of instrument along with suggestions on how children can make them from recycled materials. (For further information on this classification system, along with detailed illustrations of each type of instrument, see Diagram Group, 1976.)

Aerophones. These are instruments in which the sound is produced by blowing air into the instrument. They include flutes (e.g., end-blown and side-blown flutes, whistles, recorders), reeds (e.g., oboes, clarinets, saxophones, bagpipes), cup-mouthpiece instruments (e.g., horns, trumpets, trombones), free reeds (e.g., accordions, harmonicas), and free aerophones (e.g., buzzers and bull-roarers). Children can make simple aerophones by blowing across the mouth of a soda pop bottle (for a flute-like sound), blowing into the end of a soda straw cut into a single or double reed (for an oboe-like or clarinet-like sound), or pursing their lips and blowing into the end of a plastic tube or piece of garden hose (for a horn- or trumpet-like sound).

Idiophones. In these instruments the whole body vibrates to make a musical sound. Idiophones can be made of wood, metal, plastic, or any other type of sonorous material. They can be sounded by striking (as with wood-blocks, gongs, and xylophones), shaking (as with sleigh bells and maracas), rubbing (as with washboards and guiros), or plucking (as with jaw harps and kalimbas). Popular idiophone projects for young children include paper-plate maracas, metallic windchimes, and tin-can bells.

Membranophones. With these instruments the sound is made by the vibration of a stretched membrane or skin. There are two basic types of membranophones: drums, where the membrane is set into motion by striking with a hand, a mallet, or some other means; and mirlitons, where the membrane is set into motion by blowing or humming, as with a kazoo. Drums can be sounded by sticks, padded beaters, or brushes. Children can make drums out of tin cans with balloons or pieces of rubber stretched over the top. Mirlitons can be made with waxed paper folded over a comb, or tissue paper attached to the end of an empty toilet paper roll.

Chordophones. These are instruments in which the sound is made by the vibration of strings. Most chordophones consist of one or more strings attached to a body that serves as a resonator. Chordophones can be sounded by plucking (as with guitars, harps, and harpsichords), striking (as with pianos and hammer dulcimers) or bowing (as with violins, cellos, and psalteries). Children can make chordophones out of boxes and rubber bands, or fishing line connected to a wooden bow.

Mechanical and Electronic Instruments. These include music boxes, carillons and chimes, mechanical music makers (such as hurdy-gurdies), player pianos, mechanical organs, electric guitars, electronic organs, electro-mechanical instruments (such as vibrophones), and radio-electric instruments (such as synthesizers). With the possible exception of simple music boxes, these instruments are beyond the scope of preschool instrument makers, but can provide interesting mechanical and acoustical demonstrations for young children.

GOALS FOR CHILDREN

Our broad goals for musical-instrument making are the same as for other physical-knowledge activities—for children to be active and experimental, and to have and try out wonderful ideas. It is clear from the foregoing descriptions of types of instruments that these offer rich opportunities for many different kinds of actions on objects. Goals for children specific to experimentation with musical instruments are to

1. Become aware of differences in sounds
2. Experiment with actions and materials that produce different sounds
3. Become aware of regularities between actions and materials, and various sounds
4. Construct cause-effect relationships between actions and materials, and various sounds

The specific regularities and relationships that children can discover will vary according to their age, experience, and the musical instrument in question.

Generally speaking, however, children's understanding of musical sound is most likely to take the following form: "When I do X [for example, strike a drum], a sound is produced. When I do X [for example, strike the drum hard], the sound is more Y [in this case, louder], and when I do X [strike the drum lightly], the sound is more Y [in this case, softer]."

PRINCIPLES OF TEACHING

The principles of teaching in musical-instrument making parallel those presented in Chapter 2. The following suggestions are for making musical instruments with young children.

1. Limit Materials Available So Children Can Focus on Cause and Effect Relationships

For example, in the balloon maraca activity described below, the material used for the body of the maraca (the balloon) is initially held constant so that children can vary the contents of the balloon to produce different kinds of sounds. On another day, the teacher might want to present children with only one content (such as rice) and vary the body of the maracas by using soda pop bottles, film canisters, paper plates stapled together, and toilet paper rolls with the ends closed with tape. By controlling variables in this way, the teacher can draw children's attention to differences in the sounds that are attributable to one and only one aspect of the sound-making object, thus maximizing their ability to construct regularities and relations between the objects and the sounds they produce.

2. Allow Children to Try Out Their Ideas, Even When You Know They Will Not Work

It is through our mistakes that we are faced with the necessity to revise our thinking. This is true not only for children, but for adults as well. One of us had an experience making musical instruments that led us to construct the notion of the necessity of a resonator for a chordophone. Carolyn had been playing with two rubber bands stretched across an empty tuna can. She wanted to hold the instrument sideways and play both sides of it, thus having access to four strings instead of two, so she removed the bottom of the can. When she played her instrument, it was so soft she could hardly hear it. She had eliminated her resonator! Another adult made a similar discovery in making a stringed instrument with rubber bands stretched over a plastic

clothes hanger which she called a "hangersichord." She was disappointed
with how soft her instrument was until Carolyn suggested that she lay it on
top of an open metal box. With the metal resonator, it made a full, satisfying sound.

3. Ask Questions That Draw Children's Attention to Differences in Sounds

Young children are often fascinated with making noise and are not necessarily likely to be very analytical about the sounds they produce. It is the
teacher's role to draw children's attention to such aspects of sound as pitch
("I noticed that your rubber-band guitar has a lower sound than Tenisha's.
I wonder why that is?"), loudness ("Just a second ago, your maraca sounded
very soft and now it sounds loud. What did you do to change it?"), timbre
("I heard two different sounds coming from your rubber-band guitar—a
snapping sound and a singing sound. How did you make that happen?"),
and duration ("I can hear Jason's rubber-band guitar ringing for a couple of
seconds after he plucks it. I wonder what we could do to be able to hear it
for a very long time?").

4. Lead Children to Make Predictions About Sounds

This can be difficult with young children who are more interested in doing
something than in talking about it. But if a musical-instrument-making activity extends over time and children become familiar with it, sound can
become a topic of group time discussion. Children can bring their creations
to group time, and charts and graphs can be made to record children's predictions. For example, in making balloon maracas, children can predict
which kinds of materials will sound like thunder and which will sound like
rain. Or if a child made a maraca with only one bean and was surprised
that it made a sound, the teacher could bring it to group time and ask, "How
many people think that we will be able to hear a balloon maraca with only
one bean in it?" With young children, it is sometimes better to have the
item in question available to test right after the prediction is made, rather
than asking them to wait to test their predictions at activity time.

5. Be Prepared for, and Willing to Tolerate, a Great Deal of Noise, at Least at First

Musical instruments are noisy, and when children are first introduced to them,
they want to use them to make a lot of noise. Christie Sales, a teacher of 4-

year-olds, reported that when she first introduced a musical instrument center in her classroom, she thought she would go crazy with the noise. But after about 2 weeks, the children became accustomed to the center and began to use the instruments more selectively and purposefully. When this happened, the noise level decreased.

TWO MUSICAL-INSTRUMENT-MAKING ACTIVITIES

In this section, we describe two musical-instrument-making activities—balloon maracas and rubber-band guitars. We describe each project in detail, using examples from Christie Sales's 4-year-old class in Plainfield, Iowa, and Beth Anderson's 3- to 5-year-old class at the Malcolm Price Laboratory School at the University of Northern Iowa. Each section includes a summary of the regularities and relationships constructed by children in these activities.

Balloon Maracas

One of our first experiences with making maracas as a physical-knowledge activity was in Christie Sales's 4-year-old class. Carolyn had been visiting Christie's class on a weekly basis to explore constructivist approaches to music in early education. Her goal was to encourage children to become singers, dancers, and musicians, as well as composers, lyricists, orchestrators, conductors, instrument makers, and choreographers. The children were enthusiastic about the project.

After a few weeks of making up new melodies for old words and new words for old melodies, Carolyn decided it was time to make some musical instruments. She tells the story like this:

> During circle time, I put some rice in a balloon, blew it up, and asked the children to guess what it would sound like. Like rice? Like a balloon? We played it and listened. It sounded like rain! Since it was raining that day, we sang "Rain, rain, go away" and another song to the melody of Frère Jacques:
>
> > There is thunder, there is thunder,
> > Hear it roar, hear it roar,
> > Pitter-patter raindrops, pitter-patter raindrops,
> > I'm all wet! I'm all wet!
>
> After we finished singing, I asked the children how we might play the maraca with our thunder and rain song. Some children thought we should play the maraca all through the song; others thought we should play it only during the pitter-patter part. Children took turns

playing the maraca and singing in different ways. We found that singing and playing at the same time was hard to do.

After awhile, I brought out a bag filled with balloon maracas and handed them out. With one maraca to each child, there was "a whole lot of shakin' goin' on!" The children were so delighted with the maracas that they had trouble putting them down. So we didn't try to put them down right away, but experimented with shaking them fast and slow, loudly and softly, and so on, until everyone was ready to stop and listen.

Next we talked about how we could use the whole set of maracas in our song. Everybody wanted to play all the time, so we sang our rain and thunder song with maraca accompaniment throughout. When we were finished, somebody said, "We need thunder!"

We talked about thunder for awhile. How does thunder sound? What could we put in a balloon to make thunder? Something bigger? Something smaller? Something harder? Something softer? What might work?

The next time I came, we tried putting navy beans in one maraca and rice in another. Would they sound the same or different? We tried each one in turn. The ones with navy beans sounded like thunder and the ones with rice sounded like rain! This time I had brought a bag full of both kinds of maracas. I handed them out and we sang the song again with both kinds of sounds.

On the third day, we created a center with lots of materials to work with. We had balloons and lots of things to put in them: rice, beans, split peas, curly pasta, couscous, salt, and even some feathers. The children helped each other fit a funnel into the neck of a balloon and then put some sound-making objects inside them. After the balloons were filled, an adult helped blow them up and tie them. Then we shook them to see how they would sound.

During circle time, the children who had made maracas shared them with the group. One child had decided to fill his balloon with beans without adding any air. It made a soft, clicking sort of sound. Other children experimented with using and mixing different materials. They found that smaller, lighter materials made softer, higher sounds and that larger, heavier materials made louder, lower sounds. Some children experimented with playing the balloons in different ways (for example, by holding the tied part between their thumb and forefinger, or by cupping the whole bottom part of the balloon in their hands). Holding the tied part made a louder sound than cupping the whole balloon in one's hands. Others experimented with different sizes and shapes of balloons and different materials inside them. Later in the year we covered some balloon maracas with papier-mâché to make more durable instruments. These produced yet another sound.

The regularities and relationships that children had the opportunity to construct in this activity were the following:

1. In general, smaller, lighter items (like rice or couscous) make a softer, higher sound, and larger, heavier items (like lima beans and macaroni) make a louder, lower sound.
2. A maraca with only one item still makes a sound, although it is not very loud.
3. The addition of more items makes a louder sound, but over a certain amount does not change the sound that much.
4. Feathers do not make any sound in a balloon maraca.
5. Using a bigger balloon or blowing the balloon up bigger does not change the sound very much.
6. When you mix different items together, you tend to hear only the loudest sounds.
7. Different ways of holding the maracas can result in different sounds.

Since Carolyn's experience in Christie's classroom, we have done more experimentation with maracas, varying both the container and the things we put in them. Young children enjoy trying different kinds of containers and materials and rarely want to do much in the way of controlling variables. However, older children (middle elementary age and above) and adults sometimes expend great effort in controlling sound-making variables and derive great satisfaction from the discoveries they make.

Rubber-Band Guitars

Our first experience making stringed instruments as a physical-knowledge activity with young children was in Beth Anderson's mixed-age classroom for 3- to 5-year-olds. Over a period of 8 days, we made several different kinds of chordophones and spent time experimenting with them and playing them alone or in combination with other classroom instruments and recorded music. We also explored the physical properties of standard stringed instruments (e.g., violin, cello, mountain dulcimer, hammer dulcimer, piano, autoharp, and guitar) and learned to identify each instrument by sound.

In planning the activity, the first thing we did as teachers was to make some simple stringed instruments for ourselves. Our first instrument was made out of a box with a hole cut in the top, a cardboard bridge, and two rubber bands for strings (refer to Figure 5.1). We were delighted with our instrument and began experimenting with different ways to change its sound. First we tried varying the length, tautness, and thickness of the strings. The most dramatic effects came from variations in length and tautness, so we decided to focus on those aspects with the children first while holding the thickness of the rubber bands constant. We also experimented with the size and type of box, and the presence or absence of a sound hole in the top. These things also made a difference, so we decided to introduce these variables to the children as well. However, we decided to begin with only one size of box (a half-gallon milk carton).

Because there was so much for children to discover about making stringed instruments, we decided it needed to be more than the usual "pluck and run" activity. We met with the children six times (days 1, 3, 5, 6, 7, and 8), and on days 2 and 4, the children were free to play with their stringed instruments in any way they liked. Each day that we met with the children included a class meeting and a center activity. During the class meetings, we looked at, listened to, and played various stringed instruments and shared our questions, predictions, and discoveries with each other. During the center activities, children made, played, and experimented with various stringed instruments and shared their discoveries with each other.

During the first class meeting, Carolyn shared her interest in making and playing musical instruments. She talked about various types of instruments she had made, such as drums, maracas, and stringed instruments. Some of the children had already made drums and maracas, but nobody had made a stringed instrument. Three of the children were taking violin lessons and others had friends or family members who played guitar. The class had recently visited the high school orchestra and had seen violins, violas, cellos, and basses, and were eager to make a stringed instrument of their own.

Carolyn showed the children an instrument Betty had made out of a cardboard box, a cardboard bridge, and two rubber-band "strings." She invited several children to play it. Then she asked them whether they knew of any ways they could change the sound of the string. Some of the violin students had ideas: "Play a lower string!" "Push down on the string!" "Tune the thing!" Carolyn demonstrated some different ways to change the pitch of the string and then invited them to make their own stringed instruments.

At first, everybody wanted to make an instrument just like Betty's. But with some encouragement, they began to introduce some variations in design. For example, when Carolyn asked, "Where do you want your bridge?" one child said she wanted it on the back of her instrument. When Carolyn asked, "How many strings do you want?" another child said he wanted three. Given the choice, some children wanted sound holes and others did not. By the end of the activity period, we had a wide variety of stringed instruments to compare.

Once their instruments were made, the first thing most children wanted to do was to strum them like guitars and then take them around the classroom to show to other people. We saw this period of pretend play as an important part of getting to know the instrument. But we did not want it to end there. So after children had spent some time pretending to be cowboys and rock stars, we began to help them focus on the sounds that the individual strings made. For example, when Michael and Justin were strumming their rubber-band guitars, Carolyn asked, "I wonder what you could do to make that sound different?" Justin immediately started playing on a short section of string at the top of the carton and a short section of string below the bridge and said, "Mine goes like this."

This sort of experimentation caught on, and soon everyone was playing the strings in different places on their instruments. For example, Michael discovered that if he played his string where it was lifted from the body by the bridge, it made a different sound than if he played it on the back where it was not supported by the bridge. He walked around the classroom playing his guitar on both sides, getting a singing sound on one side and a snapping sound on the other.

On the third day, Carolyn led a class meeting in which she invited children to share their instruments with each other. For each instrument, she asked, "How is this instrument different from the one we just saw?" Once children had commented on the physical features of the instruments, she asked, "Can you show us some different ways you can play it?" and "Does that sound the same or different than before?"

Since pitch and timbre were the most salient features for the children, Carolyn decided to focus on these aspects of sound first. She described pitch in terms of "high" and "low," and timbre in terms of "singing" and "snapping" sounds. She tried singing some of the high and low sounds and invited children to sing along. Then she asked children to show the different places where they could get these sounds and followed up with questions like "I wonder why it sounds high when you play it here?" or "I wonder why it sounds snappy when you play it there?"

Sometimes children came up with surprising ideas and explanations. Devon put a rock in the hole of his guitar and shook it like a maraca. (This led to a later hypothesis that the holes in standard guitars were for storage or for adding things that would make a rattling sound.) The following conversation during the class meeting reflects Carolyn's efforts to foster children's observation and reasoning.

Jillian: (Plays all three strings on her guitar at once.)

C.H.: Do they sound the same or different?

Jillian: They're all low.

C.H.: Can you see any differences between Jillian's and Devon's guitars?

(Children notice differences in the number of strings and the placement of the bridges.)

Jillian: Me and Devon can play a song together. (They both strum their guitars together.)

C.H.: I see another difference. I wonder if anyone else noticed it, too?

Allison: A hole!

C.H.: A hole. Devon's has a hole and yours doesn't. We might want to experiment around to see if a hole makes a difference.

Jillian: [Referring to the carton] Devon's is white milk and mine is orange juice.

C.H.: I wonder if that makes a difference?

Justin: (Plays his guitar everywhere there is a place to pluck.)

C.H.: Did you make a really high sound? Where did you play that?

Justin: (Repeats the high sound below the bridge.)

Andrea: Can I do that on mine? (Tries it on hers.)

C.H.: I wonder why that happens?

Andrew: Maybe it's magic.

C.H.: It might be magic.

Alexa: I think it's because it's *lower* down there [referring to the position below the bridge] and it's *longer* up there [referring to the length of string].

Michael: (Demonstrates this with this guitar.)

Eve: (Pushes down the string with one hand and plucks with the other to get a higher pitch.)

C.H.: What do you think Eve just did?

Jillian: She plucked with both fingers!

Daniel: One finger moved!

C.H.: She pushed down with one finger and moved it to change the sound. (Demonstrates again.)

Later, Carolyn played "Mary Had a Little Lamb" on her rubber-band guitar and the children sang along. This modeling was designed to open up a new possibility—that of actually playing a song. During the center activity, children made instruments out of boxes and large and small milk cartons and played them alone and in small groups.

On the fifth day, Carolyn began group time with more sharing of instruments. One of the children showed how he had made a guitar strap for his instrument with a piece of yarn. Other children had done the same. After everyone had shared their instruments and played them, Carolyn brought out another instrument she had made—a monochord with a movable bridge made out of a piece of wood, a rubber band, and a wooden dowel (see Figure 5.2).

FIGURE 5.2. Child playing monochord

The children immediately knew how to play it. They took turns plucking the rubber band on one side of the bridge and then on the other. Then Michael came up and moved the bridge and played the rubber band on either side of it. Moving the bridge changed the sound! Then Carolyn showed her discovery: when you snap the rubber band on top of the bridge, it makes a snapping sound *and* two rubber-band sounds at the same time! After some further discussion, Carolyn played a tune on the monochord, and the children sang along.

During the center activity, children made milk carton guitars, box dulcimers, and wooden monochords (which soon turned into multichords with the addition of more strings). Some children added a second bridge to their monochord as they had seen Carolyn do to make a box dulcimer. The wooden monochords made much softer sounds than the box instruments and could hardly be heard with all the other sounds and music in the classroom. But the children played them anyway and experimented by moving the bridge(s), pressing down on the strings, stretching the strings, and snapping the strings on the bridge and on the back.

On the sixth day, Carolyn and Betty brought in a cello, a guitar, a mountain dulcimer, and a hammer dulcimer. The children identified the parts of the instruments they already knew (e.g., body, sound holes, bridges, and strings) and learned about other features of the instruments (e.g., bows, end pins, hammers, picks, necks, frets, tuning pins and pegs). During the center activity, they got a chance to play each instrument (under the close supervision of an adult). The experimental attitude they had developed during the instrument-making phase of the activity carried over to this phase as well. Children tried many different ways of playing each instrument and commented on the resulting sounds.

On the seventh day, a child brought in a stringed instrument her mother had made out of a milk carton, a yard stick, and a piece of fishing line. Another child brought in her violin, described its features, answered children's questions, and played some songs. Then everyone went up to the auditorium to see a giant stringed instrument in a black box that worked like a mechanical hammer dulcimer—a grand piano! The children identified the harp, the strings, the bridges, and other things like the hammers, dampers, keys, and pedals. Then they listened to a miniconcert by Carolyn.

On the eighth day, Carolyn brought in something that *looked* like a dulcimer, but *worked* like a mechanical guitar. It was an autoharp! Carolyn showed how she had just tuned it and several children took turns playing it with one person pushing down the buttons and the other person strumming the strings. After that, Carolyn played recorded examples of different types of stringed instruments for the children to identify (e.g., violin, cello, guitar, hammer dulcimer). The hammer dulcimer piece was so exciting that Beth invited everyone to get up and dance. The children danced, played their rubber-band guitars, and soon began to add other instruments from the music center, thus bringing our unit on stringed instruments to a spirited finale.

The regularities and relationships children had the opportunity to construct in this activity were the following:

1. The shorter the string, the higher the sound. The longer the string, the lower the sound. (You can change the length of the string by moving the bridge, or by pushing the string down with your finger.)
2. The tighter (or more stretched) the string, the higher the sound. The looser (or less stretched) the string, the lower the sound. (You can stretch the string by pulling on it, or by turning it on a tuning peg.)
3. Plucking, strumming, hammering, and bowing make different kinds of sounds.
4. Freely vibrating strings make a singing sound. Strings that are stopped by a hard surface make a snapping sound.

5. The more gently you play, the softer the sound. The more forcefully you play, the louder the sound. This is true for plucking, hammering, and bowing.
6. Instruments with box resonators are louder than instruments without box resonators. (In our noisy classroom, we couldn't hear much difference between instruments that did and did not have sound holes.)
7. Some sounds last longer than other sounds (e.g., loud sounds seem to last longer than soft sounds; singing sounds seem to last longer than snapping sounds).

Even though children had the opportunity to discover one or more of these regularities and relationships, not everyone discovered the same things. Some children described pitches categorically as either "high" or "low" while others described them relatively as "higher than" or "lower than" each other. Some children associated high and low pitches with different places on their instruments (e.g., the parts above or below the bridge; the front or back of the instrument), whereas others went on to discover why different places on their instruments made different sounds (e.g., the string is longer above the bridge and shorter below it). Nobody in the group commented on the apparent contradiction between string length and tension (when you stretch a rubber band you make it both higher and longer). This is something that would most likely be noticed by older children and adults.

By the end of the 8 days, children had used their instruments for a variety of purposes—scientific, musical, and dramatic. One child even decorated her wooden monochord with colored felt pens. Many children continued to engage in pretend play with their instruments (strumming like a rock star with all the dramatic gestures and gyrations), but for some their play was truly musical. One morning a group of children were standing in a semicircle strumming their instruments and singing an invented song with nonsense words. A teaching assistant looked up and said, "Oh, can you play me a song?" Carolyn, who had been listening, said, "They *are* playing a song." The teaching assistant said, "Oh, I'm sorry, I wasn't listening." Sometimes it is hard to listen to children's beginning efforts at improvisation. Beginning efforts often sound noisy and chaotic. But with time, random noises turn into repeated patterns that, in turn, can form the beginning of an invented song.

CONCLUSION

Making musical instruments is a rich and satisfying activity for young children. In the two examples of instrument-making activities described in this chapter, we have shown how teachers can move from Type A/B activities (where most aspects of the activity are controlled by the teacher) and Type C activities (where most aspects of the activity are controlled by the children) to constructivist Type D activities where children collaborate with the teacher and each other to make discoveries about their instruments. We hope that this chapter will encourage teachers and children to engage in their own investigations into the art and science of musical sound.

Chapter 6

Cooking Transformations

Betty Zan, Rebecca Edmiaston, and Christina Sales

Cooking is one of the most popular and satisfying activities conducted in constructivist classrooms. It appeals to children's interests, invites experimentation, and fosters cooperation among children. It also teaches children independent living skills; provides opportunities to integrate math, science, literacy, and social studies in meaningful activities that children find interesting and challenging; and fosters autonomy by allowing children to prepare and eat food in the classroom.

In this chapter we describe how cooking is typically presented in Classroom Types A, B, C, and D; discuss issues that must be resolved before bringing cooking into the classroom; and present seven principles of teaching illustrated with stories, primarily from a Head Start classroom. Finally, we describe how cooking provides opportunities to integrate across curricular domains.

COOKING IN CLASSROOM TYPES A, B, C, AND D

Although food and nutrition are important components of early childhood science curriculum, early childhood educators do not generally consider cooking itself as part of the science program. Many teachers, including those in Types A and B classrooms, tend to conceptualize science solely as content knowledge. Teachers in Types C and D classrooms regard science not only as content but also as a process of individual and cooperative hypothesis generating and testing, experimentation, and problem solving. Constructivist Type D teachers view cooking activities as opportunities to stimulate children's scientific reasoning. The approaches to cooking typical of each of the four types of teachers are described in more detail below.

Classroom Type A

Cooking rarely occurs in Type A classrooms. Children in these classrooms study the food pyramid and learn about the variety of foods within different food groups. For example, they may classify pictures of foods into the categories of fruits or vegetables. If cooking does occur, it is typically related to class parties or celebrations of special holidays and is not connected to the science curriculum. For example, children might be given the opportunity to decorate a prebaked gingerbread man with cinnamon candies or raisins at a winter celebration.

Classroom Type B

Teachers in Type B classrooms present cooking experiences as a product-oriented activity to be carried out mainly by the teacher. Although they may allow individual children minimal participation in carrying out the specifications of a batch recipe, such as adding one cup of flour to the bowl or stirring the ingredients, the teacher remains in charge of the activity. Science goals center around the nutritional aspects of food. In many Type B classrooms, teachers use cooking experiences as opportunities for children to address goals in other curricular areas such as following directions, engaging in sequencing activities, "reading" recipes, observing measurement activities, or addressing safety practices—goals clearly not related to the development of scientific understanding and knowledge. Frequently, cooking activities take on the flavor of an arts and crafts experience. For example, after reading *The Gingerbread Man*, children are instructed to replicate the teacher's pattern of a gingerbread man by counting out three cinnamon candies for buttons, two raisins for the eyes, and one piece of licorice for the mouth. This objective centers on children's counting skills and their ability to duplicate simple patterns rather than on the development of scientific knowledge.

Classroom Type C

Cooking serves a broad variety of functions in Type C classrooms. As in Type B classrooms, teachers use cooking activities to promote children's understanding of nutrition and their ability to classify foods by food groups. Cooking opportunities frequently resemble arts and crafts activities, although children are provided more opportunities to make choices and express their individual creativity than children in Type B classrooms. For example, after reading *The Gingerbread Man*, children may be given the choice to cut out and decorate their own gingerbread man. Teachers in Type C classrooms initiate young children in food preparation through cooking experiences such as Ants on a Log, in which children fill celery sticks with peanut butter and place raisins on the top. As children carry out these simple preparations, teachers also introduce basic hygiene and safety measures to young children.

Teachers in Type C classrooms often see cooking experiences as opportunities to enhance and integrate academic areas such as mathematics and literacy. For example, the teacher may write and illustrate the recipe for Ants on a Log, and encourage children to count how many celery sticks and raisins they will need. Teachers in Type C classrooms see cooking as an opportunity for children to engage in hands-on activities in which manipulating and using real objects is considered sufficient for children's development of knowledge. However, children's understanding of the regularities and relationships that can be formulated through the process of cooking is not recognized or supported. Unfortunately, many cooking activities ignore the invisible aspects of chemistry that appear to young children to be magic. For example, when cooking muffins in the classroom, teachers fail to invite children to explore why some muffins rise and others do not. As a result, children cannot see the connections between their actions and the resulting products.

Classroom Type D

Constructivist teachers in Type D classrooms include cooking as part of the science curriculum. Like Type C teachers, they recognize how cooking provides multiple opportunities for integrating curriculum, for increasing children's knowledge of food and nutrition, and for developing children's awareness of the important hygiene and safety measures related to food preparation. Additionally, constructivist educators view cooking experiences as having potential for stimulating children's scientific reasoning. Cooking activities are highly motivating to children and offer them real and purposeful opportunities to develop questions, test out their reasoning, encounter contradictions, and revise their ideas—that is, to construct knowledge. For instance, children have opportunities to notice what occurs when liquid is added to a dry mixture. Because the constructivist teacher does not insist that they follow the recipe, children may notice that their end product does not look the same as a peer's. Teachers encourage children to focus on these invisible aspects of chemistry and attempt to identify what might account for the observed differences.

Gwen Harmon, a constructivist Head Start teacher, realized that her 3- and 4-year-olds did not understand why muffins "grew" in the microwave. To them it was magic. One day when they ran out of muffin mix (see Figure 6.1), she posed the following problem: "We have a problem because we have run out of muffin mix. Do any of you have any ideas about what we should do?" The children replied that they needed more "white powder." They got a bag of flour from the pantry and proceeded to make muffins as they had in the past. However, the muffins did not "grow" and tasted terrible. Gwen

Muffin Mix:

8 cups flour
1 ½ cups dried milk
¾ to 1 ½ cups sugar (see note below)
4 tablespoons baking powder
1 tablespoon salt

Mix everything together and store in an airtight container. Makes enough mix for approximately 45 muffins.

Muffin Recipe

4 tablespoons muffin mix
(see recipe above)

3 half-tablespoons water
(not 3 and ½ tablespoons!)

1 teaspoon oil

Put everything in a small bowl and stir lightly.

Pour into a paper cup.

Bake in a microwave oven on high for approximately 45 seconds
(cooking times may vary).

FIGURE 6.1. Muffin recipe

asked if they had any ideas about how to make the muffins taste better. Over the course of the next few days the children suggested adding other white powders such as sugar and salt to the recipe and while the muffins improved in taste, they still did not grow. At this point, Gwen showed them a new white powder, baking powder. She explained that baking powder helps muffins to grow and added it to the children's muffin mix. As children made muffins that day they congregated around the microwave peering into the window. "Look, it's growing!" "Mine is getting big!" A few days later, children informed visitors to the class that it is the baking powder that makes the muffins grow. Although the children certainly did not understand all of the chemical interactions occurring as the muffins baked (neither do most adults), they no longer saw making muffins as simply magic.

BRINGING COOKING INTO THE CLASSROOM

Before introducing cooking activities in the classroom, several important issues must be considered. These concern the children's readiness for cooking, important safety and hygiene considerations, and other curriculum in place in the classroom.

Young Children's Readiness for Cooking

Even 3-year-olds can do some cooking, with support. Understanding what children are capable of doing will help when choosing appropriate recipes. Sometimes, young children are so fascinated with the ingredients of the recipe they cannot focus on the cooking aspect of the activity. A story from a Head Start classroom illustrates this point.

Near the beginning of the year, Christie Sales and her teaching partner, Gwen Harmon, were anxious to begin cooking, and chose the muffin recipe in Figure 6.1. At group time Christie demonstrated how to make a muffin. She showed the children (ages 3 and 4 years) how to measure by leveling off their measuring spoons with a wooden tongue depressor and how to measure and add water and oil without spilling. During the following few days, she sat at the cooking table during activity time, helping each child who chose to make a muffin. After witnessing successful muffin making and appropriate use of the materials, she decided to allow the children to make their muffins independently, with adults nearby to supervise the use of the microwave.

Checking in later to see how the muffin making was progressing, she noticed that few children were really measuring. Most children were just dumping ingredients in the bowl. Christie explained to Gwen that these were beginning steps and that experimentation was necessary. She predicted that when the children saw the results—inedible goo—they would begin to follow the recipe. However, a short time later a classroom volunteer called her attention back to the cooking table where one child was holding the bottle of oil upside down and squeezing. The child watched, fascinated, while oil ran everywhere.

As Christie and Gwen reflected on the incident at the end of the day, they realized that the children were not interested in measuring. They were interested in dumping! The teachers decided to follow the children's interest and filled the sand table with flour, bowls, measuring cups, measuring spoons, spoons for mixing, and other large and small containers. The children flocked to the flour table. They made make-believe pies and birthday cakes and muffins. They poured and dumped and leveled. When interest at the flour table diminished, the teachers introduced the idea of making a papier-mâché piñata. They showed the children how to make paste using water and flour. The children experimented with different consistencies and figured out the logico-mathematical relationship that the more water they added, the runnier their paste became. Likewise, the more flour they added, the thicker it became. At this point the teachers decided that the children were ready to make muffins. However, they eliminated the oil from the recipe and made them only with muffin mix and water. The children continued to experiment, but they were no longer dumping. After several weeks, when they were confident of the children's ability to follow the recipe more accurately, they returned the oil to the recipe with great success.

Safety and Hygiene

As most adults realize, cooking exposes young children to potential dangers—primarily heat, sharp objects, and germs. As teachers, our task is to minimize these dangers so that children can safely engage in cooking. Safety and hygiene are excellent examples of content that is appropriate to tell children directly because this is not something they can easily discover on their own. Young children have difficulty understanding the necessity to wash hands, utensils, and cooking surfaces because germs are not observable, and neither are the effects of not adhering to good hygienic practices. It is possible to cultivate germs in culture dishes and thus make them visible to children. However, making a connection between germs in a culture dish and good hygiene practices for cooking is beyond the comprehension of most young children. They simply do not understand why they should wash their hands before cooking or refrain from licking the mixing spoon. Even when the teacher explains the rules, these injunctions may feel arbitrary to young children. The teacher must simply insist upon them as rules for cooking.

Safety rules must also be discussed with children and enforced, and teachers must arrange the cooking environment to be safe. Disposable plastic knives are surprisingly effective for cutting up fruits and vegetables (although no knife is totally safe). Microwave ovens are much safer than conventional or toaster ovens; consequently, when a recipe requires heat, we prefer using a microwave. Electric skillets can be used in early childhood classrooms with supervision, and can be made safer. Christie constructed a wooden frame that fits over an electric skillet so that when children inevitably rest their arm on the edge of the skillet, they do not get burned. One wonderful idea that came from a child is to use children's heavyweight mittens as pot holders. They are the correct size for children and are readily available.

In addition to telling children the safety rules, teachers must provide supervision for all cooking activities that involve risk. In practical terms, this means that if one is introducing a new piece of equipment that requires close supervision at first (say, a blender), one should not have another activity taking place during activity time that also requires close supervision.

Concurrent Curriculum

Because cooking activities are extremely popular, it is especially important to provide an abundance of other interesting and engaging activities in addition to cooking. Otherwise, what will happen is a crush of children all wanting to cook at the same time. This can be a disaster and can discourage even the most experienced teacher from ever again including cooking in the classroom. To avoid this, be sure that children have other activities to capture their interest while they are waiting for a turn at the cooking center. Depending on the recipe, this may also mean the same cooking activity will need to remain available for several days or even weeks until all children have had the chance to make it several times or until interest wanes.

PRINCIPLES OF TEACHING

We have synthesized our years of conducting and observing cooking activities with young children into seven principles of teaching discussed below.

I. Choose Recipes That Offer Something Challenging for Children to Do

To do this, one must have a good understanding of what the children are capable of doing and what they would find challenging. While recipes such as Cracker Spiders (a sandwich made with 2 round crackers and peanut butter, with 8 pretzel stick legs sticking out)—a category we refer to as "cooking crafts"—are occasionally appropriate, they are generally challenging only to the youngest children. These recipes may serve other useful purposes such as providing children with the incentive to try unfamiliar and healthy foods. However, a steady diet of such recipes will not serve to promote the reasoning and construction of knowledge we have as our constructivist goals.

The general goal of constructivist cooking activities is the construction of physical and logico-mathematical knowledge. One must therefore make a thorough analysis of the recipes in order to understand what opportunities they afford children to construct regularities and relationships. As pointed out earlier, regularities are those things that always happen. They can be thought of as general laws. For example, heat changes things. This is true most of the time with cooking. Heat makes some things (such as eggs) harder, while it makes other things (such as potatoes) softer. Once they have noticed regularities, children can move on to construct relationships between what they do and the outcome they obtain. For example, children have the opportunity to discover that the longer you cook an egg, the harder it gets. This is a cause and effect relationship between the length of cooking time and the consistency of the egg. Cause and effect relationships are at the heart of scientific reasoning.

One clue to selecting a recipe that offers opportunities for scientific reasoning is whether or not the recipe is foolproof. A recipe is foolproof when nothing in it varies. With nothing to vary, nothing can happen except what is predetermined, and therefore little reasoning is necessary. Recipes such as Cracker Spiders and Ants on a Log tend to be relatively foolproof. Generally, these recipes involve placement of uncooked or precooked foods in certain arrangements so that the food preparation resembles a craft activity rather than a cooking activity. Children have few opportunities to construct cause and effect relationships in these recipes.

2. Make Recipes That Children Can Read on Their Own

Recipes should be selected and designed so that children can follow them with little help from the teacher. Depending on the age of the children, this may mean creating recipes with illustrations and few words. The fruit smoothie recipe in Figure 6.2 is a very simple recipe that can easily be illustrated. As children become familiar and comfortable in "reading" recipes, the text accompanying the recipe may be lengthened. Repeated exposure to the same recipe assists children in recognizing words that regularly appear, such as *cup*, *mix*, and *spoon*, and for some children results in a base of sight words related to cooking. For younger children it is not necessary to label the cup as one-fourth cup. It can simply be represented as one small cup. As

Put in blender

3 tablespoons yogurt

2 tablespoons orange juice

2 strawberries

¼ of a banana

1 teaspoon brown sugar

Blend briefly

Pour into cup

FIGURE 6.2. Fruit smoothie recipe

children progress to more complex recipes, the size of the illustrations can guide the children in following directions. In the muffin recipe (Figure 6.1), the size of the spoons ranges from big to small. Words such as *big*, *medium*, and *small* can be substituted for specific measurements of *tablespoon*, *half-tablespoon*, and *teaspoon*.

Recipes may be presented as posters, laminated recipe books with one direction per page, or loose-leaf recipes with one direction per page placed in sequence at the cooking station. The sequenced pages could be attached to a line with clothespins. These can be used over and over and are fairly inexpensive to make, especially if you have access to a computer, a printer, and a laminator. In Figure 6.3 we list books of children's recipes that we think are excellent. Having a recipe to follow gives children a reason to decode words and attempt to read. It also emphasizes children's autonomy in that children can regulate their actions in relation to the recipe.

3. Plan Cooking Activities That Mainly Can Be Done in Small Groups or Individually

Occasionally the teacher may want to do a whole group cooking activity such as making stone soup after reading the folktale *Stone Soup* (Brown, 1947; Forest, 1998; McGovern, 1968, 1986). In general, however, it is better to allow children to work with one or two other children (or even alone). This way, they have more opportunities to be autonomous and experimental.

Children can also work in pairs to prepare food for the entire class. With the teacher, two children decide the day before what they want to prepare (from a collection of familiar snack recipes); check to see if all of the ingredients are available; and, if necessary, make a shopping list for the teacher. The next day, they prepare enough snack for the entire class and serve it during snack time. This contributes to a sense of community as children take on the responsibility for providing food for their classmates who have a chance to express appreciation to the cooks.

Making individual portions provides opportunity to make comparisons between one's own and a peer's result. This helps children in constructing the relationships described above. An anecdote from Gwen's classroom provides a good illustration of the cooperation and learning fostered between children when they are allowed to cook side by side with little or no teacher intervention. From across the room, Gwen heard Chondra say, "You don't know what you are doing." She looked up and saw Chondra take Jerry's cup full of muffin batter out of his hand and pour it back into his mixing bowl. She stirred it until the batter was smooth and sticky, poured it back into the paper cup, and handed it back to Jerry who placed it in the microwave oven to cook. This may seem like an insignificant incident to a casual

Johnson, B. (1998). Cup cooking: Individual child-portion picture recipes.
    Beltsville, MD: Gryphon House.
Katzen, M. & Henderson, A. (1994). Pretend soup and other real recipes: A
    cookbook for preschoolers and up. Berkeley, CA: Tricycle Press.
    (This beautiful book by the author of the Moosewood Cookbook
    contains simple and healthful vegetarian recipes with easy to "read"
    illustrations.)
University of Illinois at Chicago Children's Center. (1985). I made it myself: A
    cookbook for young children. Chicago: UIC Children's Center. (This
    simply worded and illustrated cookbook contains 14 recipes that can be
    separated from the spiral binder. It can be obtained from Epicenter
    Bookshop, Chicago Circle Center, University of Illinois at Chicago,
    750 South Halsted Street, Chicago, Illinois, 60607.)
Veitch, B. & Harms, T. (1981). Cook and learn: Pictorial single portion recipes.
    Menlo Park, CA: Addison-Wesley. (This book contains illustrated,
    extremely easy-to-read recipes, many of them single portion.)

FIGURE 6.3. Cookbooks for children

observer, but to Gwen, it revealed much about the two children and the success of her curriculum. It told her that Chondra knows a lot about making
muffins and has made a relationship between the way the batter looks before it goes into the microwave and what it looks like when it comes out.
She knows that if it goes in without being thoroughly stirred, it will not make
a good muffin. This incident also showed Gwen something about how
Chondra uses her language and social skills. Rather than taking ownership
of his muffin, she handed it back to Jerry after she stirred it. This incident
also says something about Jerry and his ability to see another child in the
classroom as an expert. Jerry did not complain to the teacher, "She took my
muffin," as might be expected from a child this age. Instead, he seemed to
recognize her helpful intention and waited patiently while Chondra showed
him how to improve his muffin. All of this occurred without any teacher
intervention.

4. Do Not Insist That Children Follow Recipes Precisely

Another story about muffin making in Christie's class illustrates how devia-
tions from the recipe can result in construction of knowledge. She always
demonstrates how to make a muffin, but children frequently pay little attention to the directions and are inaccurate in their measurements. This often

results in mixtures with too little or too much liquid. When the mixtures have too little water, they are often very powdery and do not rise when they are cooked.

For several days Christie had been observing Jonathan make muffins. Every time, he either spilled most of the water out of his measuring spoon before adding it to the muffin mix or would not fill the measuring spoon all the way to the top. He would pour the crumbly batter into a paper cup, place it in the microwave oven to bake, and in 45 seconds retrieve a muffin that was no taller than it was when he placed it into the microwave. Finally, Christie said, "Jonathan, why do you think you always get such a short muffin?" "It didn't cook long enough," he answered. "Do you have any ideas about how you could make it taller?" she asked. "Cook it some more," he said. Knowing that he would not believe her if she told him this would not work, she asked, "Do you want to try that?" He nodded, put the muffin back in the microwave, and cooked it longer. Soon the room was filled with the scent of burning. When Jonathan retrieved his muffin, it was almost black in the center. He looked at it dejectedly. Christie said, "I see you are upset. Were you surprised your muffin burned?" He nodded. "Would you like to try to make another one?" He nodded again. "You know," she said, "I noticed that Lee makes really tall muffins. Maybe you could ask him what he does to get them to be so tall." Together they went to find Lee. Lee consented to show Jonathan how he makes a muffin. A few days later Christie observed Jonathan making another muffin. He very carefully poured water into his measuring spoon, filling it all the way to the top. Then slowly he moved it over the mixing bowl and poured the entire spoonful into his muffin mix. It appeared that Lee taught Jonathan the importance of measuring accurately.

This story contains an excellent example of how a constructivist teacher respects children's reasoning and fosters experimentation by encouraging them to try out their ideas. Jonathan had watched other children's muffins cook in the microwave. He had observed that as they cooked, they grew taller. He concluded that the longer you cook a muffin, the taller it gets, and that therefore he needed to cook his short muffin longer. By allowing him to burn a muffin, Christie helped him to discover for himself that his idea was erroneous.

This story also shows how cooking can contribute to the sociomoral atmosphere by promoting cooperation among children. Rather than telling Jonathan how to make a tall muffin, she referred Jonathan to Lee. This accomplished several purposes: It strengthened the relationship between Jonathan and Lee; it showed Lee that the teacher recognized his ability to make muffins; and it showed both boys that children can be teachers too.

5. Allow Children to Make the Same Recipe Many Times

It takes a long time for children to become familiar enough with a recipe to begin to notice and make sense of the regularities and relationships embedded in the activity. This familiarity is also necessary for young children (especially prereaders) to begin to "read" the recipe. The muffin recipe, for example (Figure 6.1), calls for 4 tablespoons of muffin mix, 3 half-tablespoons of water, and 1 teaspoon of oil. After children have had experience making muffins, they become aware of the seriation of the spoons (large, medium, and small).

Because children benefit more from making a few recipes many times than from making many recipes once, this means that one need not invest in massive quantities of recipes. A few basic ones are sufficient until children have mastered these and ask for more. Choice of particular recipes depends on the backgrounds of the children, the types of foods they are accustomed to eating, the foods available, and the budget. We have found that a good collection of recipes for a preschool or kindergarten class includes muffins, fruit shakes or smoothies, pancakes, french toast, quesadillas, dips (both fruit and vegetable), pudding, sauted zucchini, glazed carrots, noodle soup made with ramen noodles, and oatmeal.

6. Encourage Children to Create Their Own Recipes

When children have become familiar with a few basic recipes, they can begin to suggest variations. For example, in Gwen's classroom where the children had many experiences making banana yogurt shakes in a blender, the children decided they wanted to make a different type of shake. They had a class discussion in which they talked about several different options and decided on peaches. One child then suggested that they try ice cream rather than yogurt in the shakes; so they made a shopping list for the teacher, and the next day they made their peach shakes.

Sometimes children are simply curious about what will happen when they mix certain ingredients together. The results of these experiments are usually not successful from a culinary standpoint. This introduces the controversial subject of wasting food. For some people and some cultures, using food for activities other than meals is considered a violation of a primary value. If this is the case, then allowing children to experiment with combining and cooking different ingredients may not be appropriate. However, if wasting some food in the interest of education is acceptable, then allowing children to experiment with cooking different foods in different combinations can be fruitful.

7. Plan for Messes

Cooking generates messes under the best of circumstances. Add in young children whose motor coordination is not fully developed, and you have a recipe for possible disaster. This should not be a deterrent to cooking. Instead, the teacher can develop strategies for minimizing the mess, making clean-up go smoothly, and turning over responsibility for clean-up to the children.

Cooking is best conducted on a noncarpeted floor and, if at all possible, near a source of water. However, this is not always possible. Christie once taught 4-year-olds in a classroom without a water source. She used two small garbage cans with lids. She taught the children to fill one can by siphoning water from the sink in the bathroom and pulling the can on a cart into the classroom. The other can was for the dirty water. She placed the cans on either side of a small table and put a wash basin, a pitcher, soap, sponges, and towels beside the basin. When the children needed water, they used the pitcher to dip clean water and pour it into the basin. When they were finished, they dumped the dirty water into the dirty water garbage can. This system worked quite well.

Lots of cleaning supplies should be available to children—sponges, rags, paper towels. Diluted vinegar in a spray bottle is excellent for clean-up. It is nontoxic, cheap, and effective. A mop and bucket with a mop squeezer attached to it is invaluable for getting children to clean up floor messes and should be standard equipment in every classroom (not just for cooking). A mop handle can be cut off so that it is the correct height for children. Using the mop squeezer to squeeze water out of the mop is a physical-knowledge activity in and of itself. Also, the children love it because it makes them feel grown-up.

INTEGRATING CURRICULUM IN CONSTRUCTIVIST COOKING ACTIVITIES

Many of the skills and experiences that occur as children engage in science activities also enhance children's development in other curricular areas. Specifically, cooking provides opportunities to integrate language arts, mathematics, and social studies (as illustrated by the content web for the muffin-making activity in Figure 6.4). For example, as children follow recipes, they have opportunities to read and make sense of the words and drawings. Oral and written language skills and vocabulary are developed as children express hypotheses, discuss their experiments, and compare their results. In relationship to mathematics, children read numerals, draw one-to-one correspondences between the drawings in the recipe and the materials, seriate measur-

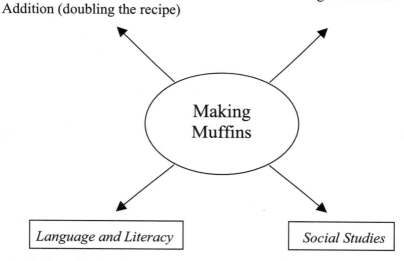

Mathematics

Measurement
1:1 correspondence
Numeral recognition
Counting (1–4)
Seriation of utensils
Addition (doubling the recipe)

Science

Forming hypotheses
Testing hypotheses
Problem solving
Making predictions
Drawing conclusions

Making
Muffins

Language and Literacy

Vocabulary: level, mix, stir, pour,
    rise, grow, texture
Group discussions
Reading recipes
Writing recipes
Sequencing their actions using photos
Representing through drawings
Phonemic awareness
Sight words (the, it, muffin, mix)
Letter–sound relationships (m)
Writing first and last names

Social Studies

Gender roles
Independent living skills
Food sources
Conserving resources
Democratic process
Social relations
  • Cooperation
  • Turn-taking
  • Sharing
  • Assisting others
  • "Teaching" others
  • Self-image

FIGURE 6.4. Web of content domains in making muffins

ing utensils, and engage in the operation of addition as they double a recipe to make enough to share with a friend. Cooking links to social studies content by promoting discussion of gender roles, development of independent living skills, and investigations of the food production and distribution system. In preschool classrooms where cooking is an ongoing part of the curriculum, integration of curriculum is easily implemented.

Literacy

Cooking provides reasons for children to engage in literacy behaviors across a broad range of developmental levels and meet literacy goals such as recognizing and writing their first names.

In Gwen's classroom, children were highly interested in making muffins, and almost everyone wanted to cook daily. Since the cooking center could only accommodate a few at a time, children decided that a sign-up list was a fair way to determine who could be in the cooking center. Jerry, who loved to cook, became very motivated to learn to write his name so that he would have a turn to make muffins. Initially he always asked an adult to write his name on the sign-up board. Gwen routinely requested that he get his nametag so she would know how to write his name. They would look at his card and discuss the letters in his name and she would demonstrate how to make his *J*. By the next week Jerry could write his own *J* and his teacher would print the other letters. A few weeks later Jerry produced his name with only minimal assistance. In addition to writing their names, children in the class learned to recognize classmates' names as they examined the list to find out whose turn was next.

One of the authors (Rebecca) who visited this classroom regularly would sometimes draw pictures or take photos of children during activity time. The children would label the pictured activities and write their names under the ones in which they had participated. This provided many opportunities to discuss the beginning and ending sounds of words and hypothesize what letters represent these sounds. For example, children labeled the cooking activity as "Making Muffins." Darnell was quick to point out that both of these words began with the same sound. When Rebecca said "Mmm, What letter do you think makes this sound?" Bridgit knew that the letter *M* came at the beginning of both words. Very quickly children began to draw attention to other words in their environment that also had letters that were in their own names. Such recognition of letters and the sounds that they represent are critical relationships children must construct in literacy development.

Some children in the classroom made books about their cooking experiences. Bridgit selected photographs that had been taken while she was making muffins, determined the appropriate sequence of the photos, and dictated the following story.

Making Muffins

By Bridgit

First I put the muffin mix in my bowl. I stirred it.
I licked the spoon.
Then I turned the page [of the muffin recipe book].
I count 1 2 3 4 [as she points to the 4 tablespoons of muffin mix on the recipe].
I count 1 2 3 [as she points to the 3 half-tablespoons of water shown in the recipe].
I put water in it.
I put 5 chocolate chips in.
Then I put it in the microwave.
I took a lick but it was too hot. So I got a drink.
Then it cooled really really long. Then I ate it all.
The End

Bridgit wrote some of the words in her book and helped identify beginning and ending letters that occurred in many of the words that she dictated. When her book was finished, Rebecca pointed out that she had one word in her story that was also in her name and circled the *it* in Bridgit. She asked Bridgit if she could find that word in her story. Bridgit proceeded to locate each *it* in her story and place a circle around it. This activity marked the beginning of sight word recognition for her. Bridgit as well as other children who authored books about cooking read them to classmates and placed copies in the class library. These books became classroom favorites and facilitated development of individual literacy goals.

Mathematics

Cooking also offers opportunities to facilitate mathematical goals across a broad range of developmental levels. Measurement, a common goal required in cooking, was meaningful for some children in Gwen's classroom, while other children were completely unaware of its role. Observations of two children, Emilio and Juan, exemplify the broad range of developmental levels observed in the class. Following the second demonstration Emilio attempted to become quite precise in his measuring. He carefully used a plastic knife to level his four tablespoons of muffin mix before emptying them into the small bowl for mixing ingredients. While measuring the required three half-tablespoons of water, he first held the spoon above his mixing bowl. When he noticed extra water spilling into the bowl, he became more careful. As he measured his next spoonful, he moved his spoon so the extra water would fall on the table rather than in his mixing bowl. Juan, on the other hand, imitated the actions of measuring without understanding the underlying reasons. Juan would pull out a heaping tablespoonful of muffin mix, hold the spoon over his small mixing bowl, level off the extra mix into his mixing bowl, and then pour the remaining spoonful on top of that! When he measured the water he always added lots of extra water to the mix. In making muffins, he intended to imitate his teacher's actions and those of his peers, but he clearly did not understand the logical reason for measurement. Inevitably, his muffins were very soggy and, according to him, not very tasty.

Operations such as addition and subtraction can also be integrated into cooking activities. The following vignette is a good example of such an opportunity. Bridgit and Summer, two good friends in the Head Start classroom, announced to Gwen they wanted to make a smoothie together. Immediately seeing the possibilities for mathematical problem solving in this situation Gwen asked, "Are you going to make enough for one person or two?" The girls decided they wanted to make enough for two. "Well," Gwen said, "this recipe is only for one person. So, how are you going to make enough for two?" She pointed to the first ingredient. "It says here you need one cup of milk. How many will you need?" "Two," the girls answered. With Gwen's support, Bridgit and Summer went through the remainder of the recipe deciding how many of each ingredient they would need to make enough for two people. When they were finished, they set out two cups and divided the shake into two equal portions.

These early experiences in mathematics provide a foundation for later, more formal investigations.

Social Studies

As demonstrated in the above vignette, social studies topics (including social and moral development) naturally arise in cooking activities. Democratic process is an integral part of a classroom in which children have a strong voice in deciding how life in the classroom should be. For example, when the children in Gwen's classroom decided to change the muffin recipe, they conducted a class meeting and suggested three possible new ingredients: strawberries, blueberries, and chocolate chips. They voted by placing their name cards under their choice. Chocolate chips won.

Cooking also provides opportunities for children to explore gender roles. Teachers can stimulate discussion by posing questions such as: "What kind of cooking happens at your house?" "Who does the cooking?" "Who cooks on the stove inside?" "Who cooks outside on the barbeque grill?" "Who cooks at the city's summer celebration in the park?" Investigations can include visits to nearby eating establishments to meet the cooks. It is entirely possible during these discussions that a child in a preschool or kindergarten class might announce that boys do not cook. Experiences such as those described in this chapter can help to dispel these stereotypes.

Finally, cooking may lead children to question where different foods come from. Investigation of this question can lead to numerous studies such as where food is grown, the roles various people play in the production of food, and how food gets to our supermarkets. Field trips to grocery stores, farmers' markets, and farms follow naturally. Because the questions are of genuine interest to children, they actively participate in identifying the answers.

CONCLUSION

Children are almost universally interested in cooking, and cooking provides them rich opportunities to be experimental. In this chapter we have attempted to show how to implement cooking activities so that they promote children's scientific reasoning and cooperation. At the same time, cooking also provides opportunities to integrate the subject matters of literacy, mathematics, and social studies, and gives children opportunities to be self-regulating. It is our opinion that cooking makes an important contribution to early childhood curriculum and should be a part of every early childhood classroom.

Chapter 7

Experimenting with Draining and Movement of Water in Tubes

Rheta DeVries, Hyang Lim Kwak, and
Christina Sales

Water play is an old standby in early education. In early childhood textbooks, justifications for water play include its contribution to children's emotional development (feelings of pleasure and mastery, outlet for aggression, and relaxation) and intellectual development (symbolic, mathematical, and language development; creativity; and problem solving). Children are said to learn "concepts such as volume, measuring, and pouring liquids" (Hildebrand, 1985, p. 220) and "implicit knowledge about buoyancy, resistance, gravity, wave motion, and other principles" (Read, 1976, p. 213). However, no detailed connection is drawn between these concepts and how children acquire them. It is as though the concepts are somehow magically learned through generalized experiences with water.

Water activities are found in Classrooms Types C and D but rarely in Types A and B. In Type C classrooms, water activities often include both those that underestimate and those that overestimate children's capabilities for learning. Those that underestimate children's possibilities include pouring, catching, and bathing dolls. Such activities are excellent for children to whom those phenomena are novel and interesting, and there are still things to figure out how to do. Sometimes they are emotionally comforting or involve rich pretend play. They may be necessary prerequisites for more complex experiences. However, these activities may be too limited for most 4- and 5-year-olds. On the other hand, teachers in Type C classrooms may sometimes overestimate children's capabilities by trying to teach concepts involving nonobservable phenomena that children can understand only as magic. For example, early childhood texts include activities such as watching a kettle boil and steam condense and observing frost patterns on windows. While children may wonder about such phenomena, they offer little possibility for experimentation. These phenomena do not meet criteria for good physical-knowledge activities as they are not producible by children's action, observable (although the results can be observed, the causal factors cannot), or variable. Children cannot figure out through their own actions how these phenomena occur. In contrast, the cognitive objectives of water activities in Type D constructivist classrooms are focused on the specific relationships involved in subject-matter knowledge. For example, rather than taking gravity as the concept to be learned, one constructivist teacher focused on the concept of draining, a result of gravity, but a phenomenon observable by children.

Most descriptions of water activities suggested in books on early education are limited to briefly listing materials and types of activities. Only a few go beyond this limited treatment to suggest how to develop, observe, and evaluate water activities in terms of children's learning. Those that do go beyond include the African Primary Science Program (1973), Elementary Science Study (1971), and the work of Zubrowski (1981), Crahay and Delhaxhe (1988), Kamii and DeVries (1978/1993), and Forman and Hill (1984). However, none of these offers detailed insight into children's reasoning as it develops over time.

In this chapter, we follow highlights of the process that a teacher and a child went through as the child experimented with water draining and the movement of water in tubes over 11 sessions during a 4-month period. Lim Kwak videotaped a constructivist teacher, Christie Sales, as she conducted water activities about once a week during activity time in a preschool classroom located in a rural public school in Iowa. Children usually came to the activity in pairs. A child could choose to participate in all or none of the activities and was allowed to come and go as desired. The focus of the case study is Tom, aged 5.5 years, selected because of his consistent interest in the activities that allowed analysis of reasoning. The description and analysis of the sessions is based on Kwak's work.

The case study presented here should not be viewed as a model except in a very general sense. It does illustrate the three parts of the definition of constructivist education: interest, experimentation, and cooperation. However, many alternative ways of doing water activities will occur to constructivist teachers as they consider their children's interests, the directions indicated by their unique experimentation, the teachers' own ideas of how to move children's experimentation forward, and children's efforts to work together to make something happen. We present simply one way it developed in one classroom. We provide a description of the emergent development of materials, activities, and objectives followed by principles of teaching.

THE EMERGENT DEVELOPMENT OF MATERIALS, ACTIVITIES, AND OBJECTIVES

Materials, activities, and objectives emerged in the course of our exploratory work with children and in collaboration with the teacher (Christie). The first activities focused on draining, and later activities, on the movement of water in tubes. According to a pilot study (Kwak, 1993), draining is an easier phenomenon for young children than movement of water in tubes. An overview of the activities in eleven sessions is as follows:

Sessions 1–2: Draining using only cups with holes
Sessions 3–4: Draining with cups hanging on a pegboard
Sessions 5–7: Movement of water in tubes, with reservoir
Session 8:   Movement of water in J- and S-shaped tubes
Sessions 9–10: Making fountains with cups, tubes, and basters
Session 11: Squirting water at a target, with variation in height of reservoir

Highlights of these sessions are described below.

Activities Involving Draining

Sessions 1–2: Draining with Cups Only. We began by offering children a water table and plastic cups with holes (shown in Figure 7.1), to focus them on the phenomenon of draining. Christie prepared these transparent plastic cups by using an electric drill to make clean holes—small (⅛"), medium (¼"), and large (½")—that would produce steady streams. The transparency of the cups enabled children to see the water level inside as well as the water flowing out. To further improve possibilities for observation, the teacher colored the water with food coloring and outlined the holes with a black marker. The cups offer children the opportunity to think about many variables. For example, they could consider the three sizes of holes, the sizes of water streams, the paths of the streams, and the cups' speeds of emptying. Many regularities and relationships may be constructed with these materials. As children experiment, they may observe that a larger or faster stream comes out of one as compared to another. They may figure out the correspondence between the large hole and a large stream, the medium hole and a medium stream, and the small hole and a small stream. These correspondence relationships may be ordered by size (seriated) and coordinated in the generalization that the larger the hole, the larger the stream (and/or the sooner it empties). In Piaget's theory this generalization is a cognitive

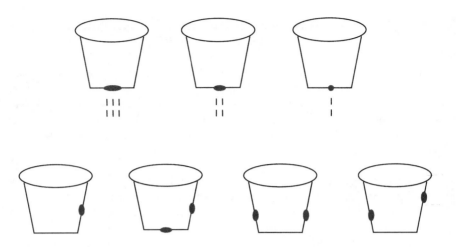

FIGURE 7.1. Cups presented in Session 1 with three sizes of bottom holes and two side positions

structure termed a *function*: a one-way relationship that can be expressed in the statement "y is a function of x" (Piaget, Grize, Szeminska, & Bang, 1968/1977). That is, the size of stream or speed of flow is a function of the size of holes. Thus the child has the possibility while experimenting with the materials to organize (structure) simple comparisons into a more complex system of relationships. Such is the nature of growth of knowledge and intelligence, according to Piaget.

With these materials children have the possibility to construct the following additional regularities and logico-mathematical relationships:

- The regularity that when the container has a hole, water always runs out of it
- The regularity that bottom-hole cups always empty completely, but side-hole cups do not
- The relationship between the position of hole and the nature of draining (that is, cups with bottom holes produce a straight stream, but cups with side holes produce a curved stream)
- The relationship between height of side hole and order in which flow ceases (that is, the higher the hole, the sooner the flow stops)

Christie introduced the bottom-hole cups first and later the side-hole cups. We expected that experience with bottom holes would offer the possibility for a contradiction with experience with side holes.

In the beginning of this 37-minute activity, Christie offers Tom a medium-bottom-hole cup and asks, "What do you think will happen if you put water in there?" Tom immediately has ideas about what to do with the cup and dips it in the water. Later, he holds a big-bottom-hole cup over the medium-bottom-hole cup and watches as the top one empties while the bottom one fills, then inspects the bottoms of the cups. He dips the two cups in water and holds them side by side at eye level as he observes the streams. Surmising that Tom is comparing the two in terms of how fast they empty, Christie asks, "Tom, why do you think this one empties so fast?" He responds, "'Cause that has a bigger hole." Later, Tom correctly predicts that the medium-bottom-hole cup will empty before the small-bottom-hole cup (without having seen this) and explains that the big-bottom-hole cup empties first "'Cause that's the biggest, that's a middle size, and that's a little size."

In order to challenge Tom with material that will lead to a new phenomenon, Christie offers him a medium-side-hole cup. Tom shows surprise when he sees that cup draining in an arc from the side. He exclaims, "Eeee!" as the water spurts unexpectedly on his arm. He quickly accommodates to the unanticipated event by turning and tipping the cup sideways so that it drains directly from its side into another cup. Subsequently, he consistently anticipates the flow from side-hole cups. He also develops a preference for big-bottom-hole cups (as drainers) that empty more quickly.

Christie adds another variable for Tom to consider by offering him a cup with medium holes in bottom and side. When the water level goes below the side hole, she asks, "Why is it only coming out one place?" Tom is clear: "'Cause it's past that hole." However, he has no prediction when she offers a new cup with two medium holes on different sides at different heights. He simply holds a big-bottom-hole cup above it and watches to see what will happen. When the teacher expresses surprise that the higher hole stops draining, Tom explains, "I know. This is the lowest and this is the highest." He seems to have quickly constructed a new practical relationship between height of side hole and order in which draining ceases, but "explains" it by describing the positions of the holes.

In Session 2, Tom and another child, Nick, hold two cups each to make one system of four cups, each emptying into the next. As we reflected on the video of this session, we decided the children needed a method of experimenting with more cups than they could hold. We therefore decided to introduce a pegboard apparatus with metal hangers for the cups (see

Figure 7.2), to make it easier for children to experiment with many cups at once.

Sessions 3–4: Draining with Cups Hanging on a Pegboard. The pegboard framed with PVC pipes was placed over a tub of water. Metal hangers allowed the children's hands to be free to arrange the cups on the pegboard. The hangers also made it possible for the children to be more systematic in their observations. When they held cups with their hands, the children often moved them without being aware of this movement. With the cups held steady by the hangers, the children were better able to observe the results of their actions. Nine side-hole cups with holes at three heights (high, middle, and low) and in three hole sizes (large, medium, and small) were added. These offered children possibilities to construct relationships between the sizes of the side holes and the speeds/sizes of flow.

FIGURE 7.2. Pegboard over tub, with hangers for cups. To make the cup hangers, a welder started with a tool hook, cut the holder part off, and attached a ring the size of the cups.

During these sessions, Christie places some hangers and cups on the pegboard, provides pitchers for pouring, and demonstrates how to arrange cups so that one drains into another. As a side-hole cup empties, the pressure lessens, and the arc of the water stream diminishes, eventually missing the catcher cup (Figure 7.3a). Christie calls attention to the fact that the stream moves away from the cup into which it is emptying. Tom tries adjusting the position of the top cup, then adds more water. Christie encourages him to figure out a way to catch the water when it misses the catcher cup. When he seems to have no ideas, she suggests putting a cup in an intermediate position. Tom does so (Figure 7.3b), adding one other cup to make a more complex system of relationships (Figure 7.3c).

During Session 4, Laura leaves an arrangement of her cups on the pegboard, and Christie asks Tom if there is any way he can make the water flow from Laura's arrangement into his bottom cup. Since Laura's arrangement does not work as a system, Tom has to think how to change it, and Christie encourages him to "move things around a little bit." With some trial and error, he succeeds and happily pours from two pitchers, first into one side of the coordinated system of nine cups and then into the other side (Figure 7.4). It is unclear whether Tom had in mind a conceptualization of the whole system before he began his series of adjustments. The practical result, nevertheless, is a coordination of spatial relationships involving both bottom flow and side flow. Christie offers to help by pouring into the right side of the system, and they pour water in both sides at the same time. As Christie's side is composed of cups with medium holes, water flows more slowly than it does on Tom's side where cups have large holes. Christie comments, "I wonder why you have to fill your pitcher more often than I do." However, this problem is beyond Tom's interest, maybe beyond his capability at this time, and he does not reply.

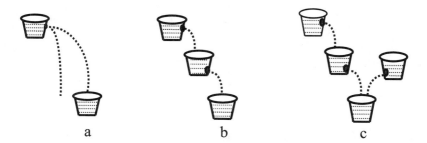

FIGURE 7.3. Coordinating all draining into one cup

Activities Involving the Movement of Water in Tubes

When interest in draining waned, Rheta and Lim planned with Christie to move to another water phenomenon they thought would interest children—the movement of water in tubes. In the first of these sessions, the children were presented with the following materials, in addition to those used previously:

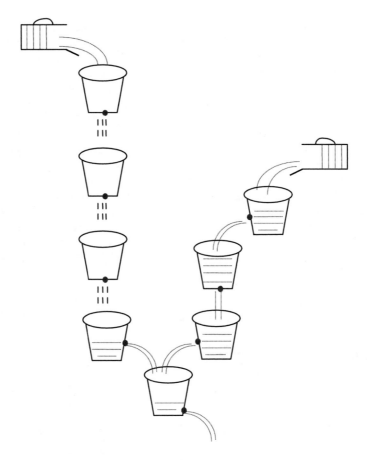

FIGURE 7.4. Tom's rearrangement of Laura's cups to coordinate a system of draining into the bottom cup

Transparent tubes 30 inches in length, ½" in diameter
Clear tube connectors (cut out of ¾" tubing), 2 inches in length
A transparent reservoir made from an inverted 2-liter soda pop bottle
    with the bottom cut off and a shut-off valve and tube attached
Hooks for tubes (commercially available screwdriver hooks)

With these materials, children have the possibility to construct the following regularities and relationships:

- The regularity that when the valve is turned in one direction, no water flows, and when it is turned in the other direction, water flows
- The relationship between the level of water in the reservoir and the movement or lack of movement of water up a portion of the tube

Sessions 5–8: Experimenting with a Reservoir, Tubes, and Cups. Tom first simply experiments with the valve and extends his pouring and catching activities to these new materials by watching the water flow through the tube and catching it in a pitcher. After a while, Christie shows him the screwdriver hooks for the tubes and suggestively places cups in hangers on the board. Tom asks for help in making the tube longer, and Christie gives him a piece of tubing and a connector. He makes the arrangement shown in Figure 7.5, turns on the valve, and watches the water flow into the cup. He continues to fill the reservoir to keep the flow going. Christie places a hook and cup near the top of the board, asking, "Can you make water go in here?" Posing this problem is intended to introduce a situation that might result in a feeling of contradiction. He puts the tube up over the cup and sees a little water flow from the tube into the cup, then stop. When the water stops, he looks at the valve and the end of the tube, turns the valve off and on, peering first at the end of the tube and then at the reservoir. His puzzlement clearly indicates a feeling of contradiction. When he bends the end of the tube downward into the cup, the water starts to flow, but when he lets go of the tube, it straightens and the water stops. He decides that he needs to extend the tube, so Christie helps him do so with connectors and another piece of tubing. He seems to hypothesize that the tube's length is a factor in water flow.

    Next he puts the free end of the tube in the top of the reservoir (Figure 7.6, top left), seeming to expect the water to recycle and flow back into the reservoir. When he sees that water does not flow from the tube into the reservoir, Tom pushes down on the top part of the tube, and it appears that that water rises a little in the tube because more of the tube is below the water level (Figure 7.6, top right). Encouraged by this movement in the direction

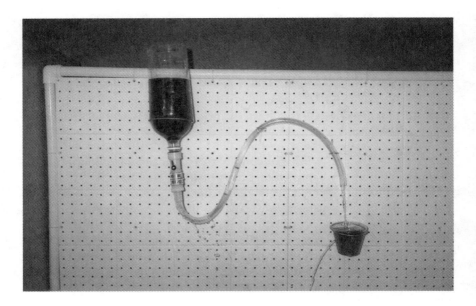

FIGURE 7.5. Making water flow from reservoir into cup

he wants the water to go, he pushes the top of the tube down as far as it will go (being restrained by the hook) without success, keeping the free end in the reservoir. Finally, he takes the free end out of the reservoir and moves it downward, and water flows out (Figure 7.6, bottom). Tom again puts the end of the tube over the reservoir several times, looking expectantly. As he does this, he turns the valve of the reservoir off and on, as if this might solve the problem. Tom clearly experiences a contradiction between his expectations and the results of his actions.

Tom explains to Christie that "When it's this way [the tube bent downward from the hook], it's shorter [he means lower] but when it's the other way, it's higher [held over reservoir], and so it's hard for the water to get up high." He clearly is struggling with his observation that the water does not flow up in some arrangements. Subsequently, Tom extends the length of the tube, but air pockets prevent the water from flowing freely. He gets more flow when he puts part of the tubing low (as shown in Figure 7.7). Thereafter, when the flow slows, he lowers the tube and adds water to the reservoir. He appears to have succeeded on a practical level, but he probably has not constructed the relation between water level in the reservoir and flow from the tube.

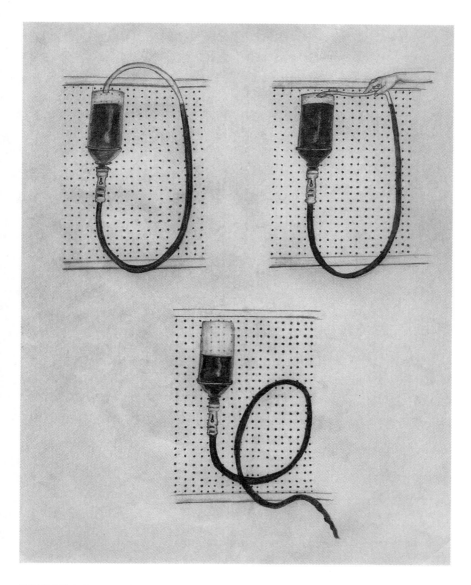

FIGURE 7.6. Trying to make water recirculate

FIGURE 7.7. Experiencing air pockets

Tom is still interested in having lots of tubing and asks for "more hoses." The teacher complies, and Tom and Nick hook several together with a funnel on one end and the other end attached to the reservoir. One notable event during this session is that when Tom sees no water coming out of the tube, he keeps on adding water to the reservoir. At one point, Tom places the end of the tube low on the board and succeeds in getting water to flow out. He "explains" to Christie, "Then the water would go down easier." Tom demonstrates his practical "know-how" that water goes down easier than up. However, the tangled length of tubing does not permit the kind of observation necessary to enable him to figure out how the system works. Thus we learned that too much tubing decreases children's ability to observe and isolate variables.

While continuing to have trouble with air pockets, Tom now has a practical solution when the water stops flowing. He simply lowers the tube. This regularity is important as an approximation to one part of the solution.

Tom holds the end of the tube just below the level of the reservoir and sees water come out, then twice tries placing the free end of the tube in the reservoir, again expecting to see water flow back into the reservoir. Although he thinks that "it is hard for the water to go up high," Tom succeeds in getting it to go up as high as the reservoir. Then why not a little higher? He is clearly not convinced that this is impossible. When he places the tube lower, he is not thinking about the height of the water level in the reservoir. He simply thinks of "lower" in terms of the tube's spatial relation to the pegboard.

We wondered whether Tom might think more easily about the water level if the materials were simplified. Therefore, for Session 6 Christie arranged ahead of time a backwards J-shaped tube and a sideways S-shaped tube on the pegboard. In the process of experimenting, children have the opportunity to observe and construct the following regularities:

- The regularity that water overflows from the short end when water is poured in the tall end of the J-shaped tube (Figure 7.8a)
- The regularity that water in the tall end will stay at the same level as in the short end of the J-shaped tube when water is continuously poured into the short end (Figure 7.8b)
- The regularity that water will not fill the S-shaped tube but will stay in the tube at the same level in the first half of the S when water is continuously poured into the left end (Figure 7.8c)
- The regularity that to make water go through the S-shaped tube, the left end needs to be made higher than the humped part on the right end (Figure 7.8d)

When he goes to the water table, Tom concentrates on the J-shaped tube. He pours water quickly into the long end and watches it spurt out of the short end. He then pours more slowly and has the opportunity to see that it comes out more slowly. Again he pours, faster. Then he pours water in the short end of the J and has the opportunity to see that water does not fill the long end and does not come out the long end. Tom and Tyler release the J tube from the hook so that the long part remains fixed on the board but the other end simply dangles. They cooperate for some time in pouring water into the fixed end and catching it at the other end with a cup having a side hole, and then catching this cup's flow with a pitcher.

The children's interest in this activity is short-lived. They seem to need more time to confirm what they already know how to do—get water to flow from the tube when they put the end lower in relation to the pegboard/reservoir. They return to what they know how to do and thus simplify the task for themselves, exercising their mastery of what they do understand.

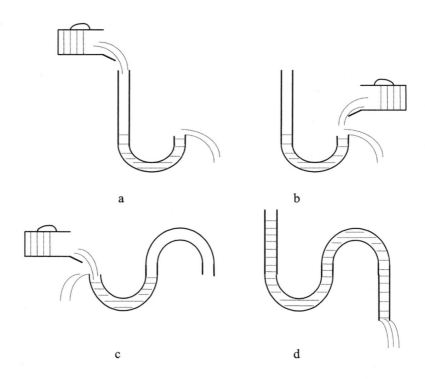

FIGURE 7.8. Pouring water in J- and S-shaped tubes

Sessions 9–10: Making Fountains. As the children still seemed interested in the flow of water through tubes into receptacles, we decided to provide a new kind of opportunity to combine draining and movement of water in tubes. In addition to materials used previously, the following materials were presented to the children in order to combine draining, siphoning, and movement of water in tubes in new ways:

Cups with two holes on opposite sides at different heights
A big clear plastic cup with two bottom holes, one of which is attached to a tube (see Figure 7.9)
Tubes: a thick one, ½" in diameter (used before), and a thin one, ⅛" in diameter, attached to the pegboard with a hanger
Basters

Added later: Cups with several bottom holes ("fountain" cup) (see Figure 7.9)

Responding to the new materials, Tom fits a hanger into the pegboard, puts in it a cup with two holes on opposite sides at different heights, and succeeds in making water flow from the big cup into it (Figure 7.9). He hooks the tube on the pegboard, adds water to the big cup, and watches the flow. Still, he twice puts the free end of the tube into the big cup that now serves as a reservoir and tries to make the water flow through the tube and up into the cup. The second time, he holds it in the cup only momentarily. By now he does not seem so surprised at this negation of his expectation. However, he still does not let go of the expectation that water will go up the tube and recycle back into the reservoir. In the eleven sessions, he never seems to conclude that this cannot occur. Repeated contradiction of his expectation does not yet seem to convince him.

In order to collect water in the cup, he plugs up a side hole with his hand, then removes it to watch the curving stream. He places the "foun-

FIGURE 7.9. Making fountains

tain" cup under the big cup to catch water (Figure 7.9). He exclaims, "I made two fountains!"

The equality relation between the levels of water in the reservoir and the tube is an idea totally beyond Tom's grasp, requiring the construction of a horizontal plane in empty space. After all, there is no direct contact between the two containers. On what basis could Tom think that one could have an influence on the other? He simply alternated between two successful methods: adding water to the reservoir and lowering the tube. At one point, Tom removes the tube from the reservoir and blows through it, delighted with his success in making water go up the tube into the cup. He invents a means of changing pressure!

Tom and Cody then experiment with the basters, filling and squirting them. Tom alternates this with going back to pour water in his reservoir to keep his fountains going. The boys squirt the basters at each other, laughing.

Session 11: Squirting Water at a Target. Christie picks up on the boys' interest in squirting the basters and sets up an outdoor situation in which they can go on experimenting. She wants to connect this to their reasoning about the movement of water in tubes and presents the following materials with the pegboard (see Figure 7.10):

A reservoir attached to a Y-shaped valve
Water squirters (made with basters attached to tubes)
Targets (inflated clowns with sand in the bottoms)

The idea is for children to try to hit the targets placed on the ground. With the intention of setting the stage for contradictions, the teacher arranges the reservoir low on the pegboard so that a child standing would not get a flow into his baster. In order to be successful, it is necessary to hold the baster close to the ground. Thus, children had the possibility to construct:

• The regularity that the baster spurts best when held in a low position
• The relationship between the water levels in the reservoir and in the tube

Tom focuses on the baster alone and simply picks it up and tries to squirt it from a standing position, without success. The teacher reminds him about turning the valve on the reservoir, squats down, and demonstrates successful squirting at the target. Nick imitates and successfully squirts the baster at the clown. Tom stands and tries to squirt, then sees no water in the baster. He repeatedly bends down to draw water directly from the tub into the baster and returns to a standing position to squirt, without realizing that most of

FIGURE 7.10. Reservoir attached to Y-shaped valve, with tubes attached to basters

the water flows back into the tube. He succeeds in squirting a little water some of the time. Here Tom uses a previous scheme that worked, drawing water with the baster. He seems not to think about the tube at all but treats the baster as if it is not attached to the tube and the reservoir. The teacher asks, "Why do you think Nick's is working and yours isn't?" Tom shrugs and continues to try to squirt the baster from a standing position. Nick responds, "Because Tom is standing." This comment inspires Tom to lower the baster and squirt it. Water shoots out. "Now it's coming out!" Then he returns to a standing position, and when no water comes out, he lowers the baster again with success. He repeats this a few more times. When Nick complains that "Mine is not fast," Tom recommends, "Put it down low." Still, he sometimes forgets and raises the baster so that it stops working. Sometimes when he does not succeed, he moves the target closer as if that is the problem. He again advises Nick, "Get down like this (bending over)." Christie tries to make the children aware of the role of the reservoir by holding it up higher than the basters. However, Tom seems not to notice the reservoir, but to revel in continued success in squirting at the targets. Christie then takes the reservoir off the pegboard to a place where the children can see it near the targets (Figure 7.11) and holds the reservoir on the ground. She also provides milk crates as supports for the targets so the children have the clear goal of knocking them off their supports. When a teacher makes it easy for children to succeed without any effort or reflection, they have nothing to figure out. It is only when the teacher changes the circumstances so the results of their actions bring a contradiction to expectation that the children have a reason to think.

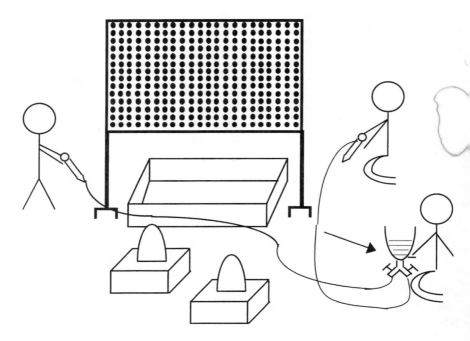

FIGURE 7.11. Reservoir moved from the pegboard to where the children can see it

Tom notices his baster is empty, and he instructs the teacher, "Turn it on." She replies that she did. Tom lowers the baster until it fills with water and then raises it up to aim, with the result that only a little bit of water sprays out, and the water goes back down the tube. Despite his advice to Nick, Tom has not understood why the baster must be held low in order to work. Not appreciating the dynamic nature of the water flow, he expects water to remain in the baster once it is there. Clearly, he does not think about the height of the reservoir or its water level although at a practical level he sometimes realizes that he must bend over in order to succeed.

Tony, who is observing the activity, volunteers to Christie, "You need to lift it [reservoir] up like you did before. You lifted it up and the water came out." The teacher consults Tom and Nick, and they agree she should try it. When Christie stands, water flows into the tubes. Tom excitedly squirts at the target. "I'm squirting it! It's coming out! I got him [the target] down!" When the teacher lowers the reservoir to the ground, Tony again suggests holding it up higher, and the children experience success. Tom then tries to squirt water from a standing position with no success. He leans down, gets water in the baster, and stands to squirt! The water squirts a little. Then Tom looks at the water that is now far down the tube, and holds the baster lower to fill it. Then he raises the baster up toward the target, and the water stops. Then he instructs Christie, "Lift it up." She lifts it up a little. "Higher," he commands, and she lifts it further. Tom is conscious merely of the correspondence between the height of the reservoir and successful squirting. This is progress in that he has decentered from the baster itself and now considers other factors in the situation. However, his actions indicate that he still does not understand the relationship between water level and flow.

PRINCIPLES OF TEACHING

In the context of a cooperative sociomoral atmosphere, Christie used the principles of teaching given below and illustrated with examples from the case study.

I. Provide Materials That Invite Experimentation, and Help Children Observe and Isolate Variables

The cups with holes immediately captured children's interest in draining. Picking up a cup automatically resulted in draining that was easy for children to observe. Observability was heightened by the colored water and the black outline of each hole. The teacher limited materials in the beginning, offering only bottom-hole cups. When she saw that Tom had constructed seriated correspondences, she offered a side-hole cup. When we saw that Tom and Nick were interested in trying to put four cups in relation to one another, we decided to make more complex experimentation possible on a pegboard with metal hangers.

In cases where materials present variables that are too complex, the teacher may need to simplify the materials. For example, when Tom's experimentation led him to work with so much tubing that air pockets developed, Christie introduced J-shaped and S-shaped tubing so that Tom would be able to observe immediately clear results of his actions.

2. Ask Questions to Increase Children's Observation of Variables

If a child seems not to notice a variable, the teacher may want to call attention to it. For example, Christie called attention to the fact that a side stream moved away from the cup into which it was emptying.

3. Ask Children to Make Predictions About What They Expect to Happen

In the beginning of the first activity, the teacher asked Tom what would happen if he put water in a cup. This offers Tom the opportunity to construct an expectation rather than act thoughtlessly and impulsively. When children immediately have ideas about what to do with materials, it may not be necessary to ask for a prediction right away. Prior to being able to predict what will happen *before* trying an action, a child may construct the regularity "When I pour water in this cup, it flows in a bigger (smaller) stream than from that cup" without noticing the contribution of size of holes in the cups.

4. Encourage Children's Purposes

It is critical that children develop and pursue their own purposes. They often have in mind certain effects they want to produce. Examples are Tom's ideas to create a recirculating system of water flow and to make water move higher in a tube. In other instances, Tom appropriated a suggestion by the teacher (for example, to try to knock over the targets using the baster attached to a tube and reservoir).

5. Encourage Children to Make Comparisons and Construct Other Logico-Mathematical Relationships

Children's construction of logico-mathematical relationships often occurs spontaneously as children explore and experiment on their own with well-selected materials. However, such constructions can also be inspired by teachers' interventions.

6. Ask Children to Think About Causal Factors

When Tom looked at the bottoms of the cups, dipped cups with big and medium holes in the water, and held them side by side at eye level, it was clear to Christie that he was comparing the two streams. She then asked a question concerning causality: "I wonder why this one empties so fast." Later she asked about a side-hole cup when the water level fell below the side hole and continued draining from the bottom hole: "Why is it only coming out one place?"

7. Model and Suggest Possibilities

This principle is followed when, for example, Christie introduces children to the new pegboard by showing them how to insert a hanger in the board and place a cup in it. She also demonstrates how to place one cup above another so it can drain into the bottom cup. When Tom has no ideas about how to solve the problem of the curved stream's missing its target cup, Christie suggests placing a cup in an intermediate position. Later, when Christie thinks Tom is ready for a new challenge, she places a holder and cup near the top of the board and asks if he can make water go in there. This opens up possibilities for new contradictions and reasoning. When children act on a suggestion and take up the idea as their own, the teacher knows the intervention inspired children to think.

8. Assess Children's Thinking by Observing Their Actions

Thinking about children's thinking provides the basis for choosing intervention strategies. Figuring out how children think begins as teachers find out what children notice, what they wonder about, and what surprises them. When Tom expresses surprise at the spurt of water from a side hole, Christie knows that it was unexpected and that it thus created a contradiction for him. As he subsequently acts to anticipate the flow from side-hole cups, Christie knows that he has accommodated this disequilibrating event.

Figuring out how children think also involves observing what children do and say when they encounter problems in creating some result. When Tom saw the curved side stream move away from the target cup, he tried to solve the problem by adjusting the top cup in its holder. This showed the teacher that he did not understand the reason for the change. Other actions revealing Tom's thinking include trying to get the water to recirculate by putting the end of the tube in the reservoir and by turning the valve on and off in an effort to get water to go up higher in the tube.

9. Back Off If a Child Does Not Respond to an Intervention

This principle is followed when, for example, Christie wonders aloud why he has to fill his pitcher more often than she does (as they pour water into two sides of a system), and he ignores this issue.

10. Create a Forum in Which Children Can Discuss Their Ideas and Share Their Discoveries with Others

Sharing of ideas occurs spontaneously at the water table, but discussion at group time can also give children ideas to try. For example, at early morning group time, Christie showed children the pegboard with J- and S-shaped tubes. When she asked what the children thought would happen, some predicted the water poured into the left side of the J would flow into the S-shaped tube. Tom's greater experience and knowledge led him to disagree. Other children thus had the possibility to think about this contradiction and to be motivated to test the theory.

CONCLUSION

The analysis of the eleven sessions of Tom's experimentation with water phenomena shows how important action is to the development of reasoning and construction of knowledge. Over time, "knowing how" gradually develops into "knowing why." It is in the course of acting on objects and observing the results that Tom constructs causal or semicausal relationships. The positive role of erroneous ideas is illustrated in the ways contradictions lead to changes in actions and conceptions. Tom is shown to become gradually conscious of his own actions and of properties of water.

Tom progressed in reasoning at the practical level for both draining and the movement of water in tubes. However, progress at the conceptual level was observed only for draining phenomena. This shows that the construction of knowledge about fluid dynamics takes a longer time than the 4 months we devoted to this study. These kinds of problems should be reintroduced to children over a number of years in order to promote understanding at increasingly complex levels.

As noted in Chapter 2, Duckworth (1996) writes that "the having of wonderful ideas [is] the essence of intellectual development" (p. 13). Many times during this study, Tom could be heard to say, "I have an idea!" The case study reported here reveals how a child may be observed to progress when the teacher accepts children's ideas and provides a setting that suggests "wonderful ideas" to children.

Chapter 8

Developing Geometric Reasoning Using Pattern Blocks

Christina Sales and Carolyn Hildebrandt

Despite the buzz of activity all around her, four-year-old Elise intently focuses on filling a frame with brightly colored pattern blocks. She places the blocks so that each one fits snugly next to the others. When Elise completes the frame, she lifts it away from the blocks and begins to fill it with other blocks. Suddenly, she excitedly announces, "Teacher, teacher, two reds make a yellow!"

Elise has just discovered that two trapezoids placed together in a particular way can substitute for a hexagon. Stimulated by this discovery, she continues to search for other ways to transform the frame's interior as she combines smaller shapes to form larger shapes and divides larger shapes into smaller shapes. After several days of working with the pattern blocks, she begins to anticipate which blocks she will need to fill certain frame shapes, showing she can visualize how specific pieces will fit together. Piaget and Inhelder (1948/1956) talk about this developmental process as the construction of mental images.

As Elise works with the pattern blocks, she is developing what the National Council of Teachers of Mathematics (NCTM) calls geometric understanding. According to the *Principles and Standards for School Mathematics* (NCTM, 2000), important aspects of geometric thought include learning about shapes and structures, analyzing their characteristics and relationships, constructing and manipulating mental representations of objects, and perceiving objects from a variety of perspectives. Besides being important in its own right, geometric knowledge can help children better understand other aspects of mathematics, such as fractions and graphs.

Piaget's developmental theory provides insight into children's developing spatial and geometric conceptual understanding. This research (Piaget & Inhelder, 1948/1956) demonstrates that young children have limited conceptual understanding of space. They construct knowledge on a practical level before they construct it on a conceptual level. The development of practical or perceptual knowledge precedes conceptual knowledge sometimes by as much as several years.

Young children cannot perform novel actions mentally without the aid of physical objects or prior experience with similar objects. Piaget states, "Young children are unable to visualize the results of even the simplest actions until they have seen them performed" (p. 453). Spatial concepts are internalized actions or images. If young children cannot create a spatial image in their minds, they cannot think about it to analyze it or imagine it a different way. Further, young children can anticipate the results of a physical action only if they can first perform that action mentally.

Piaget also suggests that experience in a content area can facilitate one's ability to internalize actions in that area. For example, it would be difficult for many people to look at a suit coat pattern and figure out how to recut it to change its style. However, tailors' prior experiences enable them to mentally perform those actions before they physically cut out the fabric and sew it together. Children, as well as adults, have more advanced conceptual understanding in content areas in which they have had a great deal of experience than in areas where they have had little or no experience.

Many mathematics educators have advocated the use of manipulatives such as pattern blocks in teaching mathematics. However, the use of manipulatives alone is not enough (Clements & McMillen, 1996; Williams & Kamii, 1986). Kamii (2000) points out that "manipulatives are . . . not useful or useless in themselves. Their utility depends on the relationships children can make, through constructive abstraction" (p. 25).

Pattern blocks are useful because they provide many opportunities for children to construct geometric relationships. The bright colors and varied shapes invite exploration and experimentation. Pattern blocks can be made even more useful and appealing by adding accessories such as pattern block frames that pose intriguing problems to solve. In this chapter, we describe the development of geometric understanding in preschool children through the use of pattern blocks and frames. We describe materials and objectives, Types A, B, and C approaches to using pattern blocks, and a Type D constructivist approach, with examples from a prekindergarten classroom taught by Christie Sales.

MATERIALS AND OBJECTIVES

A standard set of pattern blocks includes 250 ⅜"-thick pieces in six geometric shapes: 25 yellow hexagons; 50 red trapezoids; 50 green equilateral triangles; 50 blue parallelograms, each with two 60° angles and two

120° angles; 50 white parallelograms, each with two 30° angles and two 150° angles; and 25 orange squares (see Figure 8.1). All of the blocks have 1" sides, except for the trapezoid which has one 2" side.

The blocks can be combined in a variety of spatial relationships. For example, two triangles can substitute for a blue parallelogram (Figure 8.2a), and three triangles can substitute for a trapezoid (Figure 8.2b). Two trapezoids can replicate a hexagon, as can three blue parallelograms or six triangles (Figure 8.2c). Furthermore, different shapes can combine to form a larger shape. For instance, one blue parallelogram and one triangle can replicate a trapezoid (Figure 8.2d). The relationship between the two remaining shapes—the square and the white parallelogram—is more subtle. Two white parallelograms occupy the same surface area as one square, but they cannot be combined to create a square. However, when combined with the triangle to form a "house" shape, they can be used interchangeably (see Figure 8.3).

Each pattern block frame consists of a piece of wood or plastic with a design cut from the center. A standard set of commercial frames available from ETA/Cuisenaire includes eight patterns varying in difficulty. Frames can also be made by cutting designs out of the center of pieces of foamcore or wood. A frame forms an outline, challenging children to figure out how to fill it. A special feature is that once it is filled, the frame can be lifted off the design without disturbing the blocks. This allows children to find different solutions to the same problem while keeping a record of their previous work. Children thus have an opportunity to employ logico-mathematical reasoning as they create and compare solutions. Keeping a record also makes it more likely that children will share their ideas with others. A variety of solutions to one frame is illustrated in Figure 8.4.

With pattern blocks and frames, children have the opportunity to construct the following generalities concerning part-whole relations:

1. The whole can be divided into parts in various ways; that is, the same frame can have many unique solutions.

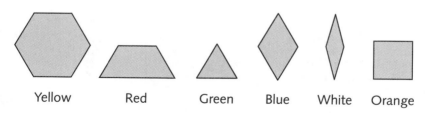

| Yellow | Red | Green | Blue | White | Orange |

FIGURE 8.1. Pattern block shapes

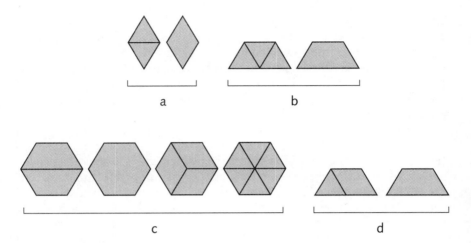

FIGURE 8.2. Examples of relationships among the hexagon, trapezoid, blue parallelogram, and triangle

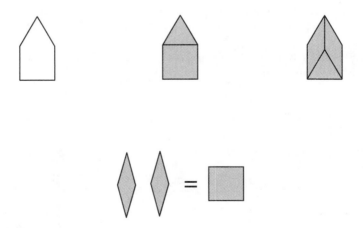

FIGURE 8.3. Pattern block relationship between the square and the white parallelogram

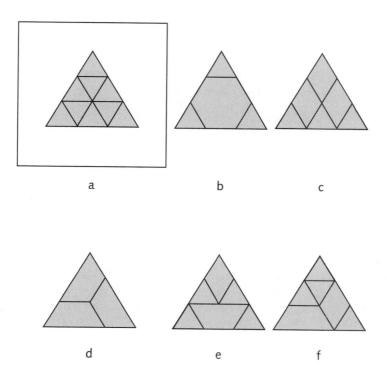

FIGURE 8.4. Examples of several solutions to the triangular-shaped pattern block frame

2. Blocks can be substituted for other blocks; that is, smaller shapes can be combined to form larger shapes, and larger shapes can be divided into smaller shapes.
3. The larger the shapes used in a frame, the fewer the number of pieces in the solution. Conversely, the smaller the shapes used in a frame, the greater the number of blocks used in the solution.
4. Designs can be symmetrical or asymmetrical.

COMPARING GEOMETRIC ACTIVITIES IN CLASSROOM TYPES A, B, C, AND D

Spatial and geometric objectives for Type A classrooms might include naming various geometric shapes, matching identical shapes, and identifying and extending patterns. Pattern blocks are rarely used. Instead, children might complete worksheets to demonstrate their knowledge of patterns.

Although children in Type A classrooms learn the names of the shapes and identify and extend patterns, they rarely have the opportunity to create patterns of their own or solve other geometric problems. Activities are directed by the teacher, with little room for experimentation and innovation on the part of the students.

In Type B classrooms, pattern blocks might be placed in one of the centers, and children might use them to complete specific tasks such as duplicating teacher-made or commercially made patterns, extending teacher-made patterns, or completing symmetrical patterns. Children might also be asked to make patterns, record them, and share them with classmates. Before moving to another center, children might need to demonstrate their ability to name shapes and colors, extend and duplicate patterns, and create new patterns.

A distinctive characteristic of Type B classrooms is that while teachers recognize the importance of designing activities that appeal to children's interests and may use the same materials used in Type D classrooms, they maintain control of the activity by instructing children to solve predetermined problems and arrive at predetermined solutions. Questioning is directed at focusing children's thinking on predetermined solutions rather than extending children's self-initiated reasoning. The following are examples of questions that teachers might ask in Type B classrooms: "Can you tell me the shapes in your design?" "What colors are you using?" or "Can you figure out how to make a pattern using six blocks?" The first two questions are tests to get information about what children know. Although it may be important for teachers to know this information, these kinds of test questions rarely help children learn anything they do not already know. Therefore, this is an assessment activity, not an activity that helps children construct new knowledge. Also, these types of assessment questions tend to establish a teacher-controlled atmosphere where children focus on giving correct answers rather than trying to figure out solutions to problems they have posed themselves. The third question could be used in Type D classrooms to suggest a new option for children to try or reject. In Type B classrooms, however, children understand there is no real choice involved, and although phrased as a question, it is actually a demand for performance. In this case, the teacher's intention and relationship with a child are critical to how the child experiences a question.

In Type C classrooms the pattern blocks and accessories such as cards printed with designs might be placed on a shelf as one of many activities children can choose to do. The accessories are provided to encourage children to match, extend, and create new designs. Sometimes children use the pattern blocks to create symbolic designs as well.

Children in Type C classrooms may discover relationships among the blocks on their own. Depending on the conversations taking place around them, they might learn the names and colors of the shapes. They might create new designs and share them with others. However, open and unconstrained space may not present challenging geometric problems, and design cards require only that children match shapes. Even though children in Type C classrooms may be interested in pattern blocks, they may not think of problems that stretch their reasoning.

Like teachers in Classroom Types A, B, and C, constructivist teachers in Type D classrooms believe it is important for children to learn to identify shapes and colors and recognize patterns. However, constructivist teachers also see pattern block activities as opportunities for children to reason about geometric and spatial problems. Observing children's actions, understanding their reasoning, and using that information to document learning and help extend thinking to new levels is an important role of constructivist teachers.

A PATTERN BLOCK PROJECT IN A TYPE D PRESCHOOL CLASSROOM

To learn more about how children use pattern blocks to construct geometric understanding, Christie conducted a project in her constructivist prekindergarten classroom in a public school in Plainfield, Iowa. Two groups of children, a morning and an afternoon group, met 3 days a week. The children ranged in age from 4 years, 5 months to 5 years, 6 months. The project was conducted during a regular 75-minute activity time. A variety of activities besides pattern blocks were available, such as construction, water, cooking, art, pretend play, ramps, books, and games. Children were free to join or leave the pattern block activity whenever they chose. Pattern blocks and frames were available every school day for a period of 2 months early in the spring semester. The pattern block sessions were videotaped for further reflection on the children's learning.

During the 2 months, Christie joined the children from time to time and made designs herself, conversed with children, and carefully observed their work. She used her observations to make decisions about how to extend the activity, encourage children to think more deeply about the problems and solutions they found, and help them pose new problems.

Information gained from this study was used to develop goals for children and principles of teaching in pattern block play. These are discussed below.

GOALS FOR CHILDREN ENGAGING IN TYPE D
PATTERN BLOCK ACTIVITIES

Our overall goal for Type D pattern block activities is for children to actively experiment with the blocks and to reason about the spatial regularities and relationships among the blocks. Specific goals for children are discussed below, with examples from Christie's classroom.

1. Create and Solve Their Own
Geometric Problems

This is probably the most important of our goals because it forms the foundation of a constructivist approach to learning. In a sociomoral atmosphere of mutual trust and respect where children are free to engage in activities that interest them, they are able to create and solve their own problems.

In Christie's classroom, children created problems for themselves when they chose to fill frames in a specific way. As Greg was working to find solutions to a triangular-shaped frame, he first solved the problem by using only triangles (see Figure 8.4a). When Christie asked him if he could tell her about his work, he announced that he had made a triangle out of triangles. It was clear that he deliberately chose to use only triangles. He then set another goal and exhibited purposefulness by repeating the activity, this time using the trapezoids to fill the triangular-shaped frame (see Figure 8.4d).

Frequently, the children posed impossible problems. Kathryn chose the same triangular-shaped frame as Greg, saying, "This is easy." After successfully figuring out several different solutions, she spent approximately 5 minutes experimenting with white parallelograms, moving them back and forth, trying to find a way to make them fit. When she was unable to do so, she removed the parallelograms and filled the frame with a hexagon and three triangles (see Figure 8.4b).

During a class meeting where children were sharing their knowledge of the relationships among the pattern blocks, Jeri held up a square block and said, "Teacher, there's no way you can do this." (That is, combine other blocks to make the square.) For her to know that, Jeri would have had to pose the problem of trying to replace the square with other blocks.

2. Create Substitutions by Combining and Partitioning

In the process of creating multiple solutions to pattern block frames, children learn to substitute blocks. They can do this by combining blocks to make a larger shape, or by partitioning (dividing) shapes into two or more smaller blocks. For example, three triangles can be combined to form a trapezoid; conversely, a trapezoid can be partitioned into three triangles.

As children created multiple solutions, they discovered a variety of substitutions. Elise, upon finishing the arrow-shaped frame (see Figure 8.5a), said, "Look what I am doing—two yellows, two reds, two blues, and two greens. I'll make it a different way, all green." After placing six triangles in the frame (Figure 8.5b), she folded her arms, looked up and said, "See, I did this, just like the yellow." She selected a yellow hexagon and placed it upon the green hexagon to confirm they were the same shape. She added more green triangles to her design and said, "Lookit, I made two just like the yellow!" (Figure 8.5c). She continued working and a few minutes later said, "I made a blue just like a yellow" (Figure 8.5d). Later still, she said, "I only used two reds like this to make a yellow. Teacher, lookit!" (Figure 8.5d).

3. Analyze and Compare Designs, Noting Similarities and Differences

Children can construct similarities and differences among designs that involve color/shape (e.g., some frames may be filled with all one color/shape, and some with different colors/shapes). Designs can also involve patterns (e.g., some designs are symmetrical and some asymmetrical; and designs include geometric shapes within shapes). These constructions set the stage for comparisons.

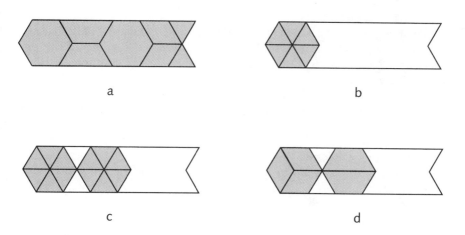

FIGURE 8.5. Elise's arrow-shaped pattern block solutions

Children had many opportunities to cooperate and compare designs in Christie's class. For example, Kent filled a frame with blue parallelograms, looked across the table at Victor and said, "Victor, you need all green, and I need all blue." Kent then filled another frame, lifted it, and replicated his design two more times. While he was working, Shelby chose an identical frame and copied Kent's design. When she finished, she said excitedly, "Kent, look, we match!"

4. Anticipate Which Blocks Will Fit Into Different Designs

Children usually begin filling the frames by trial and error. This gradually gives way to more purposeful efforts as children anticipate which blocks fit into different designs. To do this, children must think about the part-whole relationships among the blocks and the frame. Often this visualization involves mental rotations of the blocks. Once children become familiar with the blocks and their relationships, this visualization becomes more fluid and automatic. These anticipations suggest the use of mental imagery in the context of physical supports.

For example, when Sarah had a small space left in her frame, she selected a trapezoid, which was too large to fit, and held it over the space. She rotated the block to see whether the trapezoid would fit in each position. Only when she had considered and rejected all possible positions did she drop the trapezoid back into the box and choose two triangles to place in the empty space. Sarah had begun to move beyond trial and error and no longer needed to place the shape into the space before she could figure out if it would fit. However, she could not yet mentally rotate the block without rotating it physically.

After Elise demonstrated that she could replicate the hexagon in seven different ways, Christie handed her another frame (see Figure 8.6a) and asked, "What do you think would be the largest pattern block you could fit into this frame?" Elise pointed to a yellow hexagon. Christie continued, "If you use hexagons, can you figure out how many pieces you will need to fill it?" When she didn't answer, Christie suggested she try it. After placing only one hexagon (see Figure 8.6b), Elise touched the center and said, "It's going to have a triangle." She finished the frame by adding two more hexagons and a triangle (Figure 8.6c). Elise was able to visualize the image of the triangle with only one hexagon in the frame.

Some children seemed to be able to predict what the finished product would look like before placing the blocks. After Jeri filled a large parallelogram-shaped frame with several different shapes (Figure 8.7a), Christie asked if she could make it all one color. She lifted the frame from her first solution to use it again. She placed a hexagon inside, and then added a trapezoid. "Can you make it all yellow?" Christie asked. Jeri looked at the hexagon

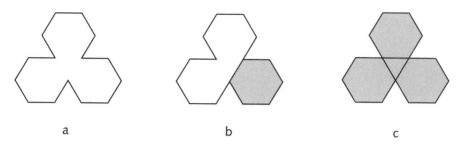

FIGURE 8.6. Elise's hexagon and triangle pattern block solution

and at the parallelogram she had already finished and shook her head. Christie continued probing by asking if she could make it all red. She responded by taking the hexagon out of the frame and filling it with trapezoids (Figure 8.7b). When she finished, Christie asked if she could make it a different color. "Yup," she said, and filled the frame with the blue parallelograms (Figure 8.7c). Elise, sitting next to Jeri, said, "A diamond out of a diamond!" Again, Christie asked Jeri if she could fill it using blocks of another color. She selected another hexagon, inserted it into the frame, looked at it and tossed it back. Finally, she chose several triangles and solved the problem by making it all green (Figure 8.7d).

Later, Jeri chose the arrow-shaped frame saying, "I'm going to make it all one color." She began by placing a hexagon in the arrow-shaped frame (Figure 8.8a). She looked at it, returned it to the box, and said, "Maybe I'll (pause) ah ha!" She began filling it with trapezoids. When she was approximately half finished, her teacher said, "Is that going to work? Are you going to be able to make it all red?" Jeri nodded and finished her design (Figure 8.8b).

5. Learn That There Can Be Many Solutions to a Geometric Problem

In working with the pattern blocks, children learn that geometric problems can have many solutions. To find new solutions, children have to think about the properties of the blocks and their substitution relationships. Experience creating multiple solutions for a single frame involves the ability to take multiple perspectives, an important skill not only in geometry but other domains as well.

Children in Christie's classroom found multiple solutions to the pattern block frames. Chris spent 43 minutes finding every solution he could invent

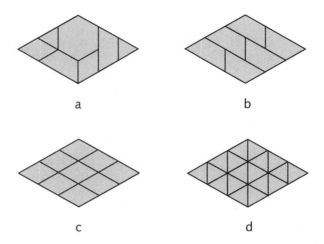

FIGURE 8.7. Jeri's parallelogram-shaped pattern block solutions

for a single frame. Shelby was particularly excited about identifying multiple solutions, exclaiming, "I'm making a hundred designs!" One day Kathryn spent 32 minutes filling almost every frame available, some of them two or three times. As mentioned earlier, she did not quit until she had tried the white parallelograms in every possible position. Chris pondered solutions to two small frames. He stayed with the problem he had created for himself until he had exhausted every solution he could devise. Not only was he persistent, he was deeply engaged as well.

6. Apply Number Concepts to Shapes and Geometric Designs

Children can use number to describe the blocks and designs in a variety of ways. For example, they can count the number of frames they have filled,

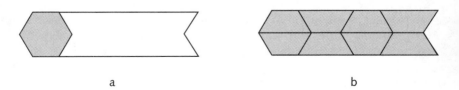

FIGURE 8.8. Jeri's arrow-shaped pattern block solutions

the number of solutions they have found to a particular frame, or the number of blocks they have used to fill a frame. They can also use number to describe the components of the shapes themselves (e.g., a triangle has three sides and three angles).

Children often applied number concepts to their designs. In describing their work, they made statements such as, "Teacher, teacher, look! One, two, three, four, five, six, seven!" "I used just one red and four blues." and "Five there and two there." When Elise had completed a duodecagon, as shown in Figure 8.9, Christie watched her place her hand across the center of her design and look at both sides. When asked why she had done that, Elise replied it was so she could see how many greens she had, "There are three greens on both sides, and three and three make six." Then she whispered in Christie's ear, "There are six oranges, too, and three blue ones." She placed her fingers on the two orange squares across from one another and said, "There are three on each side and that makes six, too." Then she touched the center of the design where she had made a blue hexagon and said, "And three blues." Elise had extended her observation of symmetry to addition.

7. Recognize and Name Blocks by Color, Shape, and Size

In working with the pattern blocks, children have opportunities to recognize and identify blocks by color (red, green, blue, orange, yellow, and white), shape (triangle, square, parallelogram, trapezoid, and hexagon), and size (larger and smaller).

At the beginning of the project, many of the children knew the colors and some of the names for geometric shapes, particularly the triangle and square. After talking about them with each other, children became more fluent

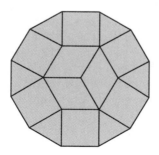

FIGURE 8.9. Elise's duodecagon-shaped pattern block solution

in their use of conventional language to refer to shapes. However, some children continued to refer to the pieces by color even when they knew the geometric names. For example, when Ellen initially needed a triangle for her frame she said, "I need one more green." But later, when Loren asked her for some triangles, she picked out a handful and gave them to him.

PRINCIPLES OF TEACHING

The following four principles of teaching are specific to pattern block activities.

1. Provide Enough Room for Several Children and an Adult to Work Alongside One Another

When more than one child is using the blocks, they often stimulate one another by sharing ideas. There are at least three reasons for teachers to play with materials alongside children. First, it helps the teacher better understand problems the materials pose, their solutions, and the relationships with which children may grapple. Second, children are often drawn to an activity in which they see adults engaging. Third, playing with the blocks gives teachers opportunities to model ways of using the blocks. This often stimulates children to try out new ideas. As teachers work alongside children, they have opportunities to think aloud and demonstrate strategies such as, "I wonder if it would work if I tried a green triangle," or "Look, I made two triangles fit where I had a blue parallelogram," or "I wonder if I can think of another way to do this design," or "This is really hard work. I can't finish this one. I guess I will have to take all the blocks out and start again."

2. Use Geometric Vocabulary in Conversations with Children

The teacher's use of geometric names for the pattern blocks and terms like *sides*, *angles*, and *symmetry* to describe attributes helps children learn geometric vocabulary and notice properties. The names of the shapes are arbitrary conventional knowledge—children can only learn them from a source outside themselves. It is important, however, to accept children's labels. Constant correction can dampen children's interest.

3. Respect Children's Choices

Although it may be tempting to show children a solution, it is important for children to discover for themselves what will work and what will not. The geometric relationships children construct are the result of logico-mathematical reasoning. If adults tell them which blocks to use, children may learn to rely on someone else for solutions rather than depend upon their own reasoning. Such interventions will thus impede children's construction of geometric relationships.

4. Observe Children Closely as They Work in Order to Know How to Intervene

Children's words and actions can provide important insights into their interests and understanding. Statements such as "I need a triangle," and "Teacher, teacher, look, two greens make a blue!" demonstrate children's knowledge of color and shape names.

Observing children's actions helps teachers understand their reasoning, recognize their "wonderful ideas," and adjust the activities and their own interventions accordingly. Constructivist teachers continually strive to find intervention methods that challenge children to invent and solve problems for themselves without giving too much or too little information.

Children often leave an activity when what they are doing is too easy or too difficult. If children seem bored, the teacher can offer a challenge by adding more complex frames or making comments such as "I wonder how many different ways there are to fill this frame." If the activity is too difficult, the teacher can make comments or ask questions that may help the child see the problem from a new perspective such as, "I wonder if it would help if you took out that yellow hexagon and tried a smaller block," or "I notice you are using only four of the shapes. Remember, there are six." The following anecdote demonstrates how Christie used information she gathered from a videotape to help Shelby see her problem from a new perspective.

Shelby stopped at the pattern block table and chose a difficult frame. She filled the edges, leaving a large square space in the center requiring four square blocks. To fill the center, she systematically and patiently tried block after block but neglected to try the square or hexagon. When none would fit together snugly, she took them all out and began again. She repeated this action again and again. After 4 minutes, she walked away. After viewing Shelby's actions on videotape, Christie concluded that Shelby had not constructed a relationship between the right angles of the square block and the right angles of the shape left in the center of the frame.

Four days later Shelby selected the same frame. Employing the same strategy, she again filled the edges and left a square in the center. As before, she began inserting blocks and taking them out. This time Christie was prepared to intervene. For Shelby to solve the problem herself, she needed to become aware of the identity relationship between the square pattern block and the square in the center of the frame. To help her do this, Christie said, "I wonder if there is a block that would fill the whole corner." Shelby looked at the corner and back at the pattern blocks. She picked up a square, inserted it into the design, looked up, and smiled. She completed the frame using three more squares. Her success encouraged her to choose another frame and begin again, in contrast to her initial experience 4 days earlier when she left the activity.

CONCLUSION

Exploring and experimenting with pattern blocks and pattern block frames provides children with many opportunities to develop geometric understanding. Children not only acquire conventional knowledge of geometry (such as the ability to name shapes) but also construct knowledge about the relationships among the blocks. This knowledge lays the foundation for future geometric and numerical understanding. In a classroom atmosphere of respect, trust, and choice, children often respond by posing challenging problems for themselves. When children are truly interested in an activity and have the benefit of appropriate adult support and guidance, they can construct powerful new ideas and share them with each other.

PART III

GROUP GAMES

Rheta DeVries, Betty Zan, and Carolyn Hildebrandt

Group games offer a motivating context in which children can develop socially, morally, and intellectually. In *Group Games in Early Education: Implications of Piaget's Theory* (1980), Kamii and DeVries define a group game as an activity in which

> children play together according to conventional rules specifying (1) some preestablished climax (or series of climaxes) to be achieved, and (2) what players should try to do in roles which are *interdependent, opposed,* and *collaborative.* (p. 3)

They advocate including group games as soon as children want to play them, usually around 4 years of age.

Games that fall most clearly into Kamii and DeVries's definition are competitive games in which children play against each other in order to win. Cooperative games are similar to competitive games except that children work together to beat the game. Children's roles are not opposed to each other but are instead opposed to whatever element they are playing against in the game (for example, a fantasy figure, as in *Max*; animals or obstacles that block a path, as in *The Adventures of Harley* or *Round-Up*; or time, as in *Harvest Time* or *Behind the Secret Door* [all available from Family Pastimes, www.familypastimes.com]).

Kamii and DeVries (1980) conceptualize three criteria of group games that promote children's learning and development.

To be educationally useful, a group game should:

1. Suggest something interesting and challenging for children to figure out how to do;

2. Make it possible for children themselves to judge their success;
3. Permit all players to participate actively throughout the game. (p. 4)

Group games contribute especially to children's motivation to reason and ability to cooperate. Cooperation is paramount because in order to play a group game, it is necessary for players to agree on the rules, abide by the rules, and accept their consequences. Therefore, the broad goal is cooperation, even in competitive games.

In this introduction to group games, we describe differences among classroom types in their use of group games, developmental stages in children's game play, possibilities for the construction of logico-mathematical knowledge, the role of contradiction, the issue of competition, and principles of teaching.

GROUP GAMES IN TYPES A, B, C, AND D CLASSROOMS

Group games are rarely found in Type A classrooms. Games may be used as alternatives to outdoor play, as rewards for performance (for example, after spending the morning taking a district-mandated standardized test), and during the short free play periods that are often given to children at the end of the day after their work has been completed. However, in these classrooms games are seen not as a part of the curriculum but as unimportant play for energy release or entertainment on a rainy day. Therefore, little attention is paid to children's games. Because of their focus on academics, teachers in Type A classrooms rarely take the time to play games with children or to observe how children play games. The teacher's intervention is primarily limited to stepping in when conflicts occur, sometimes to remove the game so that children cannot fight over it. The limited use of games in these classrooms means that children may not have the chance to become familiar with them (unless they play them in out-of-school contexts), and the full potential of games to promote development is not realized.

In Type B classrooms, the primary type of game is not a game at all. Rather, children have the opportunity (or sometimes are required) to play didactic "games" designed by the teacher to instruct children in narrow facts or skills. For example, as described in Chapter 1, children may match upper and lowercase letters on the two halves of a butterfly or put the numbered segments of a caterpillar together in numerical order from lowest to highest. Sometimes low-level games such as Memory, Bingo, or Lotto are used as drill and practice to reinforce skills, teach letters, numbers, and color and shape names. Children are often rotated through centers where they are required to do these games, and they usually have little opportunity to regulate their own play. With interest and enjoyment diminished, children simply engage in the games to satisfy the teacher and do not devote the mental energy necessary for optimal learning and development.

The goal of group games in Type C classrooms is play and enjoyment. Many age-appropriate games are made available for children's free choice. However, Type C teachers often do not know how to intervene to promote children's social, moral, and intellectual development. On those occasions when teachers in Type C classrooms do try to play games with children, they frequently become frustrated trying to teach children to play correctly. Because teachers in Type C classrooms do not understand the developmental significance of children's game playing, they have no framework for evaluating how their children play games and what they learn from them.

Teachers in Type D classrooms understand the value of group games and devote a great deal of time to choosing, evaluating, and adapting games for their particular children. They also play games with their children regularly in order to understand where children are developmentally and how to move them forward.

DEVELOPMENTAL STAGES IN GAME PLAYING

Many 4-year-olds do not understand opposing roles and do not play competitively. We know from research that the ability to compete is a developmental advance that requires taking the perspective of another and thinking about intentions (DeVries & Fernie, 1990; Piaget, 1932/1965). Piaget's research on the marbles play of boys in Switzerland led him to identify stages in children's practice of the rules of marbles. These stages are applicable to all games and can be of assistance in helping teachers observe and assess young children's game playing.

Stage 1: Motor and Individual Play

At the first stage of play (below 2 years of age), children's game playing is mainly sensorimotor. That is, they explore the game materials. Piaget describes young children piling marbles into the tufts of a chair, dropping them one after another, and pretending they are food and "cooking" them in a toy pan. Children at this stage do not even attempt to use rules to guide their play. While children's play with game pieces may become ritualized at this stage, it is not rule bound. However, the regularity of rituals can be viewed as a precursor to the regularity of rules, beginning at the next stage. Their play is also not specifically social although two or more children may play with the materials together.

Stage 2: Egocentric Play

This stage (ages 2–5 years) can best be described as "imitating the form of the game." Children at this stage attempt, as best they are able, to play according to their observations of others playing the game. However, their play conforms to the rules only in a very global sense. For example, Piaget found that children at this stage may propel their marbles to knock into another's marbles but may play without taking turns, or forget to draw the square, or be inconsistent in taking marbles that are knocked out of the square. Children at this stage are generally (egocentrically) unaware that their play does not conform to the rules of the game in question. Their play is social in the sense that they play with other children and try to follow social rules. However, they tend not to coordinate their play with one another, and it does not bother them if they are playing by different rules. Competition is not a concern to children at this stage, and even if children use the word *winning*, they tend to use it to mean finishing the game, accomplishing a particular goal (such as hitting another's marbles with their own, getting to the finish line, getting three in a row), or simply having fun. At this stage, everyone can "win."

Stage 3: Beginning Cooperation

Beginning around 7–8 years of age (or even by 5 or 6 years, in our experience), the rules increase in importance. Rules are no longer global and fluid, but are actively negotiated and mutually agreed upon. Piaget described two boys at this stage in the play of marbles who agreed that the square is necessary and that players capture marbles that have been knocked out of the square. Upon interviewing the two boys, Piaget found that they disagreed about virtually every other rule. However, they recognized the need for common rules, and spent a great deal of time trying to come to agreement. Paradoxically, the hallmark of this (cooperative) stage is the emergence of a competitive attitude. Winning is now defined in relation to the opponent (such as capturing more marbles, being first to get three in a row, getting to the finish first). By the end of Stage 3, children agree on most rules and understand the necessity of having rules to govern common play.

Stage 4: Codification of Rules

At this stage (beginning around 11–12 years of age), children become almost obsessed with the rules. They try to anticipate every possible event in the game and create a rule to deal with it. As an example of this stage, Piaget described a group of boys who, upon deciding to have a snowball fight, spend the next 30 minutes dividing into teams with captains and formulating all of the rules of the fight, leaving them almost no time for the actual snowball fight.

THE CONSTRUCTION OF
LOGICO-MATHEMATICAL RELATIONSHIPS

As pointed out in Chapter 2, constructivist teachers are concerned with children's construction of logico-mathematical relationships. Group games offer many possibilities for construction of these relationships, especially with regard to number, space, literacy, and perspective taking.

Number

Number is purely logico-mathematical in nature, even when it is used to quantify objects because number is not a property of objects. Rather, it is the knower's organization of objects into numerical relationships. In games involving dice, cards, and scoring, the use of number is embedded in the children's purposes in game play. For example, in card games such as High Card (commonly known as War), children are challenged to read numerals (or count the symbols on cards) and compare their value. The intense energy devoted to calculation in games is described in Chapter 9.

Spatial Reasoning

Spatial reasoning is involved in games such as Tic Tac Toe or Checkers, the focus of Chapter 10. Reasoning about spatial relations overlaps physical and logico-mathematical knowledge. In Checkers, calculation of the relative advantage or disadvantage of possible moves involves logico-mathematical reasoning.

Turn taking is mathematical and spatial, as well as social and moral. Young children often have difficulty with the mathematical aspects of turn taking, especially when there are more than two players. Typically, for example, the middle child of three players may reason with the "next-to" principle. Player 2 is next to Players 1 and 3 and, therefore, according to child logic, has turns after each of them, yielding a 1, 2, 3, 2, 1, 2, 3, 2 sequence in which Player 2 gets twice as many turns as Players 1 and 3. Direction of play can also be a problem in large groups.

Literacy

Constructivist teachers make a point of writing down rules for games in ways children can understand. Showcasing written rules also provides a context for literacy development. In addition, children learn to recognize numerals as well as words in the context of game play. When children make their own games, they have to struggle with how to make rules understandable from another's point of view.

Perspective Taking

Social perspective taking is inherent in all group games and requires logico-mathematical reasoning about social relations. Robert Selman's theory of perspective taking is an important framework for teachers as they evaluate children's sociomoral development. Selman (1980; Selman & Schultz, 1990) describes five developmental levels in perspective taking during negotiations and shared experiences, the first three of which are of particular interest to early childhood educators. Level 0 negotiation is impulsive, and the child treats others as objects. For example, a child might grab or intimidate by yelling. Level 1 negotiation is one-way or unilateral behavior where the child commands or controls the other. For example, a child might tell another where to put his or her marker in a board game. Level 1 characterizes most of 4- and 5-year-old children's interactions and is often appropriate even for adults. Level 2 negotiation is two-way reciprocal behavior where the child tries to persuade others. For example, a child might propose, "Let's play Tic Tac Toe," or "Which game do you want to play?" Level 2 is the "leading edge of development" in which the teacher of 4- and 5-year-old children is particularly interested.

Levels in shared experiences parallel those of negotiation. Children at Level 0 might express their impulsivity in silliness. For example, one of the boys in Chapter 10 continues to blow "raspberries" on his arm to make his partner dissolve in laughter. At Level 1, one-way shared experience might be expressive enthusiasm. For example, one child may say, "I don't want to land on him [a space where you have to move back]", and the other may echo, "And I don't want to land on him [another disadvantageous space]." At Level 2, shared experience is reciprocal (for example, "This is our favorite game!").

Perspective taking is particularly important for children's social and moral development. In games, children have opportunities to collaborate with others, think about others' points of view, and figure out how to work out problems occurring in play. (See DeVries & Zan, 1994, for further discussion of perspective taking.)

THE ROLE OF CONTRADICTION

Contradictions experienced by children in group games stem from social and nonsocial sources. Social contradiction is experienced when children are confronted with the differing perspectives of others. For example, a child may become aware that another is breaking a rule as he or she understands it. Or a child may find that another objects to his or her way of playing. These and other conflicts offer a particularly important context in which children can begin to decenter and to think about more than one perspective at a time.

Nonsocial contradiction is experienced in group games when children become aware of possible problems in how they themselves are playing. For example, in playing a path game, many children roll a die and then count as "one" the space on which they landed on the last turn (the logical error of addition). One 5-year-old was conscious of the possibility of this error yet had difficulty in overcoming it. He began saying "Mmm" instead of "one" to mark the space from which he started, and was thus able to count correctly. He actually invented the notion of zero! This was clearly an internally felt contradiction that arose from no outside source but from his own identification of a problem.

THE ISSUE OF COMPETITION

Kamii and DeVries (1980) wrote about competitive games in which children play against each other in order to win. They view such games in the broader context of cooperation. Alfie Kohn takes an opposing view. In his book *No Contest: The Case Against Competition* (1986), he argues that all competition is harmful to children's social, emotional, and intellectual development. He cites research showing the negative impact of competition in the classroom. We agree that destructive competition exists and should be avoided. However, we question whether all competition is bad for children. For example, in recent research, Stanne, Johnson, and Johnson (1999) show that these harmful effects depend on what *kind* of competition is involved (zero-sum winner-take-all competition versus appropriate competition).

The issue of competition is delicate because all teachers want to avoid the destructive competition that deteriorates relationships and causes emotional distress. However, as discussed in Chapter 2, Type D teachers seek to establish the kind of sociomoral atmosphere in which children care about one another. When this is the case, winners are sensitive to the feelings of losers, and players come to view the enjoyment of playing with a friend as more important than who wins. Our view is that the classroom sociomoral atmosphere plays a major role in how children interact with each other during games. In traditional classrooms where competition for grades, status, and teacher attention is the norm, competition may be more aggressive than in classrooms where interactions are characterized by cooperation and mutual respect. Two of us (Carolyn and Betty) are currently conducting research on this hypothesis (Hildebrandt, Bell, Zan, & Stoeckel, 1999; Zan & Hildebrandt, 2001).

While we believe that competitive play of games in the context of a cooperative sociomoral atmosphere can promote children's development, we also see value in cooperative games. However, many cooperative games described as such in the literature are not games according to the Kamii-DeVries definition, and many do not offer much intellectual challenge. The teacher can assess the intellectual possibilities of particular games by considering what children have to figure out and by considering the criteria of good group games.

PRINCIPLES OF TEACHING

We offer seven general principles of constructivist teaching that apply to all games.

1. Make Available a Wide Variety of Games from Which Children Can Choose

In Type D classrooms, a wide range of both commercial and teacher-made games are available to children for their free choice during activity time (also known as center time). Not all games will appeal to all children, so having a variety will increase the chances that children will find a game that they are motivated to play. Choices of games should include simple path games (such as Ravensburger's *Snail's Pace Race*), counting games (such as *Hi Ho! Cherry-O*), memory games (such as Concentration), board games (such as *Trouble*), card games (such as Crazy Eights and *Uno*), logic games (such as *Connect Four* and Mancala), physical-knowledge games (such as *Ants in the Pants* and *Topple*), and cooperative games (such as *Max* and *The Adventures of Harley*). To showcase games, it is useful to set aside a particular area of the classroom as a games center. Type D classrooms generally have a games table and a special shelf or cabinet where games are kept so that children can get them out and put them away when they are finished.

2. Actively Promote Game Playing in the Classroom

An activity time of at least one hour will allow children adequate time to learn a new game or play a familiar game without having to stop in the middle. When children don't know how to play a game, or when a new game is introduced, Type D teachers often invite children to play with them, so that children have an opportunity to learn how to play. The teacher may want to set aside a portion of the day specifically for game playing, at least until children become more familiar and comfortable with games. Bringing in adult volunteers or older children to teach children how to play games may also be helpful.

3. Choose Games That Address the Full Range of Developmental Levels Present in the Classroom

Games should be appropriate to the developmental levels of all of the children in the classroom so that all can enjoy playing games at their ability level. Type D teachers select games that they expect will challenge children just above their current developmental level. For example, 3-year-olds need simple games that are relatively devoid of strategies. They find it challenging simply to roll a die and move that number of spaces or place that number of markers on a grid. Type D teachers also look for games with a high ceiling, including sophisticated strategy games. These games, such as Checkers, Chinese Checkers, and Mancala, can be played at multiple levels. As children progress in their play, they continue to discover more advanced strategies. (The case study of Checkers in Chapter 10 is an example of this.) Teachers should observe and play games with their children throughout the year in order to evaluate games, removing games that are too easy and adding more challenging games as the children progress.

4. Observe Carefully How Children Play Games in Order to Know How to Intervene

Constructivist teachers are keen observers of children's game playing. They evaluate children's play and adapt games to match their skills and abilities. For example, when teachers notice children making the logical error of addition, they can make a die with 1s and 2s, so that children have many experiences of rolling a one and deciding how to move. If a particular game consistently leads to conflicts, the teacher may watch or play the game with children to try and determine the source of the problem. For example, if in *Hi Ho! Cherry-O* children are accidentally bumping each other's trees or taking cherries from another's tree, the teacher may cut up the game board so that each child has a separate tree. If a child cannot lose a game without also losing his or her temper, the teacher may play with that child and deliberately lose in order to model graceful losing behaviors. Occasionally, losing may devastate a child. At the end of a game, the teacher can say, "Great game! Do you want to play again? Maybe somebody else will win next time." During the game, the teacher can make comments like "I hope you get a good card," and "That was a great play!" Or the teacher may introduce cooperative games, temporarily eliminating the competition in order to teach the child how to play with others cooperatively. If a child consistently cheats in order to win, the teacher may play with the child in a small group in order to protest cheating and bring up the issue of fairness with the group.

5. Rewrite Rules in Language Understandable to Children

Most rules that come with commercial games are written in language that is inaccessible to young children, many of whom do not read or are just beginning to read. Therefore, the rules must be rewritten in simpler language. The rules can be augmented with diagrams and pictures in order to facilitate "reading" by the nonreaders. Even children who cannot read will often remember what each rule says and will refer to the rules during disagreements.

Some games' rules must be adapted to make the games more developmentally appropriate to young children. For example, in the game *Sorry*, young children often find it difficult to wait until they draw a "1" or "2" card to get out of their start position. The rules can be changed to allow getting out on any card. The cards that give children a choice (such as the card stating to move forward ten or back one, and the one stating to move forward 11 or exchange places with another player's marker) are often confusing to younger children. These cards can be eliminated. If children have different understandings of rules (due to playing the games at home in different ways), they can be drawn into discussions and allowed to make decisions about changing and rewriting the rules.

Children can also be invited to make new rules for games (Chapters 9 and 10 include descriptions of rules invented by 4- and 5-year-olds). This is a good introduction to the democratic process that is so important in constructivist classrooms, as children must negotiate with each other and come to agreement concerning new rules. The teacher can support children in this process by upholding the value of mutual agreement.

6. Keep in Mind the Goal of Children's Self-Regulation in Game Playing

In Types B and C classrooms, teachers often feel it is their responsibility to regulate games by prompting children (for example, "It's your turn, Jason"). If children have forgotten who played last, the teacher can say, "Elizabeth rolled, and then Jason rolled, so whose turn is it now?" With questions such as these, the teacher gets out of the role of regulator of the game and gives children the opportunity to regulate it.

Sometimes children's play of games looks peculiar. They may use rules that are difficult to understand, or no rules at all. While children should be given opportunities to learn how to play games by the rules, it is not necessary to insist that children follow those rules precisely. They may need time to explore the game materials on their own before they are ready to use them in a game situation. If children are regulating their own play, sometimes it is better not to intervene to teach the "correct" way to play unless problems occur. Instead, the Type D teacher watches children to see if they feel a need for more fully articulated rules, and is ready to step in to teach the rules.

Self-regulation is promoted when the teacher as player consults children: "What is the best thing to do?" "Where shall I put my marker?" Questions such as these enable the teacher to ask children for advice in play of the game. This minimizes the teacher's exercise of authority and promotes children's autonomy. When children act autonomously, they invest more energy in thinking about the game.

One of the things we hope children will learn from playing games is that rules can be changed when everyone agrees. Sometimes children change the rules to simplify the game or make it more challenging. Other times they unconsciously alter the rules (for example, taking two turns in a row). In this case, the teacher can say, "Oh, should we have two turns? Should we change the rule?" This helps children become aware that they have violated the rules without making cheating an issue. In fact, it is important to stress that young children often break rules without intending to cheat. The idea of cheating implies understanding of conscious intentions that is beyond many young children.

7. Use Conflict Resolution Strategies to Promote Perspective Taking

"Who wants to be first?" "How shall we decide who goes first?" "What is a fair way to decide?" These questions put to young children inevitably evoke a conflict. The constructivist teacher deliberately opens up the possibility for this conflict because it is an important experience for children to confront the opposed desires of another, begin to see more than one perspective, and learn to negotiate. Over time, the teacher helps children develop a repertoire of ways to decide fairly who will be first. Saying "Eenie, meenie, miney, moe" may work well until children figure out how to make sure they point to themselves at the end. However, the logic of this and other chants is lost on 3- and 4-year-olds who often simply recite the rhyme and then point to themselves! Scissors, Paper, Stone is a device used around the world. A stone is represented by a fist, scissors by extending second and third fingers, and paper by an open hand. Children put their hands behind their backs and on the count of three bring out either "scissors," "paper," or "stone." Scissors cut paper, paper covers stone, and stone breaks scissors. The winner is the one whose representation defeats the other's. The teacher may introduce other ways to resolve this issue (such as taking turns being first or rolling a die).

These are only a few of the interventions possible in group games. Specific interventions depend in part on the kind of game played and are illustrated in Chapters 9 and 10.

Chapter 9

Using Group Games to Teach Mathematics

Carolyn Hildebrandt and Betty Zan

Math games are an excellent way to help children learn mathematics and develop social competence. Children love games and find them extremely motivating. However, not all games are of equal value, nor are all methods for using them equally good at promoting children's social and intellectual development.

In this chapter, we address the following questions: What is a math game? and Of what value are group games in the teaching and learning of mathematics? Next we provide some general goals for children's mathematical and social learning in group games. Finally, we share some of our experiences playing math games in a preschool classroom and tell how two particular games evolved.

WHAT IS A MATH GAME?

The first thing that comes to mind in thinking about math games are games with number. Examples of commercial games involving number are Dominos, *UNO, Sorry,* and *Junior Monopoly.* Many good noncommercial games also use number (for examples, see Rosenblum, n.d.).

However, many games that do not use number per se still involve mathematical thinking. Even the simplest of games can be mathematical in nature. For example, any game involving turn taking has a mathematical component to it. As pointed out in the introduction to Part III of this book, figuring out which person goes next is not always easy for young children, especially with more than two players. Understanding turn taking and the order of play is a mathematical prerequisite to a moral understanding of fairness in games.

In addition to turn taking, other mathematical elements in games may or may not involve number. Included in this broad category are games involving space, time, speed, and logic. Tic Tac Toe, *Connect Four*, Checkers, and Chinese Checkers all involve spatial reasoning and perspective taking. In cooperative games like *Harvest Time* and *Beyond the Secret Door* children work together against time to achieve a goal. Games such as *Guess Who?* and *Set* include logic as a critical component.

WHAT IS THE VALUE OF GROUP GAMES IN TEACHING MATHEMATICS?

Math games can provide an exciting context for learning almost any mathematical concept or skill. Many teachers use math games to help children learn how to count, read numerals, compare quantities, and perform simple arithmetic operations.

Drill and practice games are common in Classroom Types A, B, and C. Examples of such games are math bees, where children compete against each other to solve math problems, or board games where children must solve a problem before they can proceed on the board. While drill and practice games may have a place in the mathematics curriculum, we believe they are limited in value from a constructivist perspective.

In our opinion, the best games are those in which children have some say about the rules and can adjust them to meet their own needs and interests. Paul Trafton and colleagues have found that children crave challenges and will pose meaningful problems to themselves if given the freedom to do so (Trafton & Hartman, 1997). In helping early primary children invent their own math games, Hildebrandt (1998b) found that children regulate the difficulty of the game according to their needs and those of their partners. They know that if the game is too easy, players will get bored and if the game is too difficult, players will get frustrated. If given the freedom to adapt games, children will gravitate toward the "flow channel" described by Csikszentmihalyi (1990). *Flow* occurs when the demands of the game are in balance with the skills of the players. Type D teachers create a sociomoral atmosphere in which children can play games according to the original rules and also adapt the rules to their needs and interests.

Developmental differences in children's understanding of number are clearly observable in games, even in those that do not directly involve number. Young children begin by describing quantities with categorical terms (e.g., big-little, long-short, fast-slow). With development, they begin to think about quantities in relational terms and use appropriate language to describe them (e.g., more-less, bigger-smaller, longer-shorter, faster-slower). This generally occurs around the time they are abandoning preoperational thought and becoming concrete operational thinkers (Piaget & Inhelder, 1969). They also begin to use number to describe quantities (for example, 5 points/10 points, 5 spaces/10 spaces). Even though children might not understand all of the logic of number at an early age, with help from adults and more experienced peers, they can begin to count objects, order them from low to high, compare quantities, and do simple arithmetic.

GOALS FOR CHILDREN

In playing math games with children, our goals are both social and academic. In the course of playing games, we would like children to learn how to do several different things, as listed below.

I. Play According to the Rules

This goal is especially important for young children who have limited game-playing experience. Group games typically include a large amount of arbitrary conventional knowledge which needs to be taught directly. How games are taught depends on the age and experience of the child. With very young children (aged 2 to 3 years), it is best to provide some time to explore the game pieces and materials, and then play "games" that involve turn taking and some type of ritualized action (e.g., taking turns picking a card and discarding another). Older children (ages 4 to 5) can go beyond ritualized actions and learn to play a simple game according to the rules.

With 4- to 5-year-olds, we find that stating the objectives of the game and describing the rules is not enough for beginners because they immediately try to reach the objectives without regard to the other players or the rules. For example, when we told a group of inexperienced 4-year-olds that the object of the game *Rat-a-Tat-Cat* was to get rid of their high cards and replace them with low cards, everyone immediately threw away their high cards and lunged for the deck. When we said that they would need to take turns, some children appeared surprised. Even after having been introduced to turn taking in several games, some children still did not understand why they should have to wait their turn. In fact, one group finally decided to dispense with the turn taking rule (as described later in this chapter).

The teacher can begin by teaching the game according to a set of rules he or she believes is appropriate to the developmental level of the children. If the game proves to be too difficult or too easy, it can be modified as long as everyone agrees.

2. Understand That Numbers Are Represented in Different Ways

Math games use many different ways to represent numbers: Arabic numerals on playing cards, dots on dice, money of various denominations, and tokens of different values. Playing math games provides children with many opportunities to form multiple representations of number. Being able to represent numbers in different ways is important for developing logic-mathematical reasoning as well as literacy.

3. Count in Various Ways

Most children aged 3–5 years can count up to 10 or higher. But what do these numbers actually mean? In playing math games, there are different ways to count and different things to count. For example, in High Card (a variation on the game War), you count how many cards you have at the end of the game to see who wins. In *Rat-a-Tat-Cat*, however, you add up the number of points you have on each card to determine who wins. In other games, you match numbers or create a series of numbers and count sets. Learning *how* to count is an important skill. But equally important are learning *what* to count and *why* you need to count it. Teachers can help by providing direct assistance in counting and many opportunities to reason about counting.

4. Compare Quantities (Numbers of Objects, Spaces, Symbols)

Children aged 3–5 years are usually able to compare small quantities, either by estimating (sometimes called subitizing) or by using numbers. For example, it is fairly easy for young children to determine perceptually that two cards are more than one, or that three cards are more than two. However, as both quantities increase, the difficulty of identifying and comparing them also increases. Comparing numbers presupposes some understanding of cardinality and ordinality. It also presupposes being able to keep more than one thing in mind at a time. Teachers can help children with the task of comparing numbers by providing manipulatives such as unifix cubes (as illustrated in this chapter with the game *Rat-a-Tat-Cat*).

5. Take Others' Perspectives (Cognitive and Social)

Group games provide a rich context for perspective taking, both cognitive and social. Many of the best game-playing strategies involve trying to figure out what your opponent is likely to do in a given situation and then acting accordingly. For example, in Tic Tac Toe, you need to think both offensively (getting three in a row) and defensively (blocking your opponent) in order to win. In both competitive and cooperative games, children need to consider the feelings of other players and include everyone in the game. Learning how to win and lose gracefully is an important skill in both types of games.

6. Think Ahead About Strategies

Thinking ahead is an important skill in games, as well as in real life. In some games, actions need to be taken in a certain order to be effective (for example, in Chinese Checkers, children can spend many turns setting up elaborate paths to jump their marbles through). Planning ahead involves causal reasoning (for example, if I do this, then that will happen). It can also involve perspective taking (for example, if I do this, then she might think or do that).

7. Invent New Rules and Adapt to New Rules Invented by Others

A constructivist approach to game playing includes opportunities to change the rules of the game, as long as everyone agrees. Even though young children sometimes do not understand the full meaning of game rules, they should be encouraged to make adaptations as they see fit. These adaptations may not make much sense to adults, but as long as they work for the children (and are safe), they should be encouraged and supported.

PLAYING MATH GAMES IN A PRESCHOOL CLASSROOM

To learn more about how young children play math games, we brought games into Amy Hird's 3- to 5-year-old class at Malcolm Price Laboratory School, University of Northern Iowa, during their 30–40 minute center time. The children were free to join the games table as long as there was room. They were also free to leave the table whenever they wished. For most of the game-playing sessions, at least one adult was at the table to assist the children (either

Carolyn Hildebrandt, Amy, a graduate assistant, or a student aide). Sometimes the adult played with the children, and sometimes he or she observed. All game-playing sessions were videotaped for future analysis.

During a 10-week period we offered five different games: two competitive board games, one for beginners, Cover Up, and one for more experienced players, *The Wild Seed Game*; two competitive card games, one for beginners, High Card, and one for more experienced players, *Rat-a-Tat-Cat*; and a cooperative board game for beginners or more experienced players, *Max*. Of these, the two most popular games were *Max* and *Rat-a-Tat-Cat*. In this chapter, we focus on these two games and how the children and teachers adapted them to meet their needs and interests.

Rat-a-Tat-Cat

Rat-a-Tat-Cat is a memory-math game by Gamewright for players aged 6 years to adult. Several 5-year-old children in the class already knew how to play and could occasionally beat their parents and older siblings. Although their mathematics and perspective-taking skills were not on a par with those of their older opponents, their memory skills were excellent, which gave them a distinct advantage.

The game consists of a deck of cards with numbers from 0 to 9 on them. Cards with lower numbers (0 to 5) have pictures of cats on them, and cards with higher numbers (6 to 9) have pictures of rats on them. Several special power cards (Peek, Swap, and Draw 2) complete the deck.

In the standard rules of play, players start with four cards face down before them in a row on the table. Before play begins, players can lift up their two outside cards and look at them. After that, they may not look at any of their cards until they make a trade.

The object of the game is to end up with cards summing to the lowest number. The sophisticated player, therefore, replaces high cards with low ones. To play, the first person picks a card from the top of the deck, looks at it, and then decides whether to keep it or not. If the player decides to keep it, he or she exchanges it for an old card (without looking at it first) and then puts the old card face-up on the discard pile. The next player either draws from the deck or takes the top card on the discard pile. Play continues until someone yells, "Rat-a-Tat-Cat!" At that point, all players turn over their cards and count up their scores. (Another version of the game allows each player one more turn after "Rat-a-Tat-Cat" is called.)

Drawing a Peek card allows the player to peek at one of his or her cards on the table. A Swap card allows the player to swap one of his or her cards for an opponent's card (without looking at either). A Draw 2 card allows the player to draw a card from the deck. This card can be kept, or the player can discard it and draw another. If a player is left with a power card in hand after "Rat-a-Tat-Cat" is called, he or she must replace it with the first card from the top of the deck.

The main mathematical challenges for *Rat-a-Tat-Cat* involve understanding order (e.g., the order in which people play; the order in which you pick a card and discard it); counting (e.g., when using unifix cubes to calculate scores, counting out the right number for each card); decentration and coordination (being able to focus on more than one card at a time; being able to focus on your own play as well as that of your opponents); comparing quantities (e.g., determining which of two numbers is higher or lower); and simple addition (e.g., adding up the number of points in your hand). An additional literacy challenge is reading and understanding the numerals on the cards, which, unlike other playing cards, have no additional symbols to indicate number on them. A mnemonic challenge is remembering where your cards are on the table, and for older, more experienced players remembering which cards your opponents seem to like or dislike (just in case you have an opportunity to swap cards with them, or to help you decide when to call Rat-a-Tat-Cat). Social challenges of the game include playing cooperatively (for example, taking turns, observing the rules), perspective taking (for example, using verbal, facial, and other behavioral cues to imagine what your opponents are thinking and feeling), and good sportsmanship (for example, being able to win or lose in a graceful manner).

Introducing the Game. When we first introduced *Rat-a-Tat-Cat*, almost everyone wanted to play, so we started with a large group that varied widely in age and experience. This did not work very well. The younger children wanted to look at all of their cards, show them to their opponents, and see what everyone else had. The older children objected. We realized in retrospect that the younger children's desire to peek and share was partly due to their developmental level and partly due to the novelty of the cards.

The "Peek" Version. Since it was hard for the younger children to resist looking at their cards, we decided to dispense with the memory component of the game and proposed a new version which we dubbed the "Peek" version. In this version, players could peek at their own cards anytime they liked but could not look at other people's cards. The younger children liked the slightly naughty idea of peeking at their cards and flocked to the game table enthusiastically. Older children who already knew how to play the "No-Peek" version shunned the new version, saying it was "cheating," "too easy," and "no fun." Whenever they played, they played the standard No-Peek version of the game.

The Peek version was fun not only for the younger children, but for the adults as well, especially those who had trouble remembering what cards they had and where they were on the table. Good-natured sharing and requests for help and advice abounded.

Andrew: (To an adult) Is a 4 good?
Adult: Well, it depends on whether you have a lower card.
Andrew: (Keeps the 4 and discards an 8).
Dicit: Hey! I got an 8, too!
Adult: (To Angela) Do you want the 8 or do you want to pick from the top?
Angela: (Picks) I picked better than a 8!
Andrew: (Peeks at his cards) Hey! I got a 0!
Eli: (Peeks at his cards) I got the *best* cards!

We took out all of the power cards for this version: The Peek cards were redundant, since you could peek at your cards anytime you wanted; the Draw 2 cards were confusing (you only drew two if you did not want the first one); and the Swap cards were upsetting (especially if someone took a card that you really wanted to keep).

Using Unifix Cubes to Figure Out Who Won. Adding up the scores turned out to be quite an adventure. When we first began to play, the younger children were not sure how to add up their scores. Some counted their cards and exclaimed, "I got four!" But since everyone had four cards, this was not a particularly good way to determine the outcome of the game. Others recited each number on their cards, for example, "1, 0, 3, 2," and then asked, "Did I win?" Others thought that if they had all cats, *they* should win.

Some of the older children were able to add up their scores, but only if the numbers were small (e.g., $2 + 1 + 0 + 1$). If the numbers were large, even the oldest needed help. To make tallying the scores easier, we got a big tub of unifix cubes and showed children how to put the right number of cubes on each card. Players combined all of their cubes into a big tower and then compared their towers. The person with the shortest tower won (see Figure 9.1).

The "Ultra-Peek" Version. As more of the younger children got interested in playing, we found that it was easiest to teach the game with all of the cards facing up so that everyone could see what was happening. We had originally meant this to be a teaching version of the game for first-time players. However, this new version became so popular that many children did not want to go back to the Peek version. So we dubbed it the "Ultra-Peek" version

FIGURE 9.1. Using unifix cubes to calculate scores in *Rat-a-Tat-Cat*

and added it to our repertoire. We gave children the choice of playing the Peek or Ultra-Peek version and often had players playing different versions at the same time (see Figure 9.2).

For the adults, being able to see everyone's cards made the Ultra-Peek version a rather humorous game. As soon as the cards were dealt, it was clear who had the lowest score and should call "Rat-a-Tat-Cat!" However, the younger children found it challenging and exciting. Having their cards face-up made it easier for them to decide which ones to keep and which ones to discard. The younger children played in parallel to each other. Although they were interested in knowing what cards their opponents had, they did not systematically compare their hands to other people's since most of them were dependent on the unifix cubes to help them count, and so could not mentally count up their own and their opponents' scores. They simply played until they felt they had a low enough score to call "Rat-a-Tat-Cat!" When the final scores were tallied, the younger children were just as surprised at the outcome of the Ultra-Peek version as they would have been if they had played the No-Peek or Peek versions of the game.

FIGURE 9.2. "Peek" and "Ultra-Peek" versions of *Rat-a-Tat-Cat*

After several weeks of playing the Ultra-Peek version, the children eventually decided to keep all of the power cards in. The Peek card had no value, but the Swap card and the Draw 2 card helped create more excitement in the game.

Child-Initiated Versions of Rat-a-Tat-Cat. The Peek and Ultra-Peek versions were teacher-initiated adaptations of the game based on children's needs and interests. In these two versions of the game, children were given freedom to play their own hands, invent their own strategies, and share them with each other. Because we were trying to teach the game, we did not allow much innovation at first. But after several weeks, we let the children decide certain aspects of the game, such as who would shuffle, who would deal, who would go first, in what order they would play, whether or not they *wanted* an order of play, and whether the highest or lowest score would win.

One day, three boys decided to play the Ultra-Peek version and invited a fourth boy, Alex, to join them. Alex had a deck of *Rat-a-Tat-Cat* cards at home, but did not appear to know how to play. When Alex learned the object of the game was to get the lowest score, he did not want to accept the cards dealt to him. He wanted to choose his own! The other boys thought that was a great idea, and all agreed to choose their own cards. Carolyn was at the table and agreed to play with them. They each took turns choosing four cards and placing them on the table. The children placed their cards face up, and Carolyn placed her cards face down. Alex liked the power cards and chose a Peek card, a Draw 2 card, a Swap card, and a 1. The other boys chose a variety of number and power cards. Carolyn chose all 0s.

Alex went first, drew a Swap card, and used it to swap his 1 for the adult's 0. Carolyn went next, drew a high card, discarded it, and called "Rat-a-Tat-Cat!" The boys were surprised that the game had ended so soon. Carolyn showed them that she had chosen all 0s. Suddenly, the boys understood why she had ended the game so soon.

For the next game, Alex spread the cards out on the table face up so that they could choose their cards again. Carolyn asked, "Who should go first?" The boys said that they wanted to choose their cards at the same time. When Daniel shoved James, Carolyn intervened saying, "This isn't going to work. Someone's going to get hurt." In this case, even though everybody agreed to the new rule, Carolyn could not allow it because it was potentially dangerous.

The Development of Children's Strategies for Playing Rat-a-Tat-Cat. One of the children who learned the most through playing the game was 4-year-old Joshua. When he first started playing, Joshua's goal was to keep the cats and get rid of the rats. He explained the game to a student assistant, Cathy, as follows:

Joshua: If you get a rat, that's bad, and if you get a cat, that's good.
Cathy: OK, rats are bad, and cats are good. What else do I need to know about the game?
Joshua: Well, the ones with cheetahs and stuff are trading cards. Who should go first?
(They discuss this point and decide that Joshua will go first so he can show Cathy how to play the game. Another adult explains how to use the unifix cubes to count up the scores.)
Joshua: Hey, you know what? The big numbers are rats and the little numbers are cats.
Cathy: So I want little numbers—and I want to get rid of big numbers?
Joshua: Yeah.

Joshua thought about the cards categorically—cat cards were little and good, and rat cards were big and bad. Zeros were especially good and 9s were especially bad. Like Joshua, other children also thought about the cards categorically. For example, if they drew a rat card, they immediately discarded it because it was "high." They did this even if they had a higher card in their hand.

In counting up their scores, children also thought categorically and tended to center on the most salient cards in their hands. Some were surprised if they had a 0 in their hand and still did not win. Others were surprised if they had a 9 in their hand and won! This contradiction between expectation and experience had clearly created cognitive disequilibrium in some of the players.

We were not surprised to see this kind of categorical thinking in this game—it is typical of preoperational thought about number (Piaget & Szeminska, 1941/1952). We were also happy to see some of the children grappling with contradictions generated through this relatively undifferentiated way of thinking about number. However, as children continued to play *Rat-a-Tat-Cat*, we became concerned that the cards might be interfering with children's ability to think in a more continuous and coordinated fashion about number. Although the *Rat-a-Tat-Cat* cards have numerals on them, they do not have any other symbols to indicate quantity, unlike the cards in the classroom's teacher-made High Card deck (which have both numerals and the exact corresponding number of circles or squares).

In order to give them a better chance to compare the numbers on the cards, we suggested playing *Rat-a-Tat-Cat* with the High Card deck. This was not a popular idea. The children missed the dramatic cat and rat cards as well as the Peek, Swap, and Draw 2 cards. So we switched to a standard deck of cards and assigned special status to face cards. This still was not as much fun as the original game. At the children's request, we went back to using the original cards.

After several weeks of playing *Rat-a-Tat-Cat* and counting up the scores, we began to see a shift in children's thinking about number. One dramatic breakthrough came when Joshua was deciding whether to keep or discard a rat card with a 6 on it. He noticed that he had an 8 in his hand. Instead of throwing away the 6, he kept it, exclaiming, "Hey, this 6 should be a cat!"

Joshua's ability to break down the larger categories of "big" and "little" cards and compare cards within those categories shows that he is beginning to construct the idea that number is a synthesis of two types of relationships: order and hierarchical inclusion (Kamii, 1982; Piaget & Szeminksa, 1941/1952). He is learning that numbers can be ordered from low to high and that certain deductions can be made from that ordering. In this case, he notes that even though 6 is a rat card (and therefore higher than the 0–5 cat cards), it is also smaller than the 8 card, which is also a

FIGURE 9.3. Cooperative game *Max*

rat. Therefore, 6 can simultaneously be high and low, depending upon what kind of card it is compared to.

Although it was originally designed for older children, with a few adaptations *Rat-a-Tat-Cat* turned out to be a fun and fruitful way for children to learn about number. Joshua and his friends made rapid progress in reading the numerals on the cards and putting the right number of unifix cubes on them to count their scores. Many continued to think categorically about number, but some, like Joshua, began to make distinctions between cards within the cat and rat categories. We also saw a shift in children's ability to focus on all four of their cards, rather than just one or two.

Max

Another popular game, *Max* is a cooperative board game by Family Pastimes for children aged 5–7 years (see Figure 9.3). The object of the game is to get three forest animals (a bird, a chipmunk, and a mouse) home to their nests before they are caught by a cat named Max. Players take turns rolling a pair of dice with a green or a black dot on each side. Two blacks means Max moves two spaces; a green and a black means Max and a forest animal each move one space; two greens means one forest animal moves two spaces, or two forest animals each move one space. If Max and an animal end up on the same space, the animal is captured!

Each animal has its own short cut. Max can take any of the short cuts, but the animals can only take their own short cut. If Max gets too close to an animal, one of four treats can be used to call him back to his house at the beginning of the path. Once all the treats are used up, Max can no longer be called back.

Even though *Max* is designed for young children, adults sometimes have difficulty saving all of the animals the first time they play. The main mathematical challenges for young children involve understanding order (knowing in which order to take turns and which direction to move the pieces on the board), understanding correspondence (establishing a one-to-one correspondence between dots on the dice and spaces/moves on the board), decentration and coordination (being able to think about all of the animals on the board, rather than just one at a time), and thinking ahead (imagining what might happen if various rolls of the dice occurred and then taking the appropriate precautions). Since the game involves dice, older children and adults may also wish to think probabilistically about the outcome of each roll (if each die has three black dots and three green dots, what is the probability of getting two greens, two blacks, or a green and a black?).

Social challenges of the game include playing cooperatively (taking turns working to save all of the animals and deciding on when to use the treats), communicating (listening as well as explaining), and negotiating (persuading as well as being persuaded).

The following examples were selected to illustrate beginning play, different developmental levels of play, changes in children's game-playing strategies, and different versions of the game invented by the children themselves.

Beginning Play. When we introduced *Max* to children who were unfamiliar with cooperative games, they tried to assimilate it to their knowledge of competitive games. The first thing we heard was "I want to be the mouse!" "I want to be the bird!" We explained that the object of the game is for everyone to work together to save the animals from Max, and that we need to take turns rolling the dice and deciding how to move the animals. When the issue of treats was raised, many children wanted to be in control of a particular treat, "I want the milk!" "I want the kibble!" Again, we explained that the treats are for the use of the whole group in calling Max back to his house, and that we need to agree on when to use the treats.

Developmental Differences. The youngest children (aged 3–4 years) normally needed assistance from an adult or an older child to play the game. If left to their own devices, they tended to play according to the rules for a short time, but then gravitated toward dramatic play (e.g., bouncing the animals around in the middle of the board or having them chase each other up and down the trees). More experienced players could often play for extended periods without assistance but sometimes had trouble playing cooperatively, at least at first. Whether to allow children to use the game pieces as a springboard for dramatic play or intervene to bring children's play in line with the game rules is a judgment that each teacher must make based on his or her knowledge of individual children. Certainly, there is no harm in using the game pieces for dramatic play. Often, if one child wants to play the game by the rules, that child will persuade the others to resume focus on the game. However, if all children are satisfied with the dramatic play, we generally do not intervene.

Because there is only one dot on each side of the dice, the mathematical demands of moving the pieces are reduced. However, the youngest and most inexperienced players still needed help determining which direction to move, and how to move one space at a time. Cory, for example, knew from watching people play board games that you roll the dice and then bounce the tokens up and down on the board. It took awhile for him to construct a one-to-one correspondence between dots on the dice and spaces on the board, and to move just one space at a time.

Other spatial and numerical challenges involve decentration and coordination. Preoperational children tend to center on certain aspects of the game to the exclusion of others. They sometimes have trouble focusing on more than one animal at a time. For example, a child may roll a green and a black, move a forest animal, and then forget to move Max. Or a group of children may pick a particular animal to save and then lose the rest in the process. For example, one group decided that since the bird was ahead, they should keep moving it so that it would be safe. Unfortunately, they neglected the mouse and the chipmunk who were soon captured.

Another challenge in playing *Max* is thinking ahead. Children need to take a careful look at the board before rolling the dice because once the dice are rolled, it is too late to call Max back. Because of all the shortcuts, Max can move very fast. If children do not stop to think about what might happen, an animal could be quickly captured. The youngest children tend to roll first and think later.

Child-Initiated Variations. We saw a number of variations of *Max* during the 10-week period. One pair of children decided to change the rules after losing one animal after another to Max. According to the new rules, when Max lands on the same square as an animal, instead of capturing it, he scares it back to a wooden stump at the beginning of the path. The children made this rule so they could play longer and would have a better chance of saving all of the animals. (One slight problem with this version is that if Max keeps moving forward, he can end up at the animals' homes and intercept them there.)

Other children simplified the game by allowing themselves to call Max back even though they had already rolled the dice. This rule change was developmentally appropriate since young children often have difficulty imagining the possibilities generated by a roll of the dice. Once they have a particular situation to think about (for example, a roll of two blacks), they can mentally move the pieces to see what might happen. With age and experience, children become able to imagine and share a variety of outcomes and act to prevent them. Playing the game cooperatively helps children imagine possible outcomes from a variety of perspectives. The ability to think hypothetically and to visualize movement in time and space is an important aspect of physical and logico-mathematical knowledge that children can develop through playing *Max*.

Development of Children's Strategies. The most dramatic development in children's strategies involved communication and planning ahead. After several disasters caused by focusing on one animal at a time, children began to look more carefully at the board before rolling the dice. They also became more open to giving and taking advice from each other. Valerie was particularly good at thinking ahead. Amy, the teacher, supported this by asking, "Do you think you should roll or call Max back?" If Valerie said, "Call him back," Amy said, "Why do you think so?" If she said, "Don't call him back," Amy asked, "Why not?" By encouraging children to think ahead and explain their reasoning to each other, Amy helped them improve their strategies of play. After several weeks of playing *Max*, children began to think ahead and spontaneously explain their reasoning to each other.

CONCLUSION

Rat-a-Tat-Cat and *Max* are just two examples of many valuable games for teaching mathematics to young children. In these games, children learn to take turns, play according to rules, read and represent numbers in different ways, count in various ways, compare quantities, take others' perspectives, think ahead about strategies, and invent new ways to play the games. In creating a sociomoral atmosphere of mutual respect, teachers set the stage for learning in a cooperative, caring environment. By observing and playing along with the children, teachers can help children adapt the rules of the games and their strategies so that they can derive the maximum fun and learning from them.

Chapter 10

Variations on a Checkers Theme

Betty Zan

The use of group games such as Checkers in preschool and kindergarten often distinguishes constructivist from nonconstructivist classes. Checkers play offers opportunities for development in the areas of spatial and logico-mathematical reasoning and interpersonal negotiation. This chapter describes a study that took place in a classroom where games were a regular part of the constructivist curriculum. One remarkable feature of this study is that the teacher's interventions, while pivotal, were few. Many of the activities described in other chapters of this book require much teacher attention. Clearly, the teacher cannot be in all areas of the classroom and interact with all children at the same time. Games such as Checkers can be a valuable addition to the curriculum in part because children can derive a great deal of benefit from them with little teacher intervention.

During one school year, Rheta DeVries and I observed closely the 4- and 5-year-old class taught by Coreen Samuel at the Human Development Laboratory School at the University of Houston. We videotaped children's game playing two mornings a week for an entire year. During our observations, we noticed two boys who were avid Checkers players. They invented several versions of Checkers and, in the process, became acutely aware of the need for shared rules. In this chapter I tell the story of their Checkers play throughout the school year and describe the development in their practice of the rules and in their interpersonal understanding.

A CHECKERS STORY

Best friends Kerrick (Chinese American) and Jordan (African American) were both ages 4 years 5 months at the start of the school year. They had attended school together since they were toddlers. They were frequent game partners, and Checkers was their favorite game. I observed these boys playing Checkers the first week of school, and their play continued throughout the school year. They played over 20 times while we were taping, either alone together or with other children. Of these incidents, only those which shed light on their understanding of the game and the rules are described here. Recurring themes include how they negotiate their play, their understanding and practice of the rules, changes they make in the rules to invent new versions of Checkers, and their developing sense of competition.

September 5: Beginning to Play Checkers

This is the first time we observe Kerrick and Jordan play Checkers. During the morning activity time, Jordan suggests to Kerrick that they play Checkers. They get the bin of checkers (more than are needed for two people to play) and sort them according to color. They talk about their knowledge of Checkers.

Kerrick: I know how to play that game.
Jordan: I know how, too. (To another child) Do you know how to?
Kerrick: . . . teach you how to play this.
Jordan: My dad taught me how to play.
Kerrick: And I know how to play the game. We both know how.
Jordan: Nobody taught me. Nobody taught me.
Kerrick: Nobody taught me, either. 'Cept my brother.
Jordan: Nobody taught me.
Kerrick: Nobody? My brother didn't, either.
Jordan: My sister didn't, either. Only my cousin. Did your cousin teach you?
Kerrick: Yeah. Only my grandfather.

After establishing that they both know something about Checkers and sharing their experience of how they learned, they disagree about who will be red. Jordan threatens Kerrick, "I won't be your best friend if you don't let me be red." Kerrick acquiesces, and they continue to divide up the checkers and move to the rug, where a checkerboard is printed in the pattern of the carpet. They place the checkers on the checkerboard, covering every square, although not in a strict division of the board. Jordan mainly covers the squares closest to him, while Kerrick covers squares on one side perpendicular to (rather than opposite) the side Jordan is covering, so that the board contains a somewhat random arrangement of red and black checkers. Their arrangement of checkers suggests that they begin play at Piaget's Stage 2, egocentric play (see the introduction to Part III of this book). That is, they seem to imitate something of what they have seen others do when playing Checkers. They know that one person gets the red checkers and the other person gets the black checkers. They know that the checkers are placed on the squares of a checkerboard, although they do not understand the pattern of three rows, black squares only.

When the board is covered, they begin to play. They do not take turns, and they move in a random fashion—diagonally, vertically, and horizontally—jumping over one or more checkers, their own or the other's, and sometimes capturing jumped checkers, sometimes not. They know that sometimes you capture your opponent's checkers, although they are not sure how that occurs. They also know that the checkers move in some fashion, although they are not sure how, and get into an argument over this. Kerrick thinks they can move forward and sideways, skipping over many spaces, but Jordan says that only kings can move like that. Their argument is unilateral and uncoordinated: That is, each child asserts what he believes to be true about the rules of Checkers, with no attempt to negotiate agreement. This form of argumentation is consistent with the egocentric stage of play, where mutual agreement with its coordination of points of view is not seen to be necessary to play the game. When all the checkers are removed from the board, thus ending the game, they make no mention of who won, but simply start a new game. This, too, is characteristic of the egocentric stage of play. Awareness of competition is a sign of the next stage, that of beginning cooperation.

It is important to note that Coreen is aware of the boys' play and does not insist that they play Checkers "correctly." Rather, she allows them to play according to their understanding of the rules. This gives them the freedom to evolve a shared understanding of the game. She does not, however, take a hands-off approach, as will be illustrated in the descriptions of subsequent sessions.

November 21: Beginnings of Cooperative Play

Since September, Kerrick and Jordan have played at least once (not captured on tape) and have learned some of the standard rules of Checkers. Obviously, they must have played or observed play of others who knew the standard rules. They set up the checkers on the rug correctly, except for one stray checker. Kerrick refers to a rule stating that red always goes first (he has black). They take turns moving diagonally, jumping their opponent's checkers but not their own. They move toward their opponent's last row, and when they get there, say, "King me." They respect the rule that only kings can move backwards. When Jordan asks if he can jump over several spaces in one jump, Kerrick says that he cannot. Jamal comes over to watch and offers his view that one can move kings diagonally an unlimited number of spaces, as long as one does not jump one's own checkers in the process. (This becomes a recurring issue, and the children come to refer to such moves as "long jumps.") They allow kings to move in this fashion. Jordan asks if kings can make a right-angle move (he demonstrates a move two spaces in one direction, then one space perpendicular to that, like the knight in Chess). Kerrick says no. Their discussion of the rules and attempts to come to agreement over what rules they will play by indicate that they are transitioning into Piaget's Stage 3, beginning cooperation. Before they are through playing, clean-up time is announced. They argue briefly over who won, indicating that both of them know that when a game is played, someone is declared the winner.

December 7: The Conflict

Their next game of Checkers is markedly more competitive than previous games. Observed by Donell, Wilson, and Trevor, who drift in and out, they set up the board correctly on the games table and play more or less by the standard rules. They disagree over how kings can move. Jordan tries to make a king jump over two spaces (the first space unoccupied, the second space occupied by Kerrick's checker), but Kerrick protests. They call Coreen over to ask her, and she tells them that, according to the rules, one can only jump one space.

When Jordan moves his king to a vulnerable space and Kerrick jumps it (legally), Jordan protests that Kerrick was moving backwards. Kerrick replies that he was not (this is true), but allows Jordan to take back the move that put his king in danger. A few moves later, when the spot is no longer dangerous, Jordan moves his king back where it was. Not noticing that Jordan has moved it, Kerrick moves into the path of Jordan's king, and on the next move Jordan jumps Kerrick legally. Since Kerrick did not notice the previous move, he thinks Jordan has again jumped over two spaces, and protests that Jordan can only move one space. Jordan tries to explain that he moved there on a previous move, but Kerrick is unconvinced. Now upset, Kerrick repeats several times, increasingly insistently, "But you can only move one space!"

The argument escalates as they grab each other's and the extra checkers, and both claim that they won the game. They sweep the checkers off the board onto the floor, yelling at each other, "I won! I got the most checkers!" When Coreen notices the conflict and comes over to ask what happened, both boys lose control. Each tries to explain his point of view to her. The yelling turns to crying, and with tears streaming down their faces and hands clamped over their ears, they wail over and over, "You took two turns!" "No, I didn't!" "Yes, you did!" "No, I didn't!"

Coreen moves the boys away from the games table so that they can no longer fight over the checkers. Jordan tries to explain to Coreen how he moved, pointing to the checkerboard on the rug with his foot, but with the yelling and the tears, his words are unintelligible. (Even as upset as he is, each time Jordan tries to explain his move he does so correctly.) Seeing that they are not making any progress in negotiating and resolving their conflict while together, Coreen explains that she cannot understand them when they are yelling at each other, and suggests that she listen to each one tell his side of the conflict separately.

Coreen takes Kerrick back to the game table, and Kerrick explains that he thinks Jordan broke the rule about only jumping over one space. Coreen looks for the written rules in the classroom, but cannot find them. She suggests that maybe Jordan wanted to change the rules. Kerrick says that you cannot change the rules. At that point, Jordan walks up and insists that he was not changing the rules. They start to yell and cry again, covering their ears. Jordan again tries to explain what happened and insists, "I have the game at my house and I know the rules." More yelling and crying follows. Coreen tells them that they need to be apart until they can regain control of themselves. Kerrick remains at the game table while Jordan leaves to go to the bathroom. Kerrick asks where Jordan is and watches for him to return. When Kerrick catches sight of him coming from the bathroom, he smiles and approaches Jordan. But Coreen, unaware that the boys have already begun to regain control, insists that they need to be separated until they can either talk calmly about what happened or clean up their mess.

Rather than moving to other centers to play (as Coreen suggests they do), they choose to sit in chairs about 15 feet apart, facing each other. A bookcase is blocking their view of each other, and Kerrick begins a game of peek-a-boo with Jordan by leaning forward until he catches Jordan's eye, and then smiling. Then Kerrick starts to blow "raspberries" on his arm, which causes Jordan to laugh. They continue this silliness, Kerrick blowing raspberries and Jordan giggling, until Coreen notices that they appear to be calmer emotionally. She asks Kerrick which he would rather do, talk about what happened or clean up. Kerrick answers that he would rather clean up, and suggests to Jordan, "Let's clean up." They both smile and sigh in relief as they return to the game table. Kerrick continues to blow raspberries, causing Jordan to collapse in laughter.

When they are almost through cleaning up, Coreen comes over and asks them if they are friends again. They both say yes, and Kerrick says, "Yeah, I started doing this (demonstrates raspberries)." Jordan adds, "Yeah, and then I started laughing." She asks them if they are still going to have problems if they play Checkers again. Jordan replies, "On my birthday we're gonna play Checkers but I'm gonna have the rules." They finish cleaning up the checkers, and then join in on a game of *Sorry* started by Coreen and another child.

This game illustrates that the boys have progressed in their play of the game. They now understand that the winner is the person who has the most checkers at the end. However, their scooping up of all the available checkers suggests that they still do not define winning as occurring as a result of following common rules. The rules are becoming more important to them, however, and they are beginning to become aware of the importance of common rules, characteristic of Stage 3, beginning cooperation.

This game also shows Coreen intervening directly in the boys' play. She tries to assist them in resolving their conflict, although ultimately they find their own strategy (silliness) to defuse the tension and restore their relationship. She shows sensitivity by starting another game in the boys' presence, thus making it possible for them to play together again before the end of the activity period. Her question about whether they are friends again focuses their attention on what they did to repair their relationship. (It is noteworthy that the boys remember this conflict and refer to it in an interview at the end of the year. For the remainder of the year, they never again get into a conflict of such intensity.) Finally, by upholding the importance of agreeing on the rules and introducing the possibility that rules can be changed as long as everyone agrees to the change, Coreen sets the stage for future development in the boys' Checkers play.

December 12: Consulting the Rules

We write and laminate the Checkers rules, and Coreen introduces them during activity time to Kerrick, Jordan, and about five other boys who are interested. Jordan starts a game with Travis, and Kerrick plays on Jordan's team (the children often play in teams, meaning that quite a few children all play together, making moves for each other and giving advice). Donell plays on Travis's team. During the reading of the rules, Coreen emphasizes the rule that kings can only move one space and jump over only one checker at a time. She demonstrates the difference between legal jumps and illegal double jumps. However, as soon as she leaves the game table, the boys again bring up the subject of long jumps. After some disagreement, they play that kings can do long jumps.

   This game is significant for the insights it gives into the boys' stage of play as well as their interpersonal relationship. Their disagreement about long jumps resembles Piaget's description of the boys at Stage 3 who did not agree on the rules of marbles. DeVries (DeVries & Kohlberg, 1987), writing about Stage 3, states that "children at this stage still have personal and incomplete rule systems, and agreement on rules tends to be limited to momentary collective coordinations during a particular game" (p. 128). This is an apt description of what is happening in the boys' Checkers play.

   The teaming of Kerrick and Jordan against Travis and Donell suggests that perhaps Kerrick and Jordan are still distressed by the conflict of the previous week and therefore do not want to risk another conflict by playing against each other. Instead, they present a unified front against Travis and Donell.

January 18: Changing the Rules

Jordan and Donell start a game that many other children join. Eventually, Travis and Tommy end up playing, with about four other onlookers, including

Jordan. This game is significant in that it is obvious the children are still unclear about how kings can move and are still arguing, trying to resolve it. When their conflict becomes loud, Coreen comes over and reads the rules to them again, emphasizing that according to the rules, kings can only move one space. However, she suggests that sometimes people play by different rules, and says, "Maybe you guys can decide ahead of time if you want to change that particular rule." She upholds the value of mutual agreement, stating, "It's okay to change the rules, as long as you agree." As an example, she suggests that maybe one day they might decide to play that it is okay to move backwards. The boys talk about playing by different rules and come to an agreement that they will play with long jumps. The boys' active negotiation of this rule suggests that they are progressing in Stage 3 toward the understanding of the necessity for common rules.

February 8: A New Game

This game marks the first time we see the boys playing what they consider to be a new type of Checkers, with a different set of rules. Donell and Jamal are playing on the rug, by what appears to be the regular Checkers rules. Jordan and Kerrick are watching, and Tommy is playing Battle with Jamal (Jamal is playing two games at once). Kerrick takes over the Checkers game for Jamal, and Jordan helps Kerrick. Kerrick does a double jump that includes jumping his own checker, and Donell protests the jump, saying that it is "too long." Jordan tells Donell that you can do that in "Double Jump." The double jump lands Kerrick on the opposite end, and Kerrick asks Donell to give him a king. Donell refuses, explaining, "You don't get kings." Jordan demonstrates to Donell how to jump his own checkers and move backwards, which Donell then begins to do. This version of Checkers, played without kings and where players can move both forward and backward and jump over their own checkers, later gets renamed "Deadly Checkers" (perhaps because, with the double, triple, and even quadruple jumps possible, it moves very fast).

February 13: Deadly Checkers

For the first time we see Kerrick and Jordan play Deadly Checkers. The game moves very fast until the players get down to only a few checkers on the board. Then they end up chasing each other all over the board. Winning at Deadly Checkers is difficult, and usually games are ended by mutual agreement, with no clear winner.

On this day, Kerrick and Jordan play alone for the most part. Each one is now quite good at making a move and then, keeping his hand on the checker (so that he can retract the move if he chooses to), evaluating what will happen if he moves there, predicting, "If I move there, then you will jump me, and then I will do a double jump on you." Other children come over occasionally to watch and comment that they are playing wrong (for example, "Hey, you can't move backwards!"), and Kerrick and Jordan explain that they are playing Deadly Checkers (implying that of course they can move backwards). Kerrick traps Jordan, and when it is obvious that he cannot win, Jordan concedes with the suggestion, "Hey, you wanna play again?" But Kerrick is not interested in another game, and play ends.

February 20: Experimenting with Rules

Early in the game, Jordan says that he wishes they were playing Deadly Checkers. They discuss which rules they want to play by, and it looks as though they are playing Deadly Checkers until Kerrick gets to the other side and asks for a king. When Jordan protests, "You don't get no kings in Deadly Checkers," Kerrick says that they are playing a different kind of Deadly Checkers. As the play continues, they combine Deadly Checkers rules with Long Jump rules (Long Jumps includes kings, a major difference between Deadly Checkers and Long Jump Checkers). This leads to a long but somewhat friendly conflict over how kings move. As each child suggests how he thinks he can move, the other replies, "Then I can do this," in a sort of jovial one-upmanship. They playfully move more than one space, make right-angle turns, and jump all over the board. Jordan protests, however, when Kerrick jumps his king, saying that it was not his turn (the turn taking has been poorly regulated and it is hard to tell whose turn it was). Finally, Jordan stops, shoves all of Kerrick's checkers that he has captured toward Kerrick and announces, "Here [are] all my men. You win. You get all these. Here." Kerrick in turn gives Jordan all the checkers that he has captured, saying, "You get all these men. Here." After pushing the checkers across the board to one another, Jordan breaks the tension by suggesting, "Let's play Deadly Checkers. You want to?" Then Jordan suggests that they play a new Checkers game called Battle Checkers (probably inspired by the lively game of Battle taking place right next to them on the carpet). Jordan makes up the game as he goes along, telling Kerrick where to set up his checkers, but the game never comes together. They stop and restart, setting up the board like a regular Checkers game, and settle into using the Deadly Checkers rules again. However, when Donell comes over and asks if they are playing Deadly Checkers, they say no. Jordan gets to the opposite side and says that he gets a king, and they start to play with long jumps again. When they are down to only a few checkers each, they decide that they both won and end the game.

   This play offers insights into the boys' thinking about rules. It is clear that they are conscious of and distinguish between at least two distinct sets of Checkers rules (regular and Deadly Checkers) and perhaps a third as well (Long Jump Checkers). At the same time, however, it appears that the rules are not fully articulated and are rather fluid (illustrated by the shifting between Long Jump and Deadly Checkers and lack of prior agreement on how to win). This is characteristic of Stage 3 in which rules tend to be limited to particular instances of games. It suggests progress in that both boys now feel free to invent new versions of Checkers (in contrast to December 7, when Kerrick told Coreen that you cannot change the rules).

February 27: Developing Strategies

Kerrick and Jordan start out playing Deadly Checkers. Jordan introduces a new rule, that if your opponent fails to notice a jump, you can take the checker that should have made the jump, blow on it, and capture it. This rule reflects Jordan's growing ability to coordinate offensive and defensive strategies. When Kerrick arrives at the opposite side, he gets a king. Then Jordan gets a king, and they play with long jumps (again switching between rules fluidly). They get into a conflict when Jordan questions whether giving the other a king constitutes a turn or not. They cannot resolve the conflict, and instead mutually decide to start a new game. They never state explicitly which rules they are using, but they appear to be playing Deadly Checkers. This time when Kerrick gets to the opposite side and asks for a king, Jordan says that they are playing Deadly Checkers (implying that therefore he cannot get a king). They reach the point in the game where neither one can win because they are chasing each other all over the board. So they decide that both should take a king, and they allow the kings to make long jumps. They continue to chase each other around the board, this time with kings making long jumps. No one can win, and they end the game by mutual agreement. A brief argument over who won is settled when Kerrick suggests, "Hey, how about you won first and I won second?" Jordan agrees, and they leave satisfied.

This game offers significant insights into the play of both boys. Jordan demonstrates his interest in rules for every occasion, illustrated both by his blowing rule and by his concern over whether giving one's opponent a king constitutes a turn or not. This concern for rules for every occasion can be viewed as an early precursor to Stage 4, codification of rules. Kerrick, on the other hand, demonstrates that his play is just barely Stage 3, beginning cooperation. One of the characteristics of Stage 3 is that players try to win. Kerrick demonstrates his less competitive attitude when he suggests a compromise—that Jordan won first and he (Kerrick) won second. This appears to be a pattern with Kerrick. Whenever there is a dispute over who won, he is willing to concede that they both won, even if he was ahead. It is also possible that Kerrick is aware that winning is more important to Jordan than it is to him, and is willing to defer to Jordan in order to preserve the play relationship.

March 1: More Deadly Checkers

Kerrick and Jordan start a game, observed by several boys who ask if they are playing Deadly Checkers. Donnell demonstrates that he knows the rules of Deadly Checkers, stating, "You can't get a king. Nobody can." The onlookers join in the game, occasionally moving checkers for Jordan or Kerrick. When Kerrick reaches the opposite side, Donnell tells Jordan to give him a king, and Jordan protests, "I don't have to. We're not playing regular Checkers." When Donnell points to an opportunity to move backwards and jump Jordan, Jordan attempts to prevent the jump by telling Donnell that he cannot move backwards. However, Austin and Donnell argue that moving backwards is permissible in Deadly Checkers. When Donnell helps Kerrick jump Jordan again, Jordan protests, "Can't help!" These brief interactions illustrate how important winning is to Jordan.

With so many children moving checkers, they lose track of turns. Jordan, becoming upset over other children making moves for him, knocks the board over, dislocating the checkers, and asks, "You wanna play over again, Kerrick? Everybody's messing us up." The other children leave, and they start a new game. Kerrick will not let Jordan be red, however, and Jordan starts the game angry, stating, "Okay, I'll be the stupid black, but my favorite color is not black." This game marks one of the rare times when Kerrick insists on getting something he wants.

March 6: Getting Better at Deadly Checkers

Kerrick and Jordan start a game of what appears to be Deadly Checkers. The game is very friendly as they suggest moves to each other that demonstrate how far they have advanced in their spatial reasoning about possible moves.

Jordan: You could hop-hop (indicates a move Kerrick could make).
Kerrick: (Starts to move as Jordan suggests, then changes his mind) Hold on, I wanna go like . . .
Jordan: Well, we both get 2 (meaning they will both have 2 captured checkers). You don't want me to get 2?
Kerrick: Do you have 2?
Jordan: I have 1. You can have 2 if you go . . . You can go like hop-hop (points out move), and I'll jump you back and you'll jump me back and I'll jump you back.
Kerrick: Nuh-uh, see, if you move right here, I'll go like . . .

Jordan: Uh-uh, no. If you move like that, I'll jump you, and you'll jump me back, and then I'll jump you (demonstrates).
Kerrick: Okay (moves as Jordan suggests).

Kerrick is winning, and Jordan complains that he has nowhere to move. Kerrick suggests, "Let's just say that I win, okay?" Jordan does not agree, and tells Kerrick to move. About 15 moves later, Jordan again complains that he has nowhere to move. Demonstrating that winning is not as important to him as playing, Kerrick moves away from a jump he could have made against Jordan and says, "You can move right here." However, Jordan appears to want Kerrick to compete. He puts Kerrick's checker back and protests, "Huh-uh, that's how you win the game. You have to jump. You wanna win the game?" Kerrick replies, "Let's just say that we both won." They agree and start a new game. They tell each other where to move, point out good moves, and when the other is in danger of being jumped, promise that they will not make the jump. Kerrick tires of the game, saying, "Let's just say we both won because I'm getting tired." But Jordan again presses for competition. He says no and points out a jump to Kerrick. Kerrick agrees and continues to play. Kerrick jumps Jordan with a fairly complicated move that Jordan protests. Jordan tries to reenact the move, but it looks as though he is trying to avoid the capture rather than explain the move fairly. Finally, Kerrick reenacts the jump accurately, Jordan accepts the jump, and play continues. They are both down to only a few checkers, and no one can win. Kerrick again demonstrates how little emphasis he places on winning by suggesting that they just call it a tie and quit, but Jordan does not want to quit and suggests more moves. Two moves later, Jordan suggests, "Let's play I say I won." Kerrick replies, "We both won." Jordan disagrees, "No, I won." Kerrick does not protest, and they begin a third game. The game is very friendly. A few moves into the game, Jordan gets ahead and laughs, "Ha ha, I got ya!" A few moves later, he announces in a gleeful tone, "I see a jump! I see a jump and I'm not gonna show you!" Kerrick misses the jump, so Jordan demonstrates, then double-jumps Kerrick. Two moves later, Jordan states, "I have five more men than you. Let's just say I won because I don't wanna play anymore." They agree to end the game, and both leave satisfied.

Kerrick's lack of interest in competition and his interpretation of what it means to win (that both players can win) could reflect the importance he places on preserving his friendship with Jordan. It could also suggest that he is still primarily at Stage 2, egocentric play. In contrast, Jordan seems solidly at Stage 3.

March 8: Another New Game

Austin and Barb, a student intern in the classroom, begin playing Deadly Checkers, but when Jordan suggests to Barb a jump that involves moving backwards, Austin protests, "We're not playing Deadly Checkers." Later, when Austin jumps backwards, Jordan tells him that he cannot move backwards, demonstrating the importance Jordan places on the rules. That is, if they are not playing Deadly Checkers (as Austin stated earlier), then Austin may not move backwards. When Austin gets a king, Kerrick (who has joined the game as an onlooker) and Jordan tell Barb that kings can do long jumps. Austin announces, "We're playing Long Jumps." This is the first time we hear the children refer to the Long Jumps version by name. New versions of Checkers are becoming part of the culture of the classroom. However, their fluid movement between the different rules for Checkers, drifting in and out of Deadly Checkers and Long Jumps, demonstrates that their understanding of the rules is still primarily at Stage 3.

March 13: A Winner

Kerrick and Jordan have already begun playing Deadly Checkers when taping begins. Jordan is winning, and Kerrick tries to leave, but Jordan protests. Kerrick points out that he is stuck and has nowhere to move, so Jordan offers to let him skip his turn. Jordan lets Kerrick skip many turns, but finally, when Kerrick points out that he is stuck and asks to skip again, Jordan refuses, saying, "No, you just want to win." Kerrick explains that he cannot move anywhere, but Jordan tells him to move anyway. So Kerrick moves, and Jordan captures all of Kerrick's checkers. This is the first game (captured on tape) that Kerrick and Jordan play to the end with a clear winner.

April 19: More Progress

Kerrick and Jordan are already playing Deadly Checkers as the taping begins. When Jordan misses a jump, Kerrick takes the checker, blows on it, and captures it. This marks the first time we see Kerrick play by the blowing rule that Jordan has been using for some time.

PROGRESS REVEALED IN CHECKERS PLAY

This microanalytic examination of Checkers provides a window through which we see progress in the two boys' practice of rules, ability to use strategies, and developmental levels of negotiation.

Practice of the Rules

The beginning of the year saw both boys' play strongly resembling Piaget's description of Stage 2, egocentric play. While they imitated the form of Checkers, they showed little need to coordinate their play with each other. They did not take turns or follow mutually agreed-upon rules, and neither one tried to win. By November, both boys appeared to be making the transition to Stage 3, beginning cooperation. Not only did they play more or less by the rules, but they also discussed what they believed the rules to be and argued over who won. Their play remained at this transitional stage, exhibiting some characteristics of Stage 2 and some characteristics of Stage 3, throughout January.

In February, they invented a new type of Checkers, suggesting that they were beginning to move to Stage 3. However, they were still transitional with regard to competition. Neither one was overly concerned over who won. Instead, they were satisfied with ending games by stating that both won, a characteristic of Stage 2. At the end of February, Jordan did something that could be considered a foreshadowing of Stage 4, codification of rules. He became concerned with whether or not giving one's opponent a king constituted a turn.

By March, Jordan was showing more concern over who won than he had previously, indicating that he was abandoning Stage 2. Kerrick, on the other hand, was still not overly concerned about winning and losing. While his use of the rules suggests Stage 3, he rarely showed more than a passing interest in winning. However, it is possible that Kerrick's lack of interest in winning was at least partly a function of his need to preserve the relationship with Jordan, who was interested in winning. Other factors possibly contributing to his relative lack of interest in winning include his personality, family attitudes toward competition, and culture.

Strategies

It is clear that both boys progressed in their play strategies from the beginning of the year. Early in their play, they figured out that in order to be able to jump their opponent's checkers, they had to allow a few of their checkers to be jumped. They became progressively more capable of anticipating moves, and as the year went on their ability to do this extended a greater number of moves ahead. Finally, they developed the ability to decenter to coordinate both offensive and defensive strategies, as illustrated by the blowing rule used first by Jordan and then by both of them. Perhaps Kerrick's reluctance to use the blowing rule reflected an inability to play both offensively and defensively simultaneously. Or perhaps he simply wanted to be nice to his friend.

Developmental Levels of Negotiation

In addition to the progress seen in the boys' ability to play by the rules and adapt the rules, we also saw progress in their ability to negotiate with each other. This progress was assessed formally through analysis of the videotapes

of ten episodes of checkers play between Kerrick and Jordan. As these results are described in detail elsewhere (Zan, 1996), I will summarize here
only those results concerning the boys' progress in negotiation.

During the data collection process, I had the impression that the boys
were using progressively more advanced negotiation strategies (see the introduction to Part III of this book). The data confirm this impression. During
the fall sessions (September–December), slightly over 20 percent of their
negotiations were impulsive (Level 0). This decreased to slightly less than 3
percent in the spring (March–April). Their reciprocal (Level 2) negotiations
increased from 13 percent in the fall to over 23 percent in the spring.

The boys also became much more adept at handling and resolving their
conflicts. In this case, a resolved conflict refers to one in which both parties
are satisfied with the outcome. In the fall episodes they managed to resolve
only 45 percent of their conflicts. However, in the spring episodes, they resolved 80 percent of their conflicts. They also became more adept at manag-
ing their conflicts without ending the game. In the fall, 40 percent of their
conflicts resulted in the game ending, whereas by spring, this occurred in only
10 percent of their conflicts.

CONCLUSION

This study provides a window into children's experience of games in Type D
classrooms where children are given the opportunity to pursue their interests. The teacher encourages game playing through the way he or she sets up
the classroom and provides access to numerous games, both commercial and
teacher-made, whenever the children want them. He or she allows children
ample time and space to play, and support when they need it. The teacher
observes children carefully and intervenes when needed. Finally, and perhaps
most importantly, the teacher establishes a classroom atmosphere based on
caring, cooperation, and mutual respect, where the quality of the interpersonal relationships makes it safe to play competitive games, free of the un-
healthy competition that sometimes marks children's game playing.

Epilogue

Rheta DeVries

We have undertaken in this book to elaborate our vision of constructivist education and, in so doing, to provide a constructivist interpretation of developmentally appropriate curriculum in preschool and kindergarten. Because developmentally appropriate and constructivist education are teachers' interpretations of theory and principles of teaching, it is important to describe the ideal at the level of daily practical experiences of teachers and children. Considering four different ways of incorporating play into the curriculum, we describe how these four approaches differ in their implementation of specific activities. We hope we have communicated a way of thinking and "a way of being with" children in constructivist classrooms. Taking seriously Piaget's (1948/1973b) criticism of an "excess of unsupervised liberty which ended in generalized play without much educational benefit" (pp. 6–7), our purpose has been to examine practices in order to distinguish what is of educational benefit and what is not.

Play is useful to children. It expresses and aids their understanding of the world of objects and the world of people as they construct relationships embedded in content. When children figure out how to partition a hexagon into triangles, how to strategize by thinking about order and inclusion in *Rat-a-Tat-Cat*, or how to make a shadow reappear after an unaccountable disappearance, they are constructing relationships that foreshadow and prepare for logical operations described by Piaget (e.g., Piaget & Szeminska, 1941/1952; DeVries, 1997). Beyond the manifest content of curriculum, we consider the underlying relationships children have the possibility to construct. From this perspective, play is not just an end in itself. It is a means, a mechanism, for development. The authors of this book believe that children must construct knowledge, but also that children are constructing more than knowledge as they play. They are constructing their intelligence, their ability to reason, their morality, and their personality.

In the Introduction to this book, I discuss the relationship between play and work in constructivist thought. Drawing upon the work of Piaget, Dewey, and Vygotsky, I argue that NAEYC's criticism of inappropriate work in early education has had the unfortunate effect of giving all work a bad name. Perhaps it is time to resurrect the idea of work and talk about *appropriate work* in early education. Both play and work can engage children's interest, experimentation, and cooperation and meet the criteria for constructivist activities. Much of what is called "play" in constructivist education is actually work. For example, children may be said to work when they try seriously to figure out how to get a shadow on the ceiling or how to organize turn taking that is fair to everyone. This is work in the context of play. In my view, we must not limit our programs to play but also encourage children to pursue purposes and activities that are more properly called "work," maintaining, however, the criterion of children's interest. By doing so, we are helping children develop the capacity for work.

The constructivist curriculum described in this book may be called transformative curriculum because it transforms teaching as well as children. It is curriculum that emerges from experimental teaching. That is, teachers create activities that follow children's interests, and they modify their interventions in terms of insights into children's thinking obtained through careful observation of children's actions. This approach to their work enables teachers to transform activities so that children can transform themselves in the course of the activities.

Virtually everyone agrees with the rhetoric of developmentally appropriate and constructivist curriculum. However, when we observe what teachers do in classrooms, it is clear that a great deal of disagreement exists at the practical level. Teachers who read this book may recognize themselves in our descriptions of the four classroom types. They may find their practices fall clearly into one type or into more than one type. Many teachers who have read drafts of this book and want to become more constructivist in their teaching have found the four types helpful in examining their own practices.

Moving from Types A or B toward Types C or D teaching requires a large leap in educational philosophy. However, the philosophical leap is not as difficult as the practical leap toward transformed practices. For many teachers the practical leap toward constructivist teaching requires a basic transformation in the sociomoral atmosphere of the classroom. The core of this change involves a transformation in the teacher's relationships with children from authoritarian to cooperative—from a "Do what I say" approach to a "Let's work together" approach. Betty Zan and I have described ways in which the teacher can change his or her actions to create a cooperative sociomoral atmosphere through consulting children and giving them a significant amount of power to determine what happens in the classroom (DeVries & Zan, 1994). The constructivist teacher is not permissive and does not give up necessary authority, but finds ways to enable children to become more and more self-regulating. With the aim of facilitating children's long-term development, constructivist teachers promote children's autonomous construction of knowledge, intelligence, personality, and morality.

The authors of this book have worked to assist teachers in their journey toward constructivist teaching. We have found it to be a process that is at times agonizing, at times exciting, but eventually satisfying. Elsewhere (DeVries & Kohlberg, 1987, Chapter 11), I have pointed out that as teachers become more and more constructivist, they give up certain ideas and replace them with others, and that progress toward constructivist teaching involves working through skepticisms, changing the physical environment, changing teaching style, and becoming autonomous. We hope that our work will help teachers find new excitement and challenge in their teaching and enable children to find new excitement and challenge in their school experiences.

Appendix

Stages in Children's Reasoning About Shadows

Rheta DeVries

Level 0: Little or No Awareness of Shadows

Many children 2 years and younger do not recognize their own or others' shadows. When toddler teachers darken the room and turn on a projector, some children invariably fail to see the shadows. When teachers point to shadows, children at this level simply look with perplexity at the screen and turn their attention to the objects instead.

Level 1: Figural Correspondence of Well-Defined Shadows with Special Objects

Level 1A: The Object-Shadow Relation of Resemblance. At this level, 2- to 3-year-olds may still have some difficulty seeing shadows. When they do see a familiar shape, they may treat it as an independent object. For example, one 2-year-old rediscovered his shadow and exclaimed, "There he is!" Another 2-year-old simply called his shadow by his own name, indicating his appreciation of the correspondence between the shadow shape and himself. Children first begin to be aware of the similarity in shape between shadows and the objects that cast them by noticing their own shadows and those of objects having a special shape such as a toy horse. At this level they are only aware of a nonspatial object-shadow relation. Some young children are reported to be afraid of shadows, especially at night when the dark shapes seem menacing to them. In this case, the shadow itself must be considered as a kind of object. When children at this level move behind the light (so that their shadow disappears) and are then asked to make their shadows again, they often are able to go back to the place where they stood when they saw it before. This is reminiscent of behavior described by Piaget at a much earlier level when babies search for a covered object by looking in the place where they found it last.

Level 1B: Coordination of the Object-Shadow and Object-Screen Relations into a Causal Relation of Proximity. Children at this level are more interested in shadows. They notice that when they stand near a certain screen, a shadow appears, and they infer (construct) falsely that shadows are caused simply by proximity to a screen. It is then a small step to another false inference that a shadow may be created in a certain place by an action of the object such as walking or leaning toward the place where one wants to see a shadow. One 4-year-old, when asked how to make a shadow, said, "You stand next to the wall." These ideas lead children to expect shadows in impossible places or under impossible conditions and create the conditions for experiencing contradictions. Surprised that shadows do not follow the "rules" they have constructed, some children conclude that the cause of shadow phenomena is magic! Usually, however, when children are faced with shadows that fail to appear and behave as anticipated, they make efforts to overcome these practical difficulties. Some children react to the fact that they cannot always control shadows by concluding that the shadow is independent and can behave autonomously: "It ran out the door."

The proximity hypothesis implies a consciousness of the screen (and the shadow-screen relation) along with the simpler object-shadow relation. However, consciousness of the role of light is absent. For example, one 4-year-old, while backing up to make his shadow bigger, collided with the lamp. He exclaimed, "Hey! What's *that* for?" in an irritated tone.

Level 2: Awareness of the Role of Light

Level 2A: Light as a Third Term in the Object-Shadow and Object-Screen Relation. At this level, children recognize that the presence of light is a factor in the appearance of shadows. However, this is not a precise relation, and children continue to expect proximity of object to the screen and/or the action of the object to be effective factors in the formation of shadows. Here we find awareness of the general condition of light in the room or of the lighted area around the shadow. Light may not be associated with a lamp but may be viewed as a kind of accompaniment to shadows without playing a causal role. One 4-year-old, for example, said "The light is everywhere and you have your shadow walking to you." When the teacher suggests trying to make a shadow on an unlighted wall, children at this level are unsuccessful because they do not think of moving the lamp.

Level 2B: Light as Specific Illumination and the Search for Spatial Solution to Practical Problems: Coordination of Object-Screen and Light-Screen Relations and Introduction of a Limited Light-Object Relation. Awareness of the light source shifts from thinking about general illumination to specific illumination of the screen on which the shadow falls. This leads to trial-and-error experimentation to find spatial solutions to practical problems. The hallmark of this stage is consciousness that the direction the lamp faces is a factor in where shadows appear, but children have difficulty in thinking of the light source and the object at the same time. Children at this level think of moving the lamp to make a shadow on the wall opposite the one where they have been seeing shadows. However, this awareness of the importance of directionality may be fragile as indicated by considerable trial-and-error efforts to change the location of the shadow. One 7-year-old, after changing the direction the lamp faced, considered only the light-screen relation as she stood behind the lamp and waved her hand. Then she accidentally waved it a little in front of the lamp, and this was enough to convince her: "You have to get in front of the light." She did not consider light-screen and light-object relations at the same time, but sequentially. Similarly, an 8-year-old suggested turning the lamp to make a shadow on the wall opposite the one where shadows were appearing, but said, "I don't think it will work, though. It might." Children at this level, however, fail to move the lamp in order to make the shadow move to the other side of themselves when seated on the floor. After all, the floor is already illuminated! It is important to emphasize that children cannot yet think of shadows as transitory because they are struggling so hard with spatial relations among light, object, and screen. Children at this level are not thinking about light as active but seem to think about these relations as if they are static. They do not think about what occurs between the light source and the illuminated area. Even when they succeed at creating shadows on new screens, what happens to an unseen shadow remains a mystery. For example, when asked what happens to a shadow when you go to bed at night, one 7-year-old said, "I guess it's just gone to bed. It just goes to sleep with you, or in the dark. . . . Nobody really knows."

Level 2C: Light as Active in the Formation of Shadows. Now children think at least sometimes of light as active in making shadows. This is notable progress because children must reason beyond the observable. Children say things like, "The light comes and hits your body," and "Light goes under the (object)." A 9-year-old likened it to wind: "It's pushing against me and making a figure behind me. When I turn around, it's pushing against my back." Sometimes not only the light but the shadow itself is considered to be active. One 5-year-old seemed to think that the light hits the object, makes it dark, and then the shadow "comes off your body." The idea of light as active does not lead children at this level to well-consolidated spatial ideas even at the practical level. They are often satisfied with generalizations that are only sometimes true.

Level 3: The Law of Spatial Relations

Level 3A: Equilibrated Coordination of Relations at the Level of Practical Intelligence. At this level children have discovered the law of spatial relations among the light source, object, and screen. They have the *know-how* to arrange the lamp and object so as to produce a shadow on any particular screen, even the floor. However, they are unable to explain the reason for their practical success. They do not *know why*. This reminds us of Piaget's (1974/1978) book *Success and Understanding,* in which he discussed his finding that practical success often precedes understanding. Because children at this level still think in somewhat mystical ways about the way in which light works, they may still reason that merged shadows blend with one another or that one covers another and that unseen shadows still exist somewhere. Lacking understanding of why the spatial relations work, children may believe that shadows simply emanate from their objects. (This idea is also found at earlier levels.)

Level 3B: Conceptual Explanation of Spatial Relations. At this level, *knowing how* is elaborated into *knowing why*. Children have a conceptual understanding of the idea of blocked light. They say that light cannot go through the object and that the object thus prevents light from reaching the screen. One 7-year-old said, "You block the light so there's no light there where you're blocking it, so that makes it dark and that's a shadow." This idea is a deduction that goes beyond the observable. Causality has progressed to logical causality. Here is a reconstruction at a conceptual level of what was understood at Level 3A on the plane of action. Still, children do not understand a shadow as the absence of light. They say that a merged shadow is still there somewhere, and they often still insist, as one 9-year-old said, "It's usually always there. It's like you, so it just disappears where you can't see it—you really don't know. It's—it might still be there and it just can be there only when the light's projecting on it."

Level 4: Deduction of Transitoriness of Shadows

Children at this level are distinguished by their insistence that unseen shadows are not there at all. As one 8-year-old explained, "If you see it, it's there, and if you don't see it, it's not." The achievement of Level 4 is what Piaget (1974/1978) referred to as the "transcendence of action by conceptualization, or . . . of the realm of success by the realm of reason" (p. 233).

NOTE

This Appendix was adapted from DeVries, 1986.

References

African Primary Science Program. (1973). *Activities for lower primary. Water.* Newton, MA: Education Development Center.

Allen, K. Z. (Ed.). (1996). *Sunshine and shadows: Delta science module II teacher's guide.* Hudson, NH: Delta Education.

Apple, M., & King, N. (1977). What do schools teach? *Curriculum Inquiry, 6*(4), 341–357.

Aristotle. (1932). *Politics* (H. Rackam, Trans.). Cambridge, MA: Harvard University Press.

Asch, F. (1985). *Bear shadow.* New York: Prentice-Hall.

Bodrova, E., & Leong, D. (1996). *Tools of the mind: The Vygotskian approach to early childhood education.* Englewood Cliffs, NJ: Merrill.

Bredekamp, S. (1987). *Developmentally appropriate practice in early childhood programs serving children from birth through age 8.* Washington, DC: National Association for the Education of Young Children.

Bredekamp, S., & Copple, C. (1997). *Developmentally appropriate practice in early childhood programs.* Washington, DC: National Association for the Education of Young Children.

Bredekamp, S., & Rosegrant, T. (Eds.). (1992). *Reaching potentials: Vol. 1. Appropriate curriculum and assessment for young children.* Washington, DC: National Association for the Education of Young Children.

Bredekamp, S., & Rosegrant, T. (Eds.). (1995). *Reaching potentials: Vol. 2. Transforming early childhood curriculum and assessment.* Washington, DC: National Association for the Education of Young Children.

Brown, M. (1947). *Stone Soup.* New York: Macmillan.

Chen, J., Krechevsky, M., & Viens, J. (1998). *Building on children's strengths: The experience of Project Spectrum.* New York: Teachers College Press.

Chenfeld, M. B. (1995). *Creative experiences for young children* (2nd ed.). Orlando, FL: Harcourt Brace.

Chittenden, E. (1991). Authentic assessment, evaluation, and documentation of student performance. In V. Perrone (Ed.), *Expanding student assessment* (pp. 22–31). Alexandria, VA: Association for Supervision and Curriculum Development.

Clements, D., & McMillen, S. (1996). Rethinking "concrete" manipulatives. *Teaching Children Mathematics, 2*(5), 270–279.

Cohen, D. H., Stern, V., & Balaban, N. (1997). *Observing and recording behavior of young children* (4th ed.). New York: Teachers College Press.

Cole, M. (1996, October). *"As long as it's fun, it's developmentally appropriate": An exploration of the educational ideology of five kindergarten teachers.* Paper

presented at the annual meeting of the Mid-Western Educational Research
Association, Chicago, IL.

Crahay, M., & Delhaxhe, A. (1988). *Agir avec les rouleaux agir avec l'eau* [Acting
with rollers, acting with water]. Brussels, Belgium: Labor.

Csikszentmihalyi, M. (1975). *Beyond boredom and anxiety.* San Francisco: Jossey-
Bass.

Csikszentmihalyi, M. (1990). *Flow: The psychology of optimal experience.* New
York: Harper & Row.

Damon, W. (1995). *Greater expectations: Overcoming the culture of indulgence in
America's homes and schools.* New York: Free Press.

DeVries, R. (1986). Children's conceptions of shadow phenomena. *Genetic, Social,
and General Psychology Monographs, 112*(4), 479–530.

DeVries, R. (1997). Piaget's social theory. *Educational Researcher, 26*(2), 4–17.

DeVries, R., & Edmiaston, R. (1999 [incorrectly printed 1998]). Misconceptions
about constructivist education. *The Constructivist, 13*(1), 12–19.

DeVries, R., & Fernie, D. (1990). Stages in children's play of tic tac toe. *Journal of
Research in Childhood Education, 4,* 98–111.

DeVries, R., & Kohlberg, L. (1987). *Constructivist early education: Overview and
comparison with other programs.* New York: Longman.

DeVries, R., & Zan, B. (1994). *Moral classrooms, moral children: Creating a
constructivist atmosphere in early education.* New York: Teachers College Press.

DeVries, R., & Zan, B. (1995). Creating a constructivist classroom atmosphere.
Young Children, 51(1), 4–13.

Dewey, J. (1933). *How we think: A restatement of the relation of reflective thinking to the educative process.* Lexington, MA: D. C. Heath.

Dewey, J. (1966). *Democracy and education.* New York: Free Press. (Original work
published 1916)

Dewey, J. (1975). *Interest and effort in education.* Edwardsville: Southern Illinois
University Press. (Original work published 1913)

Diagram Group (1976). *Musical instruments of the world.* New York: Facts on File.

Dichtelmiller, M. L., Jablon, J. R., Dorfman, A. B., Marsden, D. B., & Meisels, S. J.
(1997). *Work sampling in the classroom: A teacher's manual.* Ann Arbor, MI:
Rebus. (Original work published 1994)

Dorros, A. (1990). *Me and my shadow.* New York: Scholastic.

Duckworth, E. (1972). The having of wonderful ideas. *Harvard Educational Review, 42,* 217–231.

Duckworth, E. (1996). *"The having of wonderful ideas" and other essays on teaching and learning* (2nd ed.). New York: Teachers College Press.

Edwards, C., Gandini, L., & Forman, G. (Eds.). (1998). *The hundred languages of
children: The Reggio Emilia approach-advanced reflections* (2nd ed.). Green-
wich, CT: Ablex.

Elementary Science Study. (1971). *Teacher's guide for water flow.* New York:
Webster Division, McGraw-Hill.

Erikson, E. (1977). *Toys and reasons.* New York: Norton.

Evans, R. (1973). *Jean Piaget: The man and his ideas.* New York: E. P. Dutton.

Fein, G. (1981). Pretend play in childhood: An integrative review. *Child Development, 52*(4), 1094–1118.

Fein, G., & Rivkin, M. (Eds.). (1986). *The young child at play: Reviews of research, Vol. 4.* Washington, DC: National Association for the Education of Young Children.

Fein, G., & Wiltz, N. (In press). Play: As children see it. In D. Fromberg & D. Bergen (Eds.), *Play from birth to twelve: Contexts, perspectives, and meanings.* New York: Garland.

Fiarotta, N., & Fiarotta, P. (1993). *Music crafts for kids: The how-to book of music discovery.* New York: Sterling.

Fleege, P. O. (1997). Assessment in an integrated curriculum. In C. H. Hart, D. C. Burts, & R. Charlesworth (Eds.), *Integrated curriculum and developmentally appropriate practice: Birth to age eight* (pp. 313–334). Albany: State University of New York Press.

Forest, H. (1998). *Stone Soup.* Little Rock, AR: August House LittleFolk.

Forman, G. E., & Hill, F. (1984). *Constructive play: Applying Piaget in the preschool.* Reading, MA: Addison-Wesley.

Freud, S. (1974). *Beyond the pleasure principle.* New York: Norton. (Original work published 1920)

Freud, S. (1950). *Totem and taboo* (J. Strachey, Trans.). New York: Norton. (Original work published 1913)

Froebel, F. (1999). *The education of man.* Grand Rapids, MI: Kindergarten Messenger. (Original work published 1826)

Fromberg, D., & Bergen, D. (1998). *Play from birth to twelve: Contexts, perspectives, and meanings.* New York: Garland.

Gammons, J., & Kutzer, A. (Eds.). (1997). *Science made simple, preschool/kindergarten: The best of* The Mailbox *magazine.* Greensboro, NC: The Education Center.

Gardner, H. (1997, April). [Keynote address]. Second Annual Cornerstones Conference, Arlington, VA.

Goldstein, E. (1996). *Sensation and perception* (4th ed.). Pacific Grove, CA: Brooks/Cole.

Goodwin, W. L., & Driscoll, L. A. (1980). *Handbook for measurement and evaluation in early childhood education.* San Francisco: Jossey-Bass.

Gullo, D. F. (1994). *Understanding assessment and evaluation in early childhood education.* New York: Teachers College Press.

Gupton, P., & Cooney, M. (1997). *Children's perceptions of play: A qualitative study.* Unpublished manuscript.

Helm, J. H., Beneke, S., & Steinheimer, K. (1998). *Windows on learning: Documenting young children's work.* New York: Teachers College Press.

Hildebrand, V. (1971). *Introduction to early childhood education.* New York: Macmillan.

Hildebrand, V. (1985). *Guiding young children* (3rd ed.). New York: Macmillan.

Hildebrandt, C. (1998a). Creativity and music in early childhood. *Young Children, 35*(6), 68–74.

Hildebrandt, C. (1998b). Developing mathematical understanding through invented games. *Teaching Children Mathematics, 35*(6), 191–195.

Hildebrandt, C., Bell, T., Zan, B., & Stoeckel, T. (1999, November). *Differential benefits of competitive and cooperative games among first-graders.* Paper presented at the meeting of the Association for Moral Education, Minneapolis, MN.

Hill, D. (1977). *Mud, sand, and water.* Washington, DC: National Association for the Education of Young Children.

Hills, T. W. (1992). Reaching potentials through appropriate assessment. In S. Bredekamp & T. Rosegrant (Eds.), *Reaching potentials: Vol. 1. Appropriate curriculum and assessment for young children* (pp. 43–65). Washington, DC: National Association for the Education of Young Children.

Isaacs, S. (1966). *Intellectual growth in young children.* Routledge and Kegan Paul. (Original work published 1930)

Jackson, P. (1968). *Life in classrooms.* New York: Holt.

Johnson, D., & Johnson, R. (1989). *Cooperation and competition: Theory and research.* Edina, MN: Interaction Book Company.

Kamii, C. (1982). *Number in preschool and kindergarten.* Washington, DC: National Association for the Education of Young Children.

Kamii, C. (1989). *Young children continue to reinvent arithmetic: Second grade.* New York: Teachers College Press.

Kamii, C. (1994). *Young children continue to reinvent arithmetic: Third grade.* New York: Teachers College Press.

Kamii, C. (2000). *Young children reinvent arithmetic* (2nd ed.). New York: Teachers College Press.

Kamii, C. (Ed.). (1990). *Achievement testing in the early grades: The games grown-ups play.* Washington, DC: National Association for the Education of Young Children.

Kamii, C., & DeVries, R. (1977). Piaget for early education. In M. Day & R. Parker (Eds.), *The preschool in action* (2nd ed., pp. 363–420). Boston: Allyn & Bacon. (Original article published 1975)

Kamii, C., & DeVries, R. (1980). *Group games in early education: Implications of Piaget's theory.* Washington, DC: National Association for the Education of Young Children.

Kamii, C., & DeVries, R. (1993). *Physical knowledge in preschool education: Implications of Piaget's theory.* New York: Teachers College Press. (Original work published 1978)

Katzen, M., & Henderson, A. (1994). *Pretend soup and other real recipes: A cookbook for preschoolers and up.* Berkeley, CA: Tricycle Press.

Kent, J. (1981). *The biggest shadow in the zoo.* New York: Parents Magazine Press.

King, N. (1979). Play: The kindergartners' perspective. *The Elementary School Journal, 80*(2), 81–87.

Klein, M. (1975). *The psychoanalysis of children.* New York: Delacorte Press. (Original work published 1932)

Kohlberg, L., & DeVries, R. (1987). Psychometric and Piagetian measures of intelligence: Their nature and educational uses. In L. Kohlberg, *Child psychology and childhood education: A cognitive-developmental view* (pp. 87–177). New York: Longman.

Kohlberg, L., & Mayer, R. (1972). Development as the aim of education. *Harvard Educational Review, 42*(4), 449–496.

Kohn, A. (1986). *No contest: The case against competition.* New York: Houghton Mifflin.

Kohn, A. (1993). *Punished by rewards: The trouble with gold stars, incentive plans, A's, praise, and other bribes.* Boston: Houghton Mifflin.

Kohn, A. (2000). *The case against standardized testing: Raising the scores, ruining the schools.* Portsmouth, NH: Heinemann.

Kwak, H. (1993). *The development of an interview for the assessment of children's knowledge about water dynamics.* Unpublished manuscript.

Kwak, H. (1995). Science in a constructivist classroom: Progress in a five-year-old child's reasoning about water dynamics. (Doctoral dissertation, University of Northern Iowa). *Dissertation Abstracts International, 57,* no.02A: 0629.

Mallinson, G., Mallinson, J., Frosschaer, L., Harris, J., Lewis, M., & Valentino, C. (1993). *Science horizons (kindergarten level).* Morristown, NJ: Silver Burdett & Ginn.

McGovern, A. (1968). *Stone Soup.* New York: Scholastic.

McGovern, A. (1986). *Stone Soup.* New York: Scholastic.

Meisels, S. J., Jablon, J. R., Marsden, D. B., Dichtelmiller, M. L., Dorfman, A. B., & Steele, D. M. (1995). *The work sampling system: An overview.* Ann Arbor, MI: Rebus Planning Associates.

Montessori, M. (1956). *The child in the family.* New York: Schocken Books. (Original work published 1936)

Montessori, M. (1965). *Spontaneous activity in education: The advanced Montessori method.* New York: Schocken Books. (Original work published 1916)

Montessori, M. (1967). *The absorbent mind.* New York: Dell. (Original work published 1949)

National Association for the Education of Young Children (NAEYC). (1988). Position statement on standardized testing of young children 3 through 8 years of age. *Young Children, 43*(3), 42–47.

National Council of Teachers of Mathematics (NCTM). (2000). *Principles and standards for school mathematics.* Reston, VA: National Council of Teachers of Mathematics.

Nebraska Department of Education, Iowa Department of Education, Iowa Area Education Agencies, Head Start Collaboration Project. (1993). *The primary program: Growing and learning in the heartland.* Lincoln, NE: Authors.

Nelson, M. (1995). *You can teach yourself to make music with homemade instruments.* Pacific, MO: Mel Bay.

O'Donnell, M. P., & Wood, M. (1999). *Becoming a reader: A developmental approach to reading instruction.* Boston: Allyn & Bacon.

Perrone, V. (1991). On standardized testing: A position paper for the Association of Childhood Education International (ACEI). *Childhood Education, 67*(3), 131–142.

Piaget, J. (1954). *The child's conception of reality.* New York: Basic Books. (Original work published 1937)

Piaget, J. (1960). *The child's conception of physical causality.* Paterson, NJ: Littlefield, Adams. (Original work published 1927)

Piaget, J. (1962). *Play, dreams, and imitation in childhood.* New York: Norton. (Original work published 1945)

Piaget, J. (1964). Development and learning. In R. Ripple & V. Rockcastle (Eds.), *Piaget rediscovered: A report of the conference on cognitive studies and curriculum development* (pp. 7–20). Ithaca, NY: Cornell University Press.

Piaget, J. (1965). *The moral judgment of the child.* New York: Free Press. (Original work published 1932)

Piaget, J. (1969). *Mechanisms of perception.* New York: Basic Books. (Original work published 1961)

Piaget, J. (1970a). *Genetic epistemology.* New York: Columbia University Press.

Piaget, J. (1970b). *Science of education and the psychology of the child.* New York: Viking Compass. (Original work published 1969)

Piaget, J. (1973a). Piaget takes a teacher's look. *Learning.* October, 21–27.

Piaget, J. (1973b). *To understand is to invent: The future of education.* New York: Grossman. (Original work published 1948)

Piaget, J. (with R. Garcia). (1974). *Understanding causality.* New York: Norton. (Original work published 1971)

Piaget, J. (1978). *Success and understanding.* Cambridge, MA: Harvard University Press. (Original work published 1974)

Piaget, J. (1980). *Experiments in contradiction.* Chicago: University of Chicago Press. (Original work published 1974)

Piaget, J. (1981). *Intelligence and affectivity: Their relation during child development.* Palo Alto, CA: Annual Reviews. (Original work published 1954)

Piaget, J. (1995). *Sociological studies* (L. Smith, Ed.). New York: Routledge. (Original works published 1928–1964)

Piaget, J., & Garcia, R. (1974). Physico-geometric explanations and analyses. In J. Piaget, *Understanding causality,* New York: Norton. (Original work published 1971)

Piaget, J., Grize, J., Szeminska, A., & Bang, V. (1977). *Epistemology and psychology of functions.* Boston: D. Reidel. (Original work published 1968)

Piaget, J., & Inhelder, B. (1956). *The child's conception of space.* London: Routledge & Kegan Paul. (Original work published 1948)

Piaget, J., & Inhelder, B. (1969). *The psychology of the child.* New York: Basic Books.

Piaget, J., & Szeminska, A. (1952). *The child's conception of number.* London: Routledge & Kegan Paul. (Original work published 1941)

Pratt, C. (1970). *I learn from children.* New York: Cornerstone Library. (Original work published 1948)

Read, K. (1976). *The nursery school: Human relationships and learning* (6th ed.). Philadelphia: W. B. Saunders.

Rosenblum, V. (n.d.). *Math games for K–grade 5.* Birmingham, AL: Unpublished paper.

Rubin, K., Fein, G., & Vandenberg, B. (1983). Play. In P. Mussen (Ed.), *Handbook of child psychology: Vol. 4. Socialization, personality, and social development* (pp. 693–774). New York: Wiley.

Sabbeth, A. (1997). *Rubber-band banjos and java jive bass: Projects and activities on the science of music and sound.* New York: Wiley.

Sales, C., & Sales, J. (1994). *Using pattern block frames.* White Plains, NY: Cuisenaire.

Sales, C., & Sales, J. (1995). *Using tangram frames.* White Plains, NY: Cuisenaire.

Selman, R. (1980). *The growth of interpersonal understanding.* New York: Academic Press.

Selman, R., & Schultz, L. (1990). *Making a friend in youth.* Chicago: University of Chicago Press.

Smilansky, S. (1968). *The effects of sociodramatic play on disadvantaged preschool children.* New York: Wiley.

Spodek, B. (1977). What constitute worthwhile educational experiences for young children? In B. Spodek (Ed.), *Teaching Practices: Reexamining assumptions* (pp. 5–20). Washington, DC: National Association for the Education of Young Children.

Stanne, M., Johnson, D., & Johnson, R. (1999). Does competition enhance or inhibit motor performance: A meta-analysis. *Psychological Bulletin, 25*(1), 133–154.

Stone, J. (1996). Developmentalism: An obscure but pervasive restriction on educational improvement. *The Education Policy Analysis Archives, 4*(8). [LISTSERV @ASU.EDU]

Stone Soup. (1981). Troll Associates.

Sutton-Smith, B. (1986). The spirit of play. In G. Fein & M. Rivkin (Eds.), *The young child at play: Reviews of research, Vol. 4* (pp. 3–16). Washington, DC: National Association for the Education of Young Children.

Talbot, J. (1988). *The dragon's cold.* Martinez, CA: Discovery Toys.

Trafton, P., & Hartman, C. (1997). Developing number sense and computational strategies in problem-centered classrooms. *Teaching Children Mathematics, 34*(4), 230–233.

Turner, P., & Hamner, T. (1994). *Child development and early education: Infancy through preschool.* Boston: Allyn & Bacon.

Upitis, R. (1990). *This, too, is music.* Portsmouth, NH: Heinemann.

Upitis, R. (1992). *Can I play you my song? The compositions and invented notations of children.* Portsmouth, NH: Heinemann.

Van Rynbach, I. (1988). *The stone soup.* New York: Greenwillow Books.

Vygotsky, L. (1966). Play and its role in the mental development of the child. *Soviet Psychology, 12,* 6–18. Also in J. Bruner, A. Jolly, & K. Sylva (Eds.) (1976). *Play: Its role in development and evolution,* (pp. 534–554). New York: Basic Books. (Original work published 1933)

Wasserman, S., & Zola, M. (1977). Promoting thinking in your classroom. *Childhood Education, 54*(1), 2–7.

Weber, E. (1969). *The kindergarten: Its encounter with educational thought in America.* New York: Teachers College Press.

Wien, C. (1995). *Developmentally appropriate practice in "real life": Stories of teacher practical knowledge*. New York: Teachers College Press.

Wiggins, G., & McTighe, J. (1998). *Understanding by design*. Alexandria, VA: Association for Supervision and Curriculum Development.

Williams, C., & Kamii, C. (1986). How do children learn by handling objects? *Young Children, 42*(1), 23–26.

Williams, R. A., Rockwell, R. E., & Sherwood, E. A. (1987). *Mudpies to magnets: A preschool science curriculum*. Mount Rainer, MD: Gryphon House.

Wing, L. (1995). Play is not the work of the child: Young children's perceptions of work and play. *Early Childhood Research Quarterly, 10*(2), 223–247.

Zan, B. (1996). Interpersonal understanding among friends: A case study of two young boys playing Checkers. *Journal of Research in Childhood Education, 10*, 114–122.

Zan, B., & Hildebrandt, C. (2001, April). *Children's interpersonal understanding in cooperative and competitive games*. Paper presented at the meeting of the American Educational Research Association, Seattle, WA.

Zubrowski, B. (1981). *Messing around with water pumps and siphons: A children's museum activity book*. Boston: Little, Brown.

Index

About the Authors

Rheta DeVries is a developmental psychologist with a Ph.D. from the University of Chicago. Currently, she is Professor of Curriculum and Instruction and Director of the Regents' Center for Early Developmental Education at the University of Northern Iowa. Previously, she has held faculty positions at the University of Illinois at Chicago, the Merrill-Palmer Institute, and the University of Houston where she was also Director of the Human Development Laboratory School. Research interests include study of constructivist education and its effects on children and cognitive and sociomoral development in children. Rheta DeVries has written several books, including *Constructivist Early Education: Overview and Comparison with Other Programs* (with Lawrence Kohlberg), and *Moral Classrooms, Moral Children: Creating a Constructivist Atmosphere in Early Education* (with Betty Zan).

Betty Zan is Assistant Professor of Curriculum and Instruction at the University of Northern Iowa where she is a Research Fellow with the Regents' Center for Early Developmental Education. She received a B.S. in Human Development and Family Studies and an M.A. and Ph.D. in Developmental Psychology from the University of Houston. She is the coauthor, with Rheta DeVries, of *Moral Classrooms, Moral Children: Creating a Constructivist Atmosphere in Early Education*, published by Teachers College Press. Her research interests include constructivist early education, young children's social and moral development, game playing, and friendship.

Carolyn Hildebrandt is Associate Professor of Psychology at the University of Northern Iowa and a Research Fellow with the Regents' Center for Early Developmental Education there. She received a B.A. in Music from the University of California at Los Angeles, an M.A. in Educational Psychology from the University of California at Davis, and a Ph.D. in Human Development and Education from the University of California at Berkeley. She has published articles on cognitive, social, moral, and musical development in children, adolescents, and adults, as well as articles on constructivist approaches to education. Her current research interests include cognitive, social, moral, and musical development in young children and constructivist approaches to early education.

Rebecca Edmiaston is an Assistant Professor in Curriculum and Instruction and a Research Fellow in the Regents' Center for Early Developmental

Education at the University of Northern Iowa. She received her Ph. D. from the University of Texas in Special Education with an emphasis in Early Childhood Education and Learning Disabilities. Dr. Edmiaston has published articles on assessment, inclusion, and literacy in professional journals. Her research focuses on including children with special needs in constructivist classrooms and facilitating children's language and literacy development in preschool and primary programs.

Christina Sales is a Research Associate at the Regents' Center for Early Developmental Education at the University of Northern Iowa. She received her B.S. in Child Development from Iowa State University and her M.A. in Curriculum and Instruction with an emphasis in Early Childhood from the University of Northern Iowa where she is currently a doctoral candidate. She has been a teacher of young children for more than 25 years and has a special interest in developing early childhood constructivist mathematic and science curriculum materials. She invented the pattern block frames discussed in Chapter 8.

8354